W9-DHI-680

Destinies Shared

U.S.-Japanese Relations

Destinies Shared

U.S.-Japanese Relations

EDITED BY

Paul Gordon Lauren
and Raymond F. Wylie

Introduction by Ambassador Mike Mansfield

Westview Press
BOULDER, SAN FRANCISCO, & LONDON

Westview Special Studies on East Asia

Copyright © 1989 by Westview Press, Inc.

Published in 1989 in the United States of America by Westview Press, Inc., 5500 Central Avenue, Boulder, Colorado 80301, and in the United Kingdom by Westview Press, Inc., 13 Brunswick Centre, London WC1N 1AF, England

Library of Congress Cataloging-in-Publication Data
Destinies shared: U.S.-Japanese relations / edited by Paul Gordon
  Lauren and Raymond F. Wylie; introduction by Mike Mansfield.
     p.   cm.—(Westview special studies on East Asia)
  Bibliography: p.
  Includes index.
  ISBN 0-8133-0631-0
  1. United States—Relations—Japan. 2. Japan—Relations—United
States. I. Lauren, Paul Gordon. II. Wylie, Raymond Finlay, 1941–
III. Series.
E183.8.J3D47   1989
303.4'8273'052—dc19   89-31145
                                                                              CIP

Printed and bound in the United States of America

The paper used in this publication meets the requirements of the American National Standard for Permanence of Paper for Printed Library Materials Z39.48-1984.

10   9   8   7   6   5   4   3   2   1

For
Ivan and Mary Lou Lauren
and
Sheelagh and Teresa Wylie

Contents

Acknowledgments

It gives us great pleasure to acknowledge the many individuals who have contributed in one way or another to this book. In addition to the Mansfield Center and the contributors themselves, we extend gratitude to

- members of our advisory committee—Roy Anderson, Albert Borgmann, Thomas Huff, James Flightner, James Lopach, Leo Moser, John O. Mudd, Dennis O'Donnell, Howard Rheinhardt, Daniel Smith, and Philip West—for conceptual design and organizational help

- members of our foundation's board of directors—Max Baucus, Christopher Dodd, Tom Foley, Richard Gerstner, Gerald Grinstein, James Hodge, James D. Hodgson, Henry Kissinger, James V. Koch, Daniel Lambros, Brian Powers, Kenneth B. Pyle, Paul Schmechel, Ted Schwinden, Lloyd Schermer, Bruce Sievers, Lester Thurow, Paul Volcker, and Charles Young—for direction and assistance

- the Burlington Northern Foundation for financial support

- Bill Brown, Virginia Braun, Mary Ann Campbell, Susan Carlson, Jeff Demestrescu, Bev Decker, Donald Habbe, Claudia Johnson, Tovah LaDier, Al Madison, Ron Klaphake, Jim Raphael, Kate Saenger, Howard Skaggs, Brian Spellman, and Stephen Wing for various forms of assistance

- Irene Finley for outstanding staff support

- Libby Barstow, Barbara Ellington, Miriam Gilbert, Bruce Kellison, Kathy Streckfus, and Brenda Satrum of Westview Press for publication advice and help

- our wives, Susan and Sue, for their patience and encouragement.

Paul Gordon Lauren
Raymond F. Wylie

Introduction

Reflections on the United States and Japan

Mike Mansfield

As we approach what is often called the Age of the Pacific one fact is clearly before us: The next century will see the United States and Japan standing together at the dynamic center of a new global economic structure. Together, along with the other advanced nations, we will share—even more than we do today—the awesome responsibility for the economic future of the entire world.

Bearing the responsibility for shaping much of the world's economic structure is not new to the United States; it is what the Marshall Plan and much post–World War II U.S. history is all about. But sharing this responsibility *is* new, and here we have the challenge. We must learn to see things in new ways, to understand the nature of our interdependence with Japan, and to reconceive our national interest in light of what we understand of this relationship.

In this Introduction, I wish to reflect upon some themes that have interested me in my work over the years in Tokyo and to sum up my thinking about this valuable partnership we have with the Japanese. I hope that from this endeavor, a picture will emerge outlining the ties between our two nations and delineating where I think we ought to go and some ways that we need to prepare, on both sides, to get there.

The Beginnings

As I look out my window over the Tokyo skyline, I marvel at what has been accomplished here since the devastation of the war. This economic miracle that surrounds me here in Tokyo is the result of a people who saved—even when they had very little to save—who put off recreation and personal pleasures for the sake of rebuilding, who worked with an astounding efficiency and determination in a manner not seen in the United States since the darkest days of World War II.

These patterns of domestic independence, frugality, and diligence applied so successfully in Japan during the postwar period, with the support and encouragement of the United States, have served the Japanese well. But it became clear in the 1970's that these patterns, coupled with a uniquely aggressive export orientation, were creating more and more difficulties for the United States. The U.S. economy simply was not prepared for interaction with an emerging economic superpower that maintained the ethics and economic practices of a less developed nation. In tracing the history of the U.S.-Japanese relationship, we can see the development of two paradoxical economic themes: growing international interdependence and increasing economic frictions.

In the early years of this relationship we were fortunate indeed to be led by men of vision: Prime Minister Shigeru Yoshida, and Secretaries of State George Marshall and John Foster Dulles. But I believe even these men of great foresight could not have predicted how deep and far-ranging our relationship would develop.

To be sure, we started with a good framework. The Treaty of Mutual Security and Cooperation, signed in 1951, gave us the promise of a strong and peaceful Asia with an independent Japan free to pursue its political and economic destiny. In those early years of working together, we learned much about each other. Americans learned that the Japanese have an enormous capacity for resilience, for hard work, and for succeeding in the face of adversity. I believe that during this period, many Japanese learned that Americans have virtues that they also respect, plus an optimism about the future and a willingness to roll up their sleeves and share the work.

Over time, despite our vastly different languages and cultures, despite our geographical distance and divergent histories, and despite the war, we became friends. There just seemed to be something about the Japanese and American characters that made our peoples come to like and respect each other.

As we look back on these early years, we can see in the pages of the *Congressional Record* a chronicle of discussion and debate in the U.S. Congress about this growing relationship, described with a mixture of admiration and pride for the role the United States played in Japan's postwar development. Again and again in this journal we find praise for Japan's commitment to democracy, for its vital artistic traditions, and for the successful efforts to rebuild its economy.

As the U.S.-Japanese relationship grew over the years, new themes began to emerge. Younger generations with no memories of the war began to move upward in both societies. In the United States, the pattern of immigration of peoples into the country began to change: First the West Coast and later the entire country began a process of shifting its attention from Europe to the Far East. At the same time, the mighty engine of the Japanese economy, fueled by some of the most dedicated, educated, and resourceful workers in the world, began to provide us first with novelties, then with low-cost conveniences, and finally with state-of-the-art technological and industrial products that have become part of the daily life of every household in our land. For our part, the United States has contributed to Japan the products of its abundant and efficient agricultural system; equipment for production, information processing, and medical use; and hi-tech innovations and ideas from its unmatched research and development sector.

Yet sadly, while our relationship now has grown to the point where we are partners in nearly every aspect of international human endeavor, it is in the area of economics where nearly all of our problems lie.

Sources of Friction

There are a number of reasons why we find ourselves so often in economic confrontation with Japan: First of all, because we have not yet found a better way, we continue to deal with each economic issue between our two countries as a new international crisis. While dealing with one after another short-term economic or trade problem, we must also learn to devote time and planning to developing a mechanism for handling these problems with less disruption to our overall relationship. This goal calls for examining problems in a broad framework and looking for long-term solutions. We cannot allow the urgent to continually drive out the important.

Second, we should remember that the economic problems we encounter grow out of our interdependence, and it is, after all, this close relationship that nurtures both our peoples. As I have said before, though the waves may sometimes be high, we cannot condemn the sea.

Third, as patience is not particularly an American virtue, neither is haste a Japanese characteristic. We must show more regard for the ways in which each country perceives, approaches, and attempts to solve our common economic problems.

Fourth, the stereotypes that form the tone and context of many of the issues we face hinders their resolution. Japan can no longer be seen as a poor country lacking natural resources and blessed only by the skills of its hard-working people. At the same time, it cannot be seen as a ruthless economic giant bent on the domination of all future technological innovation. On this last point, I would like to elaborate on why our peoples often perceive each other as a threat. Perhaps by looking at the emotional aspects of these problems, we will find ways of solving them.

Japan is seen as a threat by many Americans because its rapid economic expansion has forced unwanted and painful adjustments in the United States. When change comes as a result of the loss of traditional markets and jobs to a foreign competitor, it matters little to those who lose them that new demands for goods or services, and therefore also jobs, are being created elsewhere in the economy. It also matters little that the adjustment is an easy medicine for an economist to prescribe but a difficult one for a patient to swallow. On this subject, I believe my Japanese friends also have considerable recent experience.

Second, Japan is seen as a threat by some Americans because its success is somehow falsely interpreted as our decline. We simply must find ways to help our citizens understand the nature of the interdependence of our relationship—to understand that in the game of international economics, it *is* possible for all to win.

Third, as James Fallows suggested in an article in *The Atlantic*, perhaps Japan is fundamentally different from the United States. It has long-standing cultural and historical traditions that have hindered its adaptation to the modern international market system. Its rise to economic superpower status has been incredibly rapid and has created pressures for speedy and dramatic adjustments. Some Americans doubt the willingness and sincerity of some Japanese leaders to adapt Japan's economic practices to conform to those of its trading partners around the world. This perceived refusal to adapt—in their terms, Japan's willingness to accept the benefits of a modern international trading system while sharing little of the domestic costs of such a system— is threatening to these critics. But there should be no underestimation of the difficulties involved in such adjustments; such changes do not come easily, and they involve not only economic but also enormous political costs.

Of course, some of these threats are, to a greater or lesser extent, felt on the Japanese side as well. In addition, some Japanese apparently feel that the United States is intent on preventing Japan from enjoying the fruits of its justly earned prosperity. They believe, understandably and in large part correctly, that Japan's present prosperity is the result of excellent organization and much hard work. Some have even gone further and, tying together unrelated incidents in an area of intense

U.S.-Japanese competition, the electronics industry, have put forth the theory that there is a conspiracy afoot to destroy this economic sector in Japan.

That theory, of course, is nonsense. If we understand the true nature of our interdependence, we know that action taken against one of us will only damage the other. This principle will become even more obvious as we continue to grow closer in the years to come.

It is these elements of emotionalism which have entered our economic debate that are to me most troubling. On both sides we often fall into the mistaken notion that our own country is somehow the victim and the other nation is the aggressor. The messages that we are sending our young people as a result of these continuing economic shocks are profoundly disturbing to all of us who see every day the immense benefits that both our societies obtain from our partnership.

The Escalation of the Debate

The emotionalism in these international disputes, coupled with the ready availability of the tools of public relations and mass media, has proved an effective mix on both sides for turning particular economic issues into major political confrontations. In a short time, Americans and Japanese alike have become remarkably effective at identifying, publicizing, and focusing international attention on problems in specific trade areas. To the degree that they help us quickly resolve such problems, these methods are to the good. To the degree that they lend momentum to a trade war, they are dangerous.

Having served for a good length of time in both houses of Congress, I am familiar with the appeal that this type of confrontation has for a member of Congress or a senator eager to be seen in the press as standing up for the welfare of his or her constituents. No matter how conscientious and balanced a representative may be, there is no question that he or she is under a kind of pressure from the media and from various interest groups that is unique to Washington.

When pushed to this level, individual trade issues acquire an emotional baggage that turns them into issues of national pride, and therefore they become infinitely more difficult to solve. We end up requesting our respective heads of state to deal with specific trade issues at summit conferences because we in our embassies, departments, and ministries and our colleagues in business have failed to reach effective solutions. This approach is unfortunate, not only because it damages the vital relationship between us, but because it represents a lost opportunity. We expend enormous amounts of time and energy on problems for which the solutions are simple and technical. Instead, this time and energy could be spent planning ways in which our partnership could ensure a more stable future for Asia as well as economic development for those regions of the globe that are now in desperate need of help.

In the course of my duties in recent years I have met with nearly all of our state governors and I have found an extraordinary difference between their perspectives on the U.S.-Japanese relationship and those of the scores of members of Congress with whom I have spoken during my time in Japan. I know that our governors are not one bit less concerned than Congress about the impact of Japanese imports on the workers in their states. But they also seem to know very well what our relationship with Japan provides for these states—that Japan consumes 80% of our exported beef, 65% of our exported fish, 15% of our aircraft, and so on. To be sure, the governors want a level playing field as much as, if not more than, any other American. But they seek quiet and effective solutions to specific problems—solutions often involving trade-offs in one area for gains in another. Many of these governors are becoming extremely effective in these types of negotiations. These individuals have much to teach us about the process of quiet and effective negotiation, and we should all listen to them carefully. Of course, one can find many parallels in the way in which the Japanese political system reacts to trade issues. Perhaps the same lesson can be learned on that side as well.

Defense

Although it is often pointed to as a source of bilateral friction, defense is one of those areas in which we should take greatest pride in our joint achievements with the Japanese. The road has not always been smooth, but look how far we have come. Between our two countries and within each country has emerged a significant degree of consensus on our common defense. This understanding is predicated on the terms of the 1951 Treaty of Mutual Security and Cooperation. The United States remains content with the basic arrangement and division of defense roles and missions, and I believe that most Japanese are satisfied as well. Our alliance is strictly bilateral and Japan's role purely defensive, but it is essential to the maintenance of peace and security throughout the region.

No alliance exists in a vacuum. In response to changes in the regional security situation, the two nations have worked to strengthen their partnership. Japan, for its part, decided on several important initiatives—including Prime Minister Zenko Suzuki's 1981 commitment to defend the sea-lane approaches out to a distance of 1,000 nautical miles, the Mid-Term Defense plan, the technology transfer agreement, the decision to make direct purchases of major weapons systems such as the next generation of fighter-support aircraft known as the "FSX," and participation in Strategic Defense Initiative (SDI) research. Also, the United States is pleased by the concern shown and actions taken by the Japanese government in the wake of recent unauthorized sales to the Soviet Union in violation of the regulations of the Coordinating Committee for Export Control (COCOM). Japan's laws and procedures in this regard are tougher now, and I believe the Japanese government is determined to enforce them strictly. Furthermore, Japan is now committed to helping the United States repair the damage that was caused.

But perhaps the most important measure taken by the Japanese government was its decision to fund approximately 40% of the costs of the U.S. military presence in Japan ($2.5 billion out of a total cost of $6 billion—or the equivalent of $45,000 for every Japan-based U.S. military person). U.S. forces in Japan serve as a deterrent to any aggression directed not only against Japan but also against others throughout the Far East. Indeed, U.S. bases in Japan are essential to the defense of the United States itself. Thus, Japan's cost-sharing— the most extensive of any U.S. ally—has been a major plus, not only for Japan and the United States, but for global peace and stability as well.

Japan itself now has a defense budget comparable in size to that of any of our major North Atlantic Treaty Organization (NATO) allies. U.S. leaders will be looking for continued efforts by the Japanese government to further strengthen its Self-Defense Forces and extend its cost-sharing arrangements, but as it stands now, if there is any "free ride" on American defense, I do not see it occurring in Japan.

Overseas Development Assistance

Another area in which Americans have been quick to criticize Japan concerns its lack of overseas development assistance programs. There is considerable truth to the opinion that Japan has come rather late into the business of foreign aid. It is, of course, understandable that a nation dedicated to self-reliance, reconstruction, and economic development should place a low priority on providing external assistance. The fact is, however, that this perspective has changed dramatically in recent years. Not only has the realization grown among Japanese leaders that they must contribute more in this area, but already the figures themselves bear notice.

In 1988 the United States budgeted some $10.1 billion for nonmilitary foreign aid. The figure for Japan was $10.37 billion. Furthermore, I am confident that the Japanese figures will increase in the years ahead.

Our Task

It is no secret that we Americans have a big job ahead of us. We need to save more, consume less, and continue to restore our competitive strength. We need to get our "twin deficits"—the massive red ink in our federal budget and our trade deficit—under control. We must remember that Japan is not the only source of our deficit problem. We have deficits with all of our major trading partners. The trade deficit is a national concern, and it is we who must decide how to deal with it.

We are making some progress there. Trends in U.S.-Japanese trade, with the help of the upward revaluation of the yen, are moving in the right direction and accelerating. For the first time in a decade we are seeing export-led economic growth in the United States. The payoff from these rising exports has been manifested in new jobs and has yielded the lowest unemployment rate in a decade and a half.

In addition, the United States is taking serious steps to bring the federal budget under control. U.S. industries are streamlining and adopting forward-looking management strategies. We as a nation and our corporations still need to learn a great deal about the importance and the techniques of exporting effectively. We have been complacent with our domestic market for too long. This is changing.

We have a long way to go, but we must keep working at these problems if we do not intend to be a permanent debtor nation dependent upon capital flows from abroad to finance our lifestyles. I believe we Americans must, for the sake of this vital relationship, continue to learn and strive to discipline ourselves.

The Japanese Task

Farsighted Japanese leaders have also forthrightly acknowledged that they have a job to do. Just as the United States must get on with its attack on the "twin deficits," Japan needs to complete "twin adjustments." Namely, Japan needs to pursue an adjustment of its economic structure and an adjustment of its view of itself to correspond to the reality of its status as an economic superpower.

The standard of living the world has now achieved owes much to the global trading system that has matured since World War II. A nation that is organized to export, to use the proceeds to add productive capacity, and to export still more, we have learned, is ultimately highly destabilizing to that trading system.

We can understand a single-minded drive to build export volume by developing nations, for how else can they catch up? Furthermore, their exports are normally exceeded by massive imports of capital goods. In time, however, the successful developing country devotes more and more of its gains from trade to improving the living standards of its own people. So that other nations can afford to buy from it, it will import a growing fraction of the goods it needs from abroad. It will do so, ironically, even though it may have become very good at making almost everything it needs. As David Ricardo pointed out 150 years ago, two-way trade is a game that puts everyone ahead.

This is indeed the premise that animated a visionary report issued in Japan during 1986. It was produced by a distinguished group under the chairmanship of Governor Haruo Maekawa. The Maekawa Report is a blueprint for the structural adjustment of the Japanese economy in pursuit of two fundamental goals: first, to assure that Japan may live in harmony with its friends and allies, and second, that the people of Japan may enjoy the fruits of their tremendous efforts over the past forty years. This report provides the philosophical underpinnings of Japan's much-heralded shift to a more domestic-oriented economy—an economy that will absorb more of Japan's products at home rather than export them to the rest of the world.

In the interim, the United States offers one message to its Japanese friends: access, access, access. In looking at a wide variety of business opportunities in Japan over the years, I have come to the conclusion that the Japanese market is much more open than most Americans believe. At the same time, it is clear to me that the Japanese market is not as open as most Japanese believe.

Japan has long maintained, for cultural and historical reasons, some marked inefficiencies in its distribution, construction, and agricultural sectors. As our relationship has grown, these inefficiencies have come to take on a symbolic significance as proof of Japan's economic pro-tectionism. The Japanese realization of the costs of these inefficiencies is widespread, and in modern sectors of the Japanese economy, many of these approaches have already been eliminated. Now the debate in Japan concerns how the remainder of these obstacles to free import might be dismantled. For the health of our relationship, I urge that those remaining areas where foreign access to Japanese markets is restricted be liberalized quickly. The costs of doing so now are relatively small. The cost of not doing so may be far greater.

Looking to the Future

In a recent speech delivered in Tokyo, Robert McCormick Adams, secretary of the Smithsonian Institution, outlined the future impact of technology on the U.S.-Japanese economic relationship. He described a world with growing reliance on high-speed processing, storage, and transmission of information; evolution toward multiple centers of manufacturing; and a change in the nature of markets from "places" to "networks" so that work increasingly becomes detached from place, operations from their central headquarters. Commodity mixes will shift rapidly, falling within new corporate entities and being abruptly introduced and dropped in response to an increased volume and accelerating flow of information. With the specter of redundancy and justifiably declining faith in job security, individual as well as aggregate economic well-being will depend upon adaptability—a concept that increasingly has to be defined in terms of making new accommodations to an information-oriented world.

Thus it is obvious, Adams noted, that our basic, mutual interdependency can only grow as each nation seeks to maximize its own competitiveness and reduce its own vulnerability. In short, as we realize the full impact of information technology on our economic systems, if we fail to develop effective methods to resolve economic conflicts, we are in trouble. The new systems will involve not a series of individual trade disputes, but rather, shifting waves of them as fluid production centers electronically ferret out and target the pockets of consumers in each other's markets.

We already have the technology that enables a salesperson in Hamamatsu to order products from Dallas or Detroit as easily as from Osaka. We are coming close to the day when geographical distance will be nearly meaningless to the conduct of commerce.

Will we fight this new wave of technology by continuing to impose tariffs, by protecting inefficient economic sectors, and by preserving antiquated rules and regulations that discriminate against the goods and services of other nations? Or will we be farsighted enough to realize what freedoms and benefits we can gain from this communications revolution? If we choose the latter course, we can begin now to develop a system of trade and commerce that lives up to the promise of the new technology, a system that can bring the family in Butte, Montana, or the family in Yokohama the same wide range of products and services at the lowest possible prices.

Preparing for Even
Greater Interdependence

We have some tools at hand that give us a start toward this vision of the future. A strong General Agreement on Tariffs and Trade (GATT) organization can help us prepare our economies for this increased interdependence. GATT can give us a common set of rules of the road to keep us from colliding with each other while we seek our separate national destinations. Moreover, special-purpose organs and mechanisms, such as the market-oriented sector-selective (MOSS) talks, which dealt with electronics, medical equipment, and other specific types of bilateral trade issues, can provide a helpful method of dealing with problems before they reach crisis proportions.

Also, in my view, one of the ideas that was not endorsed by the Reagan administration but deserves a closer look is the notion of a free-trade agreement between Japan and the United States. I do not fool myself into thinking that a free-trade agreement could be worked out simply or in a short time. It took us several years to negotiate one with Canada. But we ought to study whether one might be possible, or at least whether some features of such an agreement could be helpful in defining the economic goals of our relationship. It is better to face up to the whole of a policy than to submit to "nickel-and-diming" on every single issue.

The Forest and the Trees

On both sides, we tend so easily to lose perspective. As the blind man perceives only that part of the elephant he can touch, so do some Americans perceive the U.S.-Japanese relationship as fundamentally involved with only the Japanese import restrictions on some agricultural or industrial product. Similarly, there are Japanese who see the relationship essentially in terms of domineering U.S. pressure to eliminate traditional village economies or job security systems.

We must learn to see this partnership in its entirety—and not only what is now, but the promise that it holds for both our peoples. We must understand that this relationship has given us regional peace and stability; that it has enriched the cultural and educational lives of our citizens; that it has helped—and will increasingly help—to focus more resources and constructive efforts on less fortunate countries. We should also remember the small but manifold ways in which we as individuals derive tangible benefits from these ties. Each day nearly every household in the United States derives pleasure from the products of Japan's consumer electronics industry; likewise, millions of Japanese are delighted by the products and ideas from the U.S. food industry. These are only two of countless examples.

It is an extraordinarily rich and varied relationship that our two nations share. It is built on the foundation of hundreds of thousands of individual relationships and friendships among peoples who, regardless of vast national differences, have come to respect and like each other. Nowhere can we see this more clearly than in the fabric of U.S.-Japanese cultural and educational exchanges.

Building on Cultural Ties

If we look at the cultural relationship between the United States and Japan, we find—as befits two democratic nations—a complex weaving of private and government exchange programs and cultural exchanges that touch every conceivable area of achievement and inquiry.

We now share with Japan nearly 200 Sister City pairs, and it seems that a new contract is drawn up nearly every month. The vast majority of these relationships are active ones. They encompass exchanges of exhibits and of students, government officials and businesspeople. The most active of these exchanges have fostered joint research on urban planning and problems and have paved the way for mutual trade and business opportunities. It has become nearly automatic for our embassy staff to begin discussions with Americans wanting to know about trade and university exchange opportunities with the question "Do you have a sister city?" These ties frequently provide the social connection so important in the Japanese context and the cultural and linguistic bridges vital to the American visitor.

I am also pleased to note the continuing development of sister states and prefectures and sister institutions of all sorts. Each of these relationships has a substantial contribution to make in building the trust, friendship, and confidence needed to overcome economic dis-agreements.

Moreover, a tide of visitors annually washes over both our shores. Last year more than 2 million visitors from Japan came to the United States, and we expect more this year. Foremost among these visitors from Japan were their imperial highnesses, the new Emperor Akihito and Empress Michiko. These charming emissaries from Japan traveled throughout the United States displaying a warmth and friendliness that captivated crowds of Americans and whetted their appetites to see Japan and learn more about it. Their visit was a delightful reminder of how much goodwill we share.

Also among these 2 million visitors last year were nearly 20,000 Japanese students who came to study in U.S. schools and universities. This number too will increase in coming years, in part because of a welcome initiative by the Ministry of Education that allows credit toward a high school diploma for exchange student experience. Japanese scholars now contribute intellectually, culturally, and financially to colleges and universities across our land. Here it is appropriate to cite the role of the Japan-U.S. Educational Commission (JUSEC, or the

Fulbright program in Japan), which, jointly funded by both governments, stands as a symbol of the resolve of both nations to increase their knowledge of each other and to focus many of the best minds in the respective countries on issues related to our common future.

In this educational exchange process, the role of young people is particularly noteworthy. We know that Japanese parents can give us no greater gift than to allow us to participate in the education of their children. It is a testament both to the Japanese regard for Americans and to their recognition of the excellence of the American system of higher education.

My only wish here is that the flow of visitors could be more balanced. The yen revaluation has made this wish unattainable for many American families for the time being. Nevertheless, the flow of American educators, businesspeople, journalists and, even now, tourists is impressive.

I am also pleased at the way the Japanese government at various levels has moved forward with new and innovative programs to increase exchanges and to prepare Japanese youth for the future of Japan's relationship with the United States and its new prominence in international society. I speak here specifically of the Japan Exchange and Teaching Program (JET), which places hundreds of U.S. college graduates and their colleagues from other English-speaking countries in secondary schools and government offices throughout Japan for a year or longer in order to provide a living resource for students of the English language and American culture as well as of other foreign cultures.

Recently, I was also pleased to participate in a ceremony for the first group of young Japanese graduates who, under a work-study program sponsored by the Hokkaido International Foundation will seed some sixty U.S. and Canadian colleges with Japanese language teachers.

It is my hope that creative approaches such as these will fuel the initiative already under way in colleges and high schools throughout the United States to give to Japanese language and cultural studies the emphasis they deserve. Such an emphasis is necessary in order to prepare the next generation of Americans to help guide and shape this vital relationship.

So, while our economic forces collide and confrontations continue to alienate blocks of workers and farmers in both countries, our cultural exchange network continues to expand. I trust that these exchanges will continue to succeed in creating an even closer tie between us and to create—in the words of the motto of one such organization—"one friendship at a time."

As a former college teacher myself, there is a message I would like to direct toward my colleagues on campuses around the nation: If you are sincerely interested in making a contribution to help your country and to build a better future, a good place to start is by encouraging your most promising students to learn about Japan. The United States will need new leaders who know Japan, and I believe you will be helping them to find an important and satisfying role in world affairs.

To sum up, despite the imbalance in the flow of visitors, our cultural relationship is sound and, as with our security relationship, it is an achievement in which both sides can take much pride. Moreover, these exchange programs have given us a key, if we only care to use it. They teach us that in order to seek solutions to our disagreements, we must first know and respect each other.

And that, after all, is what it boils down to: treating the other fellow the way you'd like him to treat you. I have found that the Japanese respond to that idea as well as Americans. With a little time and a little mutual respect, we can make this relationship fulfill its promise. In that promise we will have found "a pearl without price," not only to enrich American and Japanese lives, but also to contribute to the well-being of future generations everywhere.

As we stand on the edge of the new Age of the Pacific and look ahead, we see the inevitable and relentless intertwining of our national destinies. What will the U.S.-Japanese relationship be? Will we go forward bickering with each other, hesitant and fearful, lest someone, somehow, should take advantage of us? Or will we, Americans and Japanese, go forward as friends and equals to explore this future and its promise for us and for all humankind? This is what we must decide.

Suggestions for Further Reading

Adams, Robert McCormick, "Science, Technology, and 'Progress': Reflections on the Historical Relationship," speech of 18 May 1988 delivered in Tokyo.

Fallows, James, "Japan: Playing by Different Rules," *The Atlantic* (September 1987):22–32.

Frost, Ellen, *For Richer, For Poorer: the New U.S.-Japan Relationship* (New York: Council on Foreign Relations, 1987).

Maekawa, Haruo, et al., "The Report of the Advisory Group on Economic Structural Adjustment for International Harmony, Submitted to the Prime Minister, Mr. Yasuhiro Nakasone, on 7 April 1986" (Maekawa Report).

Mansfield, Mike, *No Country More Important: Trials in a Maturing Japan-U.S. Relationship* (Tokyo: Simul Press, 1984).

Romberg, Alan D., ed., *The United States and Japan: Changing Societies in a Changing Relationship* (New York: Council on Foreign Relations, 1987).

United States–Japan Advisory Commission, *Challenges and Opportunities in United States–Japan Relations: A Report Submitted to the President of the United States and the Prime Minister of Japan* (Washington, D.C.: Government Printing Office, 1984).

1

U.S.-Japanese Relations: From the Past to the Present

Raymond F. Wylie
and Paul Gordon Lauren

On many occasions Ambassador Mike Mansfield has described the relationship between the United States and Japan as "the most important bilateral relationship in the world, bar none."[1] This bold assertion challenges us to consider not only whether there are any other contenders that might possibly vie for the title but also just how much power and influence Japan and the United States actually have to exert. Today, the United States and Japan have, respectively, the first and second largest national economies in the world. Together they command a significantly disproportionate share of the world's intellectual and material power. Their combined personal wealth, industrial capacity, military strength, educated population, stable governments, and cultures have the ability to alter the present and the future of the globe. Consequently, as Mansfield suggests in his reflective Introduction to this volume, the current state and the future of the bilateral relationship between Japan and the United States produce compelling interests and provoke vital concerns that far transcend these two countries alone and directly affect Asia, the Pacific region, and the world at large.

The U.S.-Japanese relationship is characterized, however, by far more than the remarkable strength of its combined economic, military, political, and cultural resources. Another feature is that both countries share so many important goals at home and abroad. Despite their differences, Japan and the United States share a strong commitment to democracy, to market-oriented economic growth and prosperity, and to political stability in the Asia-Pacific region and in the international system as a whole. Basic agreement on such fundamental principles

17

by two such powerful states gives their bilateral relationship even greater significance.

Another distinguishing and influential characteristic of the relationship is the intensity and magnitude of interdependence. For Japan, the United States is its former benefactor, the linchpin of its national security, the leader of the free world, its largest foreign market, and an attractive magnet for capital investment. It is also a critical source of food and raw materials, a pacesetter in scientific research and development, and a major influence upon popular culture. For the United States, Japan is its former protégé, its most stable and reliable ally in Asia, a major link in the U.S. global defense network, a partner in foreign affairs, and its largest overseas market. Japan is also an important partner in research and development, a key player in global financial flows, the largest direct foreign investor, a source of high-quality consumer goods, and the home of a sophisticated culture. "The two countries have become so closely intertwined that forced separation would be wrenching and probably impossible," wrote Ellen Frost of the Council on Foreign Relations. "They are in it for good, so to speak, thrown together for richer or poorer."[2]

Yet, despite the strength, common goals, and interdependence of the bilateral relationship between Japan and the United States, in recent years that relationship has exhibited another feature: friction and conflict. No two nations have ever found complete accord and unanimity on all issues, and hence it is too much to expect total harmony between these two powerful states. Nevertheless, relations are increasingly strained by massive bilateral trade imbalances that greatly favor Japan and by complaints in the United States that a favorite ally is not carrying its "fair share" in security burdens and not "playing fair" in trade. Particularly in the sensitive area of economics, there has been a rapid shift in the relative wealth within the relationship as Japan has become richer and the United States has become poorer. This development has seriously strained the partnership by eroding goodwill and mutual trust, fostering recrimination and resentment, provoking "Japan bashing" in Washington and emotional outbursts in Tokyo, and sparking public statements about ruthless and devious competitors engaged in a "trade war."

Given the tremendous power and influence of the U.S.-Japanese relationship it is not surprising that nations and peoples around the globe are watching these developments closely. How and when Japan and the United States manage their relationship, resolve their growing disputes, readjust their partnership, translate their economic strength into political muscle, and reassess their respective places in the emerging international system will affect the world—for good or for ill. For this reason, it is difficult to dispute the inherent and critical importance of the U.S.-Japanese relationship to the interests and the shared destinies of us all.

History of the Relationship

Japan and the United States have a history of relations that dates back to the middle of the nineteenth century, and some of that history continues to shape the relationship to this day. Often their ties have been friendly and mutually beneficial to the peoples of both countries. At other times, suspicions and hostilities have risen to the fore, leading to serious economic, political, and military conflicts. When the relationship between Japan and the United States has been strong and constructive, it has brought peace and prosperity not only to those two countries but to others as well. When the relationship has been weak and confrontational, however, it has brought war, most notably the bitterly fought Pacific conflict during World War II. Throughout their shared history, ordinary Japanese and Americans, even as they have struggled to overcome immense barriers of distance and culture, have remained fascinated with each other and with the nature of their special and influential relationship.[3]

Early Relations

The doors of modern Japan opened to the United States in 1853 when Commodore Matthew Perry took command of the U.S. Pacific fleet and set sail for Edo (Tokyo) Bay. His mission was ambitious and ultimately successful: to outflank the British and the Russians in the "opening" of Japan to the West, to demand the opportunity for trade, and to place U.S. relations with Japan on the basis of a firm treaty. This goal was achieved by 1857 when U.S. envoy Townsend Harris negotiated the U.S.-Japanese Treaty of Amity and Commerce with the reluctant Tokugawa shogunate, the military regime then ruling Japan. For the United States this new treaty with Japan was a triumph; it placed America at the forefront of the Western penetration of Japan and the Far East and served as a stirring symbol that "Manifest Destiny" was stretching out across the Pacific. For Japan, the treaty threw the country into turmoil over whether to accommodate or to resist the United States and other imperialist powers; this controversy finally led to the restoration of the symbolic power of the emperor and the end of the Tokugawa line.

With this dramatic change precipitated by the impact of the West, Japan began its process of modernization. The Meiji Restoration of

1868 issued in a new generation of "enlightened rule" that was to transform Japan from a traditional, agricultural, and isolationist country into an innovative, industrial, and expansionist power in the Western mold. During the remaining decades of the nineteenth century, the Japanese took to Western ways with great speed and success. In this process they looked to the United States as one of their principal "foreign teachers." Dr. William S. Clark, for example, a well-known American educator, left his mark on the development of Hokkaido, Japan's northern home island. When he was about to return to the United States in 1877, he is reputed to have admonished his young students: "Boys, be ambitious!"[4]

In the last decades of the nineteenth century the Japanese were forming ambitions of their own, not all of which would have been approved by Professor Clark. With great success behind them in industrializing and modernizing their society, the Meiji leaders sought to stabilize change at home and to secure a new relationship of equality with the Western powers abroad, including the abolition of the unequal treaties imposed earlier by the West. Japanese self-confidence was enhanced immeasurably with a stunning victory in 1894–1895 during the Sino-Japanese War, fought largely over the issue of who would dominate Korea and Taiwan. With the once-imposing Chinese empire so decisively beaten and falling rapidly into disunity, it appeared to many Japanese that the mantle of leadership in East Asia and the Pacific had been placed on their shoulders.

The United States, meanwhile, was growing uneasy with this new ascendancy of Japan in the Far East. Americans had watched with fascination and growing apprehension Japan's defeat of China and annexation of Taiwan, its rising power in Korea, and, even more alarming, its scarcely hidden ambitions to incorporate Hawaii into the expanding Empire of the Rising Sun. Indeed, it is one of the great coincidences of history that Japan and the United States became great powers at almost the same time. For the United States, the historical turning point was the Spanish-American War of 1898, which humiliated Spain and left the United States as an Asia-Pacific power with control over Hawaii and the Philippines. For Japan, the moment came in 1904–1905 when it challenged imperial Russia's power in Manchuria and Korea. Japan's triumph over Europe's largest empire drew gasps of astonishment from the Western powers and the colonies they ruled in Asia. It was the first time in modern history that a "colored" people had triumphed militarily over a great Western "white" nation, and even colonial peoples who knew little of Japan could not but take heart at its decisive victory over Russia in the Far East.[5] The United States and Japan now faced each other in Asia and the Pacific, and the state of their relationship would determine much of the future.

The Road to Pearl Harbor and War

While Europeans grew apprehensive about Japan's seemingly relentless rise to power in the Far East, Americans viewed this development with deep alarm. Having recently consolidated its grip on the Philippines, the United States was in no mood to be edged out of Asia and the Pacific by Japan. During the latter part of World War I, 1914–1918, Washington and Tokyo fought as nominal allies and emerged as common victors, but this alliance could not disguise the mutual suspicions that began to undermine their relationship. In Japan there was increasing talk of saving "Asia for the Asians," while some Americans espoused the then-fashionable notion of the "yellow peril" as a rationale to stand fast against further Japanese encroachments in Asia and the Pacific.

Eventually, the competing visions and ambitions of Japan and the United States came to focus upon China, which recently had moved from empire to republic via the Revolution of 1911 only to fall into the chaos caused by competing warlords. For the Japanese, China represented a prize of immeasurable value and opportunity: an outlet for territorial expansion and colonization, a source of food and raw materials, a target for investment and industrialization possibilities, and a check on the growth of Western (including Russian) power in the Far East. The United States, on the other hand, saw China as a vital market for continued trade and investment and as a troubled and beleaguered giant in need of succor from a "special friend." Thus, while Washington may have acquiesced in Japan's annexation of Korea in 1910, it was not so disposed toward the Japanese conquest of Manchuria in northeast China during 1931. U.S. Secretary of State Henry L. Stimson, for example, announced that the United States would adopt a policy of "nonrecognition" of all Japanese inroads into China. In 1937 when Japan launched a full-scale invasion of China, Tokyo was in no mood to seek Washington's opinion—let alone approval—on its growing ambitions in Asia and the Pacific.

The Japanese believed at this time that they could act with impunity in the Far East, for opposition from the United States amounted to little more than diplomatic posturing and some reluctantly imposed trade embargoes. But Tokyo's decision to deploy a "southern strategy" against U.S. and European positions in the Philippines and throughout Southeast Asia was another matter completely. With the Europeans locked into bloody World War II launched by Adolf Hitler in 1939, and with the Soviet Union effectively neutralized by a 1941 nonaggression pact with Japan, only the United States stood in the way of Japan's ambitions for the conquest of all Southeast Asia.

The Japanese attack on U.S. naval facilities at Pearl Harbor in 1941 was a calculated preemptive strike designed to gain the initial military advantage in the Pacific and possibly to dissuade the United States from entering the war at all. Admiral Isoroku Yamamoto, who was charged with planning and executing the attack, was himself a reluctant convert to its wisdom. But, wise or not, the attack on Pearl Harbor snapped the tenuous threads that held the U.S.-Japanese relationship together and plunged the two nations into a devastating and disastrous war that tragically ended only with the atomic clouds over Hiroshima and Nagasaki.[6]

The Occupation and Its Aftermath

With the U.S. occupation in 1945, Japan crossed a major watershed in its own history and relations between the two countries entered a new and most constructive phase. Overall, the occupation was a tremendous success and remains to this day a monument to U.S. magnanimity and Japanese good sense. Certainly no previous occupation has been so dedicated to political and social reform. Few other societies have been so thoroughly transformed in so short a time as was Japan between 1945 and 1952. Japan's response was also all the more remarkable since the country had never before experienced a defeat in war that brought foreign occupation to its own soil.

Japan emerged exhausted and devastated from the war. More than 3 million Japanese had lost their lives. Incendiary raids on its cities and the explosion of two atomic bombs had destroyed 30% of Japanese homes and crushed industry to one-quarter of its prewar potential. The yen was barely a hundredth of its prewar value. For almost a year Japan had been virtually cut off from sea communication, and inland transportation had all but collapsed. Acute shortages of food brought much of the country near starvation.

Out of this rubble of defeat Japan made a remarkably swift and impressive recovery due to the hard work of its people and the benevolent nature of its relationship with the United States. The process was marked by a virtual transformation of Japan along Western, democratic lines. Some reforms focused upon demilitarization, which meant stripping Japan of its wartime gains and abolishing the institutional supports upon which the military establishment rested. Others involved economic issues, such as seeking to decentralize the economy, enact land reform, and promote prosperity. Still other reforms involved changes in the Japanese educational system. Perhaps the most important reform of the entire period, however, was the establishment of a new constitution. Adopted under the careful guidance of the United States, the Constitution of 1947 fundamentally altered the political structure of Japan, creating a truly representative form of government in which the locus of sovereignty was placed in the hands of the Japanese people. It established a cabinet, made both houses of the Diet elective, instituted an independent judiciary, extended the right to vote to all men and women over the age of twenty, guaranteed basic human rights, and through Article 9 created the now-famous provision for the disavowal of warfare except in self-defense.

Japan's recovery in the international arena also was facilitated by the United States. In 1951 the United States joined forty-seven other nations in signing a formal peace treaty with Japan that restored Japan's sovereignty. During the same year, the United States and Japan also negotiated one of the fundamental elements of their bilateral relationship: the U.S.-Japan Treaty of Mutual Security and Cooperation. This security treaty and an administrative agreement entered into force in 1952. It provided for the continuation of U.S. military bases in Japan and committed the United States to protecting Japan in case of war. Both countries thus bound themselves closely together on the mutually advantageous issue of peace and security in Asia and the Pacific.[7]

The 1950s and 1960s witnessed a steady maturing of the bilateral relationship. Emphasis was placed upon external security abroad and political stability and economic growth at home. It was largely assumed that for many years to come, an almost defenseless Japan would remain dependent upon the militarily strong United States, Japan's influence in the world would be regional at most, Japanese economic growth would be steady but slow, manufactured goods from Japan would never present serious competition in the international market, and "little" Japan always would remain in the shadow of its powerful and wealthy American partner. These complacent assumptions proved to be short-sighted. By 1968 Japan had risen from a defeated and despondent nation to assume third place among the world's industrial powers, yet this amazing achievement in such a short period marked just the beginning of the transformation of Japan and of the U.S.-Japanese relationship.

Challenges and Opportunities in the Relationship

For a wide variety of reasons discussed in the chapters that follow, many of the assumptions from the past no longer apply to the U.S.-

Japanese relationship. Unforeseeable events and accelerated developments of the 1970s and 1980s brought a new focus of cooperation to
Japan and the United States, but also brought a series of new problems
and sources of conflict. Moreover, these developments changed the old
asymmetry between Japan and the United States and thereby significantly
altered the relationship itself. Today, at a time of constant warnings
that the United States is on the decline, Japan—above all other nations—
is dramatically and conspicuously on the rise. "There is no reason that
Japan will not continue to grow," says Paul Kennedy of Yale University,
historian and author of *The Rise and Fall of the Great Powers.* "Its
economic drive is pushing it toward center stage."[8] Most experts agree
with this assessment. "The American century is over," claims Clyde
Prestowitz, a former deputy assistant secretary of commerce in the
Reagan administration and author of *Trading Places: How We Allowed
Japan to Take the Lead.* "The big development in the latter part of
the century is the emergence of Japan as a major superpower."[9]

In assessing the U.S.-Japanese relationship, it is instructive to consider
the following factors:

- Japan is now the world's largest creditor, with net foreign assets
  of $240 billion. The United States, in contrast, is the world's largest
  debtor, with a net foreign debt of more than $500 billion.
- For 1989–1990 Japan budgeted over $10 billion for foreign aid, a
  7.8% increase, displacing the United States as the world's most
  generous donor.
- The Japanese have fifty-three destroyers to protect their home
  islands, more than twice as many as the U.S. Seventh Fleet has
  to patrol the entire western Pacific and the Indian Ocean.
- Japan now contributes nearly 11% of the United Nation's budget,
  second only to the United States.
- Japan, in its uneven balance of trade, currently enjoys a trade
  surplus with the United States that amounts to nearly $60 billion.

These factors, among others, reflect the current state of the U.S.-
Japanese relationship and are likely to affect the inherent challenges
and opportunities of that relationship in the future. Clearly, now is a
time of challenge: Japan's rapid rise to world financial power relative
to the United States is forcing both countries to reassess the nature
of their relationship and their respective places in the emerging
international system. But there is opportunity too, for out of this highly
controversial and often public reassessment can emerge a new understanding of each other's needs and a renewed commitment to work

for what we share in common. In light of the tremendous power and influence inherent in the U.S.-Japanese relationship, it is not surprising that other nations in Asia and the Pacific and around the world are watching closely. They know, too, that their own interests and destinies are very much at stake as Japan and the United States seek to reassess their bilateral relationship and set out a new course for the future.

To address these issues, we have assembled the opinions of some of the most prominent and highly respected statesmen, business leaders, diplomats, and scholars on both sides of the Pacific who write with knowledge, personal experience, and special insight. Collectively, the chapters that follow address a wide variety of different but related issues concerning the U.S.-Japanese relationship. These include assessments of the perceptions and cultural differences that influence relations between the two countries (Christopher), of the political and security debates over shared responsibilities and charges of "free rides" (Armacost and Wylie), and of the controversial and highly publicized balance-of-trade problem (Okita and Morita). The text continues with discussions about the importance of U.S.-Japanese relations to economic development in the Asia-Pacific region (O'Donnell), a view of the U.S.-Japanese relationship from the perspective of East and Southeast Asia (Koh), an overview of differing approaches to education in Japan and the United States (Cummings), and an analysis of cooperation and competition in the vital area of science and technology (Lynn). The final chapter (Morse) explores issues that may arise in the future as Japan and the United States move their relationship and their shared destinies toward the twenty-first century.

Notes

1. This expression is used frequently by Ambassador Mansfield. See, for example, his speech of 1 June 1988 at the American Club in Tokyo.

2. Ellen Frost, *For Richer, for Poorer: The New U.S.-Japan Relationship* (New York: Council on Foreign Relations, 1987), p. 2.

3. An influential, if somewhat dated, introduction to the U.S.-Japanese relationship is Edwin O. Reischauer's *The United States and Japan*, 3rd ed. (Cambridge: Harvard University Press, 1965); see also his more recent *The Japanese* (Cambridge: Belknap Press, 1981); John Whitney Hall, *Japan: From Prehistory to Modern Times* (Tokyo: Tuttle, 1983); and the Bibliography, which lists many books on U.S.-Japanese relations.

4. See the entry under "Clark, William S. (1826–1886)" in the *Kodansha Encyclopedia of Japan* (Tokyo: Kodansha, 1983), vol. 1, p. 321.

5. For more detailed discussion of this racial factor, see Paul Gordon Lauren, *Power and Prejudice: The Politics and Diplomacy of Racial Discrimination* (Boulder, CO: Westview Press, 1988).

6. A recent study of the Pacific conflict is Akira Iriye, *Power and Culture: The Japanese-American War, 1941–1945* (Cambridge: Harvard University Press, 1981).

7. For an up-to-date account of the occupation, see Michael Schaller, *The American Occupation of Japan: The Origins of the Cold War in Asia* (New York: Oxford University Press, 1985).

8. Paul Kennedy, as quoted in "Japan: From Superrich to Superpower," *Time*, 4 July 1988.

9. Clyde Prestowitz, as quoted in ibid. See also "The Pacific Century: Is America on the Decline?" *Newsweek*, 22 February 1988.

2

Cultural Dimensions of the U.S.-Japanese Relationship

Robert C. Christopher

Any review of the current state of U.S.-Japanese relations must include a consideration of some of the cultural dimensions of the relationship and their possible implications for the future. Other contributors to this book deal with such important substantive issues as trade, security, education, and technology in a comprehensive and definitive manner. Yet, as we all know, substance can be affected by style, and so it is worthwhile to reflect on how the differing emotional, intellectual, and social predispositions of Japanese and Americans seem to influence their dealings with each other.

Predispositions and Cultural Differences

In the search for a healthier U.S.-Japanese relationship, the most important challenge facing the ruling establishments of the two countries is not that of promoting cross-cultural understanding; rather, it is finding the courage and strength to induce their respective populations to face up to some unpleasant truths. The people of the United States must be persuaded that their country cannot indefinitely continue to consume more wealth than it creates without endangering the entire world economic order. By the same token, the Japanese people must be persuaded that they too will imperil that order (as they did in the past) if they continue to rely to such an extent on exports to fuel their nation's economic growth.

In making these statements, the purpose is neither to provoke controversy nor to burden readers with the obvious. Rather, it is to highlight the idea that one must be very cautious about concluding that cultural attitudes alone can explain particular national policies or problems.[1] Sometimes, to be sure, that is clearly the case. Thus, it seems reasonable to assume that the disdain with which the people of China traditionally regarded foreigners was at least one of the major factors that precipitated the disastrous decline of Chinese power in the nineteenth century. And it is self-evident that the deep-seated American conviction that theirs is a providential society has repeatedly found concrete manifestations in U.S. foreign policy—manifestations ranging from the irredentism of Woodrow Wilson to the Carter administration's preoccupation with human rights. Nonetheless, in a great many instances, it is simplistic and misleading to regard cultural attitudes as the sole—or even the primary—determinant in economic and political developments.

Similarities or differences in national behavior, particularly in regard to economics, cannot automatically be assumed to reflect similarities or differences in cultural patterns. Clearly, for example, the great influx of married women into the labor forces of both Japan and the United States in recent times reflects not an identity of attitudes on sexual roles but rather the impact of similar economic forces upon the two peoples.

That disclaimer made, however, it is undeniable that cultural factors *do* in many cases play a significant role in determining how different societies respond to similar economic or political circumstances. Consider, for example, the fact that Japan coped with the successive oil crises of the 1970s notably faster and more smoothly than did the United States and that opposition to the construction of nuclear power plants has been far less fierce in Japan, the only nation ever to suffer major casualties from nuclear weapons.

It would be easy to ascribe both these phenomena to the fact that Japan is much more dependent upon foreign energy supplies than the United States and that, as a result, the Japanese had no rational choice but to make a swift and complete adjustment to the changes that have occurred in the global energy equation. But there is more to it than that.

It was at least in part the group orientation of the Japanese—their sense of overriding responsibility to the collective—that enabled them to adapt more readily to post-OPEC constraints on oil consumption than was possible for Americans, who are brought up with the assumption that society exists to serve the individual. And that same cultural difference, reinforced by the fact that the Japanese have traditionally had a more acute sense of collective vulnerability than Americans, also helps to explain why the Japanese people are more willing to resign themselves to the risks inherent in a reliance upon nuclear energy.

In short, it appears that the different economic and diplomatic realities that Japan and the United States confronted in the 1970s cannot by themselves fully explain the two countries' different responses to energy concerns. And that same principle holds true even more firmly when it comes to the different ways in which the two countries have responded to radical shifts in world trading patterns and hence in their economic relations with each other over the past fifteen years or so. A large—if largely unconscious—cultural component has been evident in the behavior of both Japan and the United States, and there is no reason whatever to doubt that this component will continue to affect the conduct of U.S.-Japanese affairs in the months and years immediately ahead.

Before I identify some of the cultural factors that play a significant role in determining how Japanese and Americans deal with each other at the national as well as at the personal level, it needs to be stated that, for the purposes of this discussion, I am not concerned with whether the particular attitudes and behavior patterns we shall consider are inherently desirable or undesirable in some abstract moral sense. The intention is simply to explore what they are and how they may express themselves in the policies that Japan and the United States pursue toward each other in the future.

In order to explore this topic, it will be necessary to indulge in some generalizations. That, of course, is an inherently risky process, and I do not for a moment want to suggest that all Japanese or all Americans can be fitted into tidy cultural pigeonholes. Nor do I want to create the impression that the behavior patterns that seem to be broadly prevalent in each of the two societies today are in any sense immutable. (In fact, there are distinct signs of rather major changes occurring in some aspects of Japanese society—for example, in attitudes toward work and leisure.) But neither are these patterns going to change overnight, and precisely for that reason, any attempt to foresee what lies ahead in U.S.-Japanese relations must take them into account.

One of the most important cultural differences between Japanese and Americans is the degree of vulnerability that they ascribe to their respective societies. In this regard, the two peoples are at opposite ends of the spectrum, a fact which contributes to a built-in cause of mutual misunderstanding. What too few Americans recognize is that in the collective psyche of the Japanese, potential catastrophe is an ever-looming presence. Earthquakes, typhoons, tidal waves, high population density, skimpy natural resources, and the threat of domination by nations with far greater inherent economic and military strength— these are the historical realities that shaped the Japanese world view and that still powerfully influence it. Yet in the United States it is rarely recognized that underlying Japan's international economic thrust is an enormous sense of insecurity. To most Americans, in fact, any suggestion that the United States should show consideration for the vulnerability of a nation that, in a blinking of history's eye, has emerged as the world's second greatest economic power seems at best disingenuous. And that attitude is likely to remain intact even if Japan actually does begin to suffer major economic distress as a consequence of U.S. policies.

The other side of the coin, of course, is the uncommon confidence that Americans possess in the strength and resilience of their own society. For this attitude, too, there are objectively valid reasons— among them our abundance of natural resources, our vast land mass and low population density, the protection against foreign conquest so long afforded us by geography, and a proud record of economic and technological innovation. Yet at a time when U.S. economic and industrial leadership is increasingly in question, it is easy for the Japanese to perceive our self-confidence as mindless arrogance. And when, as has already begun to happen and will no doubt happen more frequently in the future, the Japanese suggest that we might do well to pay more attention to our own shortcomings than to theirs, we Americans tend to perceive that as arrogance.

But it is not just in economic affairs that the Japanese sense of vulnerability and the relative sense of invulnerability in the United States tend to create misunderstandings that adversely affect the relationship between the two countries. That difference also helps to account for the fact that, while both societies have a strong sense of their own uniqueness, the ways in which they perceive their nationhood are almost diametrically opposed.

While there are, to be sure, other factors involved, it is at least partially because of this sense of vulnerability to malign outside forces that the Japanese remain essentially tribal—tribal, that is, in the sense that the only way to win acceptance as a member of the Japanese community is to be born Japanese; one cannot simply be assimilated. Americans too often fail to recognize the full depth of this Japanese sense of insecurity. What sometimes appears to Americans to be aggressive Japanese racism is fundamentally a defense mechanism— an attempt to find reassurance in the assertion of cultural and ethnic distinctiveness. In this one instance let me depart briefly from my promise to maintain a nonjudgmental stance and offer the opinion that although these historical factors help explain the race consciousness so frequently visible in Japan, that explanation does not render this attitude any more acceptable to non-Japanese nor any less worrisome as a potential source of tension between Japan and other nations.

There is real danger in the fact that the Japanese so often fail to recognize the degree to which the national confidence and pride of Americans rests on the idea of an inclusive and pluralistic society— and in that, one might add, the Japanese are not alone. In an article he published recently in the *New York Times Magazine*, a Hong Kong– based journalist named Ian Buruma abandoned his habitual "Japan-bashing" long enough to give a kind of backhanded endorsement to Prime Minister Yasuhiro Nakasone's much criticized public comment in 1986 on the educational attainments of American blacks and hispanics. Nakasone's observation, Buruma asserted, had produced what he de-scribed as a "yelp" from Americans because it had hit us in "a soft spot."[2] But Buruma and the numerous Japanese who without doubt privately agree with him have misunderstood the outcry that Nakasone's comment provoked in the United States. This outcry was inspired not by any complacency over the way in which our educational system currently serves our black and hispanic citizens but rather by Japan's apparent ignorance of an important feature of U.S. society and culture. That is, the unique strength of U.S. society, as most Americans conceive it, lies not only in its demonstrated capacity to bring once-disadvantaged groups into the mainstream of national life but, above all, in the diversity of the American population.

That this divergence in our views of nationhood will continue to disturb U.S.-Japanese relations at least in some degree for years to come seems all but inevitable. And it will do so in part because of another psychological and cultural difference between the two peoples. Culturally speaking, Americans are possessed by the missionary spirit, whereas the Japanese for much of their history have been preoccupied with maintaining their own identity. Indeed, for forty years now they have consciously shrunk from trying to influence the attitudes and behavior of societies other than their own.

The potential for conflict created by this particular difference is obvious. Because they are insufficiently aware of the psychic trauma that the Japanese experienced as a consequence of World War II, Americans tend to see Japan's reluctance to exercise strong international influence not as a matter of "once burnt, twice shy," but rather as a shirking of global responsibilities. The obverse of this coin is that, as Japan's national self-confidence has grown, the Japanese have increas-ingly come to perceive U.S. exhortations concerning the proper conduct of their national and international affairs as naked cultural imperialism. More than once, young Japanese of my acquaintance—men and women quite knowledgeable about the United States and capable of moving easily in American society—have remarked with obvious bitterness and using almost identical words, "Sometimes it seems that what Americans are trying to force us to do is to stop being Japanese and become Americans." Here again, let me emphasize that for the purposes of this discussion it is not of central importance whether either (or both) of these national attitudes is desirable. What is important is that they exist, that they have increasingly colored the national dialogue between the United States and Japan—and that they are likely to color it even more strongly hereafter as Japan's international role continues to grow.

Conflicting National Behavior Patterns

Potentially dangerous as this particular factor is, however, it is overshadowed by a whole nexus of conflicting national behavior patterns that stem directly or indirectly from the very different ways in which Japanese and Americans characteristically regard the relationship between the individual and the group. It would be presumptuous to offer a pat and necessarily oversimplified restatement of the conventional wisdom concerning the group orientation of the Japanese versus the individualism of Americans. But there are some specific manifestations and consequences of that broad truism that deserve brief discussion because, just as they have in the past, they seem all but certain to complicate the interaction between Japan and the United States in their shared destinies for the future.

The first of these factors involves the nature of the decision-making process found in the two countries. Rooted as they are in a society that regards the maximum assertion of individual authority as not only the privilege but the hallmark of an effective leader, Americans frequently find it very hard to accept the consensus-seeking process that prevails inside the Japanese government. At best, Americans are apt to regard the *nemawashi* (root-binding) process as inordinately time consuming, and not infrequently, they see it as a deliberate delaying tactic or mechanism for deceit. And even though American sophistication on this point has been growing, it would be folly to believe that we will not, in the years ahead, continue to hear U.S. politicians and negotiators accuse the Japanese of bad faith in situations where what is actually involved is a painful effort on the part of Japanese politicians and bureaucrats to forge a consensus.

A second source of continuing misunderstanding, I think, is supplied by the very different ways in which Americans and Japanese regard the relationship between patron and protégé—a difference capsulized in the much analyzed Japanese dependency syndrome known as *amae* (sense of obligation). It is not at all uncommon in the United States for individuals to have a patron in their company, university, or other organization. But in Japan, while such relationships are much more common, they take a slightly different form. In the United States, a protégé is at least tacitly expected to repay the preferment received through a patron's intervention by advancing the interests of that patron as actively as possible. But under the *amae* concept, the relationship is in a sense more binding on the patron than on the protégé. So long as the protégé remains loyal, sincere, and dutiful, he or she is entitled to continued support from the patron even though the patron gains nothing from the arrangement or actually suffers positive disadvantage from it. In the eyes of many Japanese, particularly older ones, Japan's long dependence on the United States economically and militarily imposes a responsibility upon the American people that we betray when we take action that is harmful to Japanese interests. In the meantime, of course, a great many Americans are persuaded that the Japanese have betrayed *us* by repaying all the help we have extended to them over the years by "taking a free ride" in terms of national defense and resorting in a massive way to "unfair trade practices," as discussed elsewhere in this volume.

Obviously, there is enormous potential for future conflict to arise out of these divergent attitudes—and still more conflict may arise out of the profound cultural gap implicit in the increasingly frequent American use of that word "unfair" in relation to Japanese behavior. As individualists, Americans tend to be intellectual absolutists, convinced that it is only possible to determine what is fair and unfair or moral and immoral according to some set of abstract principles. But the Japanese, on the other hand, tend to be relativists, convinced that the greatest immorality lies not in violating some rigid code of commandments but in failing to meet the reasonable expectations of other members of the group to which one belongs.

One effect of this difference is that, while Americans like to think of themselves as pragmatists, they tend, in reality, to be prisoners of ideology to a much greater extent than is customarily the case with the Japanese. In the United States, when a policy fails to achieve its intended results or proves to have extraordinarily painful and unforeseen side effects, the reaction is often predictable. It is to rebuff any suggestion that the theoretical foundations of the policy may be unsound and obdurately insist that the way to cure the problem lies in administering a stronger dose of medicine out of the same ideological cabinet as before.[3] By contrast, in the Japanese view, the fact that a policy is ideologically or theoretically admirable is of scant importance if that policy clearly has harmful practical consequences.

This difference in approach and some of its implications were very strikingly revealed in April 1987 when President Ronald Reagan decided to intensify the growing semiconductor war by imposing punitive tariffs on a number of Japanese products. According to the *New York Times*, this move elicited from one Japanese government official a reaction of both bitterness and bewilderment. "We can understand the importance of the semiconductor industry for the national security of the U.S.," he said. "But if for that reason the U.S. needs protection in semiconductors, then why not ask Japan frankly to agree? Why accuse us of violating an agreement that many people believed from the start could not possibly work anyway?"[4]

The answer to the Japanese official's questions is, of course, obvious. In the Japanese context, there is no political stigma automatically attached to pursuing policies that are dogmatically inconsistent with each other—provided that each of those policies achieves the desired results. But in the United States, the Reagan administration, with its avowedly unshakable commitment to free trade, could not publicly concede that it is prepared to resort to protectionism in certain cases without undercutting its basic political position and opening itself to all sorts of unpleasant charges, among them, duplicity.

On the surface, to be sure, nothing more than a matter of differing national political styles appears to be involved here. But in reality, very serious ramifications are involved that go well beyond that. To the Japanese, a change in political or economic course does not necessarily imply that one's past course was evil or even foolish; it merely means that it has now become advisable to accommodate to changed circumstances or to the changed expectations of one's friends and allies. Hence, a change of policies is acceptable. Yet, when the Japanese make changes in their trade policies in response to pressure from the United States, we Americans with our insistence on ideological consistency all too often point to those concessions as confessions of past guilt or error on the part of the Japanese. And by so doing we have created—and will continue to create—increasing resentment in Japan itself.

That fact, however, does not seem to trouble U.S. politicians and officials, many of whom make no bones of their belief that "the only way to get the Japanese to move is to keep the pressure on." But here too there are significant cultural differences and misperceptions involved. As individualists, Americans in general assume that, provided it is kept within reasonable bounds, confrontation is healthy and useful. But the Japanese, with their dedication to group harmony, for the most part have an almost instinctive distaste for confrontation and will go to considerable lengths to avoid it. And, to indulge in gross oversimplification, precisely because it is fundamentally alien to their culture, it has been my experience that when the Japanese do adopt a confrontational style or are forced to do so, they generally do not handle it skillfully.

It is this last observation which could make the American taste for confrontation a major stumbling block in U.S.-Japanese relations in the years ahead. Our national assumption that confrontation can be valuable rests in the last analysis on the belief that, in negotiations between responsible people, rationality and self-interest will ultimately prevail over purely emotional reactions. And that, in the eyes of a great many movers and shakers in the United States, means that because Japan's relations with the United States are so vital to the Japanese, the United States can continue to put pressure on Japan with impunity almost indefinitely.

The difficulty with this theory, however, is that Japanese history abounds in examples, both individual and collective, of what to Western eyes appear irrational reactions to confrontational situations. Because confrontation seems to most Japanese distasteful and inherently anti-social, a frequent Japanese response to what is perceived as a continuing pattern of slights, injuries, and abuses is to endure such treatment relatively politely for a prolonged period—and then to explode abruptly in a frenzy of destructive rage with no heed for consequences. These statements are not at all designed to predict that this is the direction in which U.S.-Japanese relations are inexorably heading. But such an outcome is not an inconceivable eventuality either—and no one responsible for the conduct of U.S. relations with Japan should ever forget it.

The truth is, unhappily, that when one considers all of these cultural factors it is not at all hard to construct a thoroughly unpleasant scenario concerning future economic relations between Japan and the United States. In such a scenario, the United States, instead of adopting the domestic economic policies and measures necessary to alleviate our trade deficits, would continue to take more and more steps injurious to the Japanese economy. This approach, inevitably, would render the Japanese increasingly resentful until eventually they would decide that they had little to lose by taking retaliatory economic action against the United States.

Under such circumstances, moreover, there would be scant hope that the adverse consequences could be confined to the economic sphere alone. Already, as is demonstrated by the recent argument over who will build the FSX fighter plane, economic tensions have begun to impinge on the security relationship between Japan and the United States and such conflicts could prove merely to be the tip of the iceberg. How likely is it, in fact, that one country could find itself in what amounted to a state of economic hostility with another country yet still feel safe in relying on that nation for its basic military security? Clearly, if one major aspect of the U.S.-Japanese relationship were destroyed, it would only be a matter of time before the sense of mutual interest disappeared and other aspects of that relationship also deteriorated.

As already discussed, it is all too easy to construct a scenario of this kind in purely intellectual terms. But I myself remain enough of an optimist to think that in reality things will work out differently. There are enough responsible and farsighted leaders in both Japan and the United States—people whose primary dedication is to the national interest rather than to some selfish parochial one—to ensure the adoption in both countries of policies that will not only forestall disaster but promote ever more fruitful interdependence.

Some Positive Cultural Factors

To suggest what those policies ought to be would obviously range far beyond the scope of this chapter. But it might be useful to present briefly some cultural considerations that might encourage both Japan and the United States to adopt policies that will prove mutually beneficial rather than mutually destructive.

The French sometimes describe a person as having the defects of his virtues. In a sense, the cultural factors just described, which Japanese and Americans sometimes see as defects in one another, also represent the greatest virtues of the two countries.

This is emphatically true of the Japanese tendency to perceive the effectiveness of a piece of public policy as infinitely more important than its consistency with some overall ideological construct. Not infrequently, Americans interpret this attitude as betraying a lamentable lack of principle. It seems more accurate, however, to interpret this approach as an intelligent adjustment to objective realities. This attitude, reinforced by keen awareness of the incalculably great economic and political stakes involved, renders it probable that Japan will prove far readier than most Western nations would conceivably be to make major—even onerous—changes in its policies in order to accommodate to legitimate U.S. interests. In similar fashion, it is not unlikely that what the Japanese not infrequently see as a somewhat hypocritical American obsession with "fairness" will in certain respects work to Japan's advantage in the end. To be more specific, it is clearly unfair to imply that the worldwide U.S. trade deficit is primarily the fault of the Japanese, and ordinary Americans are not as unconscious of that fact as some of the more disingenuous politicians and self-serving industrial "patriots" in the United States might like to believe. Indeed, the anti-Japanese hubbub in Washington essentially reflects the response of politicians to special interest groups rather than to the electorate in general. There is little evidence that "Japan-bashing" and protectionism have overwhelming support among the populace at large; rather, the polls supply considerable evidence that there is remarkably little public hostility toward Japan. One suspects that protectionism is more popular among special interest groups than it is among American voters as such.

But whether or not that judgment is valid, there is one phenomenon that undeniably has benign implications for the future of U.S.-Japanese relations. This is "cultural convergence." This expression does not imply that the Japanese are becoming Americanized or Americans Japanized. Rather, it means that in certain respects both peoples are moving toward a common ground in which neither traditional Japanese behavior patterns nor traditional American ones fully obtain.

There are obvious reasons why this should be the case. Cultural attitudes, after all, are not genetically acquired. In the very long run they essentially reflect adaptations to various external forces and circumstances. And the external forces and circumstances to which the Japanese and American peoples have to adapt—here one thinks particularly of the level of economic development and the conditions of material life in the two countries—become more and more similar with each passing year. And though they will not invariably do so, these circumstances seem to be producing an increasing similarity in Japanese and American behavior. Many examples could be cited here, including several from the field of business.

Several years ago in my book *The Japanese Mind*, for example, I made certain generalizations about differing approaches in Japan and the United States to such things as corporate promotion policies, standard patterns of career development, and executive job-shopping.[5] Those generalizations, largely based on observations in the late 1970s and very beginning of the 1980s, were perfectly valid at the time they were written. But when I began research for a book on U.S. business operations in Japan, I discovered that with the increasing internationalization and complexity of Japanese economic life, some of the behavior patterns and attitudes characteristic of Japanese industry were undergoing major changes.[6] In some cases these changes were occurring with astounding rapidity. By the same token, certain patterns once the norm in U.S. businesses were no longer so universal. And without exception, the changes were in the direction of greater commonality of attitudes and behavior on the part of businesspeople in the two countries.

Perhaps most interesting of all, I discovered that the degree of convergence was greatest among younger businesspeople in both countries. For example, not long ago a young man working toward a doctoral degree in cultural anthropology consulted me about a comparative study he is making of Japanese and American students at the graduate school of business at his university. The point of his study was to identify in as scientific a fashion as possible culturally determined differences in the ways Japanese and American executives and entrepreneurs respond to identical problems. To this purpose, he distributed to his sampling of business school students a set of scenarios carefully designed to play on what have traditionally been accepted as distinctively American and distinctively Japanese business approaches. To his initial dismay, however, my friend discovered that there was almost no difference in the responses he received from the majority of the students involved, regardless of whether they were Japanese or American. Fearful that perhaps Japanese students at a U.S. graduate business school might be in some sense a self-selected group, he then extended his investigation to the members of what he assumed would be a more heterogeneous group—Japanese executives from a variety of backgrounds then assigned to New York by their companies. The results of this survey were not yet complete by this writing, but, to my friend's mounting fascination, the preliminary indications were that what proved to be the case for the business school students also holds true for nearly all Japanese executives under thirty-five, regardless of whether they ever attended universities in the United States.

Another piece of evidence can be offered from my own observations of the academic world. Twenty years ago anyone studying the Japanese language at a U.S. university was almost certainly preparing for a scholarly career. Today, however, that is no longer the case. As it happens, I am currently a member of a committee that awards two traveling fellowships each year to recipients who must possess three qualifications: reasonable fluency in Japanese, some journalistic experience, and the intention of making a career in some branch of the media. As recently as a decade ago, I think it would have been unusual in any given year to find even one candidate among the 170 students at the Columbia Journalism School who met all three of these requirements, but this year we had no fewer than nine highly qualified applicants. Similarly, at the Columbia Business School, students with a command of spoken Japanese and considerable knowledge of Japanese society, while not commonplace, have become far from unusual.

Again, such changes do not mean that these young Americans have been in any sense "Japanized." But it is clear that they have far more understanding of—and far more in common with—Japanese of their own age and professional background than is true of the vast majority of Americans now of an age to be responsible for the management of national affairs.

This fact constitutes a hopeful portent for the future and supplies the note on which this chapter should end. It suggests that the people who will be in charge of our national affairs in the future, both in Japan and in the United States, will have considerably more understanding of each other and will have somewhat more convergent attitudes than has been the case in the past. This prediction is extremely encouraging.

Yet, for anyone to pretend that there will not be some rocky and perilous passages ahead where U.S.-Japanese relations are concerned would constitute self-deception of the most dangerous kind. Take, for example, the question of Japanese nationalism. There is no doubt that there is a nationalism both latent and expressed in Japan. Currently, the number of people who overtly promote extreme nationalism is quite small. The number of people in Japan who privately would like to see a greater degree of nationalism expressed in Japanese policy, and particularly in military policy, is hard to measure, but they do exist, occupy influential positions, and believe that Japan should acquire a significant military capacity. Some even believe that Japan should develop nuclear weapons. Nevertheless, it will take a long, long time before these people are able to surmount the basic reluctance and nervousness of the great majority of the Japanese people on that score.

The one thing that might encourage a revival of nationalism would be a breakdown in relations with the United States with a related economic reversal in Japan. If that were to occur, the consensus behind the present kind of democratic system in Japan might begin to collapse. That, in turn, would produce very dangerous political consequences that would encourage the nationalists. In a sense, that is what happened before World War II. Most people perhaps forget, but there was considerable progress toward democracy in Japan in the 1920s. But then came the Great Depression—and the extreme nationalists rose to power. The danger obviously still exists. However, this danger is likely to remain relatively modest, provided the United States does not tip the chessboard over.

If the United States and Japan can successfully navigate the difficult passages ahead of us during the next few years—as we can legitimately hope they will—we should in due course move into the calmer waters of a world in which, without having sacrificed their own unique identities, the Japanese and American peoples can approach their mutual problems and shared destinies with far surer insight into each other's motivations and values than they sometimes display today.

Notes

1. The literature on cultural attitudes and patterns continues to grow. See, among others, Asahi Shimbun, comp., *The Pacific Rivals: A Japanese View of Japanese-American Relations* (New York: Weatherhill, 1971); Lewis Austin, *Saints and Samurai: The Political Culture of American and Japanese Elites* (New Haven: Yale University Press, 1975); Akira Iriye, ed., *Mutual Images: Essays in American-Japanese Relations* (Cambridge; Harvard University Press, 1972); Hiroshi Kitamura, *Psychological Dimensions of U.S.-Japanese Relations* (New York: Cambridge University Press, 1971); Takie Sugiyama Lebra, *Japanese Patterns of Behavior* (Honolulu: University of Hawaii Press, 1976); H. Paul Varley, *Japanese Culture* (Honolulu: University of Hawaii Press, 1984); and Kenichi Yoshida, *Japan Is a Circle: A Tour Round the Mind of Modern Japan* (New York: Kodansha International, 1975).

2. Ian Buruma, "A New Japanese Nationalism," *New York Times Magazine*, 12 April 1987.

3. There are times when the behavior of U.S. Congressional representatives and other leaders reminds me of something I observed as a young man when I first went to Washington, D.C. I came from snowy New England and when I got to Washington there was a bad storm. I noticed that Washington drivers in general, as they approached a hill or slippery spot, would gun the engine, and then when the wheels began to spin, they would gun the engine still faster. This approach produced no particular effect except to burn up more rubber. There are times when our political and economic behavior as a nation effectively recalls this scene to me.

4. Susan Chira, "Japan to File a Protest," *New York Times*, 16 April 1987.

5. Robert Christopher, *The Japanese Mind: The Goliath Explained* (New York: Linden, 1983).

6. Robert C. Christopher, *Second to None: American Companies in Japan* (New York: Crown, 1987).

3

A View from Washington

Michael H. Armacost

In viewing relations between the United States and Japan, it is critically important to keep in mind three fundamental ideas. The first is that the twenty-first century will be the Age of the Pacific. The second is that the U.S.-Japanese relationship is the most important bilateral relationship in the world and is taking on added significance with each passing day. The third is that the value of that relationship is measured not merely by the benefits it brings to our two nations but also by the capacity we possess jointly to ameliorate and resolve regional and international problems.

These are important truths. It is useful to remember them at a time when trade disputes dominate virtually all discussions of our relationship. The air seems filled with accusations, threats, and recriminations. The U.S. Congress is contemplating a plethora of protectionist bills, many aimed specifically at Japan, most containing threats of sanctions. Organized labor and many businesspeople speak of Japanese competition with awe, irritation, anger, a sense of grievance, a conviction that Americans do not enjoy "fair" access to Japan's markets, and fear of a rising tide of imports, not only in the manufacturing sectors but also in high-technology products, where, historically, the United States has long enjoyed a comparative advantage. In Japan, meanwhile, impatience with what is perceived to be the inconsistency of U.S. policy is increasing. Moreover, frustration with what are considered high-handed American pressure tactics is growing—even among those Japanese who reluctantly concede that without pressure, change comes too slowly.

Yet U.S. relations with Japan go well beyond the current trade frictions. The political, economic, and strategic interdependence between our countries has grown dramatically in recent years. Concerns about the equitable sharing of the burdens as well as the benefits of this relationship are quite natural and inevitable. Such concerns exist in relationship to any major country in the world with whom the United States has close ties. But a fair judgment of those equities is possible only if we consider the wider dimensions of our interaction with Japan.

Japan's Growing Weight in the World

Historians of the future are likely to regard former Prime Minister Nakasone as a towering figure. He guided Japan through a series of administrative and economic reforms designed to prepare his nation for the next century while assuming a wider range of international responsibilities. Japan's industrial and commercial prowess is now universally respected. But we sometimes forget how quickly those truly stunning achievements have been accomplished. Less than twenty years ago, Japan's per capita gross national product (GNP) was twentieth in the world; today it matches that of the United States. Japan alone produces fully one-tenth of the world's GNP. Together, the United States and Japan account for 60% of the output of the industrialized nations.

As a trading nation, Japan has few peers. In 1987, it ran an account surplus of nearly $97 billion. Japan is not only the major overseas trading partner of the United States but also surpasses all others in its bilateral trade with virtually every Asian country. Japanese companies are increasingly transnational. In 1985, Japan's nine top trading companies achieved more than $80 billion in offshore sales; that is, more than the total of their exports from Japan itself. Japanese industries are building much of their new manufacturing capacity outside Japan in order to capitalize on locally available raw materials and lower wages. In the process, they are spurring the export-led growth of many neighbors, contributing to the stability of East Asia, and becoming a provider as well as a beneficiary of technology transfers.

Japan has also become a major source of overseas investment. The yen has become a major form of international currency, and Tokyo is now a key financial center in the world economy. Yen-denominated Eurobonds now account for 15% of all Eurobonds issued. Twelve percent of international bank loans in 1987 were denominated in yen—a threefold increase since 1982. Seven of the ten largest commercial banks in the world are Japanese. Japan is the world's leading creditor nation, holding roughly $700 billion in overseas assets. More than one-fifth of that total may currently be invested in U.S. government securities, thereby helping to finance the U.S. fiscal deficit. Total capitalization of the Tokyo Stock Exchange exceeds that of the New York Stock Exchange. Nomura Securities, Ltd., is now the largest securities broker in the world. The lure of Japanese funds has proven so attractive that the Chicago Commodities Exchange initiated night trading several times a week to improve access for Japanese investors to U.S. commodities markets. Predictably, as Japan's financial power has increased, its stake in the economic stability and prosperity of other nations has grown.

Japan's influence on international economic policy deliberations also has increased. For example, Tokyo launched the General Agreement on Tariffs and Trade (GATT) round of tariff reductions in the 1970s. Japan is often a key participant in the summit meetings of the industrial democracies, and it was a prime mover in organizing the Uruguay Round of multilateral trade talks. It is a central player in the Group of Five (G-5) financial club, which handles sensitive financial issues, and has established a prominent presence wherever central bankers gather. You can be sure that the Japanese are present on the international stage and that they are very influential players.

Japan has become a prominent, indeed the preeminent, provider of assistance to developing countries. Its foreign aid budget has steadily expanded. Over the past five years, after the United States, Japan has been the largest aid donor in the Organization for Economic Cooperation and Development (OECD). In January 1989, the Japanese government announced its intention to increase its foreign aid budget to more than $10 billion. This will make Japan the largest donor and lender of development assistance in the world. In the past, Japan's aid effort was characterized by critics—with some justification—as an export subsidy program. Increasingly, its assistance efforts are being directed toward humanitarian and political aims as well as commercial objectives and the improvement of the global economic environment in which Japan— along with the rest of us—must live and work.

Japan, finally, is gradually assuming larger security responsibilities. To the relief of its neighbors, it continues to forswear the role of a great military power. Yet, stimulated by awareness of its growing economic status, buoyed by a sense of national pride, sensitive to U.S. pressures for a more equitable sharing of mutual defense burdens, and aroused by the continuing Soviet military buildup in Asia, Japan has steadily increased its defensive military capabilities to assume responsibility for its own conventional defense.

Today Japan's defense expenditures rank fifth in the world. The Japanese recently abandoned their traditional 1% of GNP ceiling on defense spending. Although Japan's Self-Defense Forces remain short on readiness and sustainability, they possess state-of-the-art equipment for command and control and maritime and air defense systems. The Japanese deploy more tactical fighter aircraft than do U.S. forces in

Asia, their navy fields more destroyers than does the U.S. Seventh Fleet, and they are developing a new front-line fighter aircraft.

The Japanese have broadened their self-defense missions to include sea-lanes up to 1,000 nautical miles south of Tokyo. They have embarked on a cautious but steady defense buildup aimed at acquiring the capabilities necessary to fulfill somewhat more ambitious roles and missions. Most important, Prime Minister Nakasone clearly placed Japan within the Western camp. In 1981, inclusion of the word "alliance" in a communiqué issued at the end of a visit by Prime Minister Suzuki to Washington nearly brought about the downfall of his government. At the Williamsburg summit in 1983, however, Prime Minister Nakasone asserted without any equivocation that "Japan is now firmly a member of the West," and he increasingly associated Japanese efforts with the broad aims of the Western alliance.

There are other indicators of the growing impact of Japan upon the world and of the world upon Japan. Twice as many Japanese travel abroad now as did so a decade ago. The number of Japanese businesspeople working overseas has more than tripled, as has the number of Japanese scientists serving abroad. The numbers of foreign businesspeople, students, and teachers residing in Japan have increased in a comparably dramatic fashion.

What is clear is this: Japan is no longer merely reacting to the vicissitudes of the external environment. It has become a powerful player on the international political and economic scene. It has identified itself with the Western industrial democracies. It is becoming "internationalized" in the sense that it recognizes not only that it has responsibilities to the international community but also that its self-interest requires it to meet those responsibilities.

Impact on U.S.-Japanese Relations

The transformation of Japan's international role is quite welcome in the United States, though some Americans appear to believe that it is "a day late and a dollar short." The biggest changes have come in the economic arena, where the relative balance of power between Japan and the United States has shifted dramatically. Even there, the impact has been mixed. For one thing, there is universal admiration for the quality of Japanese products. Consumers vote with their pocketbooks, and Japanese manufacturers have won a resounding endorsement. Then, too, an infrastructure for supporting imports from Japan has emerged involving those in marketing distribution, service and maintenance, and financial institutions. These sectors of the U.S. economy have an active and tangible interest in keeping the U.S. market doors open to

Japan. The strength of Japan's trading position and the size of its bilateral trade surplus with the United States has provoked strong reactions, stimulated a searching look at Japanese trading practices at home and abroad, and fueled protectionism—particularly in the unions, in the business community, in the Democratic party, and in Congress. Hypotheses regarding the root causes of the trade imbalance abound, ranging from crude shibboleths to sophisticated theories. The former frequently dominate public discussions and typically focus on complaints that Japan is never willing to open its market or, on the other end of the spectrum, that U.S. businesspeople are not trying hard enough to crack the Japanese market.

The Reagan administration shunned both simplistic explanations and simple-minded remedies when faced with this situation. It was guided by the following general premises: (1) trade deficits of the magnitude we have run in recent years are neither politically nor economically sustainable, and adjustments must and will be achieved; (2) in promoting a more balanced trade, we should rely on measures that expand rather than contract commercial exchanges; (3) we should preserve open markets and shun the regulation or cartelization of trade.

In keeping with this approach, the administration undertook a variety of efforts to redress the bilateral trade deficit. Voluntary export restraints were instituted to cope with the rapid expansion of Japanese car imports in the early 1980s. Voluntary restraints were also utilized to protect critical industries like machine tools and steel. In 1985, the United States initiated a series of sectoral negotiations—the market-oriented, sector-selective (MOSS) talks—designed to open up the Japanese market in fields such as telecommunications, forest products, electronics, pharmaceuticals, and medical equipment—products in which the United States is competitive if the playing field is level. U.S. exports in these sectors are clearly up. Major efforts have also been devoted to achieving greater market access in Japan for leather and tobacco products, and sanctions have been invoked to induce compliance with an agreement on semiconductors.

Of greater significance, the United States has worked to encourage adjustments in the relationship between the dollar and the yen—a factor that affects U.S. trade competitiveness across the board. Since 1985, the yen has appreciated by 60% against the dollar, or conversely, the dollar has depreciated 60% against the yen. It is important to remember in all of this, of course, that the market is producing these changes. Something like $170 to $200 billion is traded on any given day in the markets in Tokyo, New York, London, and other security markets. Any government may at most intervene with sales or purchases of, say, $0.5 billion to influence currency fluctuations. This amount obviously does not add up to very much given the magnitude of private transactions. For this reason, these changes are not susceptible to significant manipulation by the U.S. government or by others; instead, they reflect market reactions to the underlying shape of economic power. Although the expected impact on the trade deficit has been slow in appearing, major adjustments are inevitable, and recent statistics suggest they have begun to occur.

As concern about the trade imbalance grew, the Reagan administration's attention turned increasingly to structural imbalances in our respective economies that affect our trading relations. Of paramount importance in Japan is the imbalance between the rate of domestic savings, which remains very high, and domestic investment, which is relatively low. This persistent imbalance reinforces Japan's time-honored reliance upon the export sector to sustain high growth. Japanese economists and officials have belatedly acknowledged this imbalance. The highly regarded Maekawa Report concluded that the Japanese government should shift to a greater reliance on domestic demand for growth. While the report occasioned laudatory editorials, its conclusions are only now beginning to be implemented by policymakers.

During former Prime Minister Nakasone's last visit to Washington, he foreshadowed a $35-billion supplemental budget request to the Diet to stimulate domestic demand. News reports subsequently indicated Cabinet approval of a slightly higher fiscal stimulus package to the tune of $42 billion in increased public works spending and a tax cut. Prime Minister Takeshita appears to be continuing this encouraging development.

We know, of course, that the U.S. fiscal deficit has an impact on U.S. competitiveness in international markets. The Gramm-Rudman-Hollings legislation reflects congressional awareness of this problem. The Reagan administration certainly recognized that the fiscal deficit must be brought under control, and it did begin the task of addressing systematically how adjustments of public policy in other areas (e.g., education, research and development policy) could help restore U.S. competitiveness.

Finally, the United States joined with Japan and others to promote the Uruguay Round of GATT trade negotiations and made certain that the issues of greatest U.S. concern—such as services trade, high-technology goods, and agriculture—were high on the agenda of those negotiations. We can assume that the new administration of President George Bush will continue this approach.

These efforts have not yet succeeded in restoring a balanced trade with Japan, although the size of the deficit is on its way down. The underlying problems are being addressed, however, and the steps taken are beginning to produce results. It is therefore perplexing that Congress keeps rushing to pass protectionist legislation that would disrupt trade and place bilateral cooperation between the United States and Japan on other fronts in some jeopardy. Trade clearly has been the area where the United States has felt the biggest impact of the growth of Japan's power.

A second major adjustment in U.S.-Japanese economic relations stems from the growing volume of cross-border investment. Japanese investment in production facilities in the United States is growing rapidly; U.S. investment in Japan is also increasing, albeit at a slower clip. This two-way flow of investment funds creates jobs, blunts protectionist pressures, and familiarizes the people in each country with the management practices and labor relations traditions of the other. This process is breaking down economic barriers and should, in time, dampen some of the tensions stimulated by trade frictions. This, too, is a very positive development.

Japan's status as a major aid donor is a third development affecting our bilateral relationship. Japan's augmented assistance efforts increasingly compensate for recent shortfalls in our own foreign aid budget. The Japanese, who recognize the constraints on their ability to assume a major military role, regard their economic assistance as a contribution to Western security, because it enhances the stability of critically important Third World countries. Japanese assistance to important Asian nations like Korea, the Philippines, Indonesia, and Thailand, as well as nations farther afield (e.g., Pakistan, Turkey, Egypt, Zambia, Zaire, Kenya, Jamaica, and Honduras) represents evidence of this "comprehensive security" policy approach in action. The drastic congressional cuts in U.S. foreign assistance have made Japan's rapidly expanding economic assistance all the more critical to developing countries facing crushing debt burdens.

Finally, as Japan's defense capabilities grow, our mutual security arrangements with Japan will become a more operationally relevant feature of the balance of forces in East Asia. U.S.-Japanese defense cooperation has grown impressively in recent years. Host nation support for U.S. forces in Japan has increased dramatically. Japan provides homeports for the only U.S. carrier battle group based abroad. Joint planning—virtually unthinkable in the early 1970s—has become routine. Joint exercises have increased in number and scope. Technology-sharing agreements have been negotiated that assure a two-way street in defense research and development efforts, and professional relations between our military establishments have been placed on a firm footing.

While Japan has assumed more ambitious self-defense roles and missions, the broad contours of our strategic division of labor remain intact. These are worth reciting. The United States supports Japan by extending a nuclear umbrella, by protecting long-distance sea-lanes of communication and trade, and by maintaining a military presence in the western Pacific to assure an adequate regional deterrent. Japan, meanwhile, has assumed responsibility for its own conventional defense, is providing growing financial and other support for our residual military presence—thereby facilitating the efficient and cost-effective projection of U.S. power into East Asia and the western Pacific and Indian Oceans— and is contributing to mutual security interests by extending generous aid to other U.S. allies such as South Korea, the Philippines, and Thailand and front-line states like Pakistan and Turkey beyond the rim of Asia. Defense and international political cooperation has grown, despite the accumulation of frictions.

Our Present Dilemma

It is perhaps notable that whereas in the past complaints about Japan's so-called "free ride" in defense have been symptomatic of trading problems, this time both nations, for reasons of their respective interests, have managed to segregate defense cooperation and trade issues rather successfully. Within the U.S.-Japanese relationship, what we have seen is a growing economic and strategic interdependence. Our mutual commitments are so extensive and our destinies so closely tied to each other that we have virtually no alternative but to muddle through any present difficulties. But clearly, we are going through a rough patch. Mainly, this difficulty reflects the fact that U.S. expectations of a new pattern of international burdensharing have outpaced the rate at which Japan has taken on new international responsibilities. The result is frustration, a preoccupation with questions of fairness, and a need to take a harder look at ways of redressing the balance of benefits and burdens in the relationship.

Within the U.S.-Japanese alliance, we have constantly had to reconfigure the distribution of political burdens. In the past, Americans shouldered a disproportionate share of those burdens, and we were willing to do so. But the bilateral balance of economic strength has changed. A growing trade deficit, the political pressures stimulated by intense Japanese competition, and the restrictions of our federal budget have all increased pressures for more rapid adjustments in the redistribution of international burdens than the Japanese political system has thus far produced.

In Japan, meanwhile, growing economic strength is inspiring a more ambitious vision of Japan's international role, yet it also fuels resistance to criticism and advice from abroad—particularly when such advice is offered publicly. The Japanese have also begun to offer more forthright expressions of their own assessments of U.S. economic performance and international strategy. The potential for friction grows as U.S.-Japanese interdependence expands. These tendencies are natural, but knowing this does not make the adjustment any easier.

Japan has achieved remarkable stability and growth through reliance on consensus-building techniques of policymaking. Opposition to new initiatives is worn down, coopted, encircled, and enveloped. The results have been impressive. But it is a time-consuming process, and Americans are an impatient people. The problem is not that Japan has refused to accept new international responsibilities, but that there is a disparity between what the United States sees as a set of reasonable expectations—and what the political process in Japan is able to produce. The heaviest burdens of adjustment tend to fall to the strongest nations. With Japan's growing strength, it is natural to expect some acceleration in the pace at which it takes on broader responsibilities.

The Future Agenda

Over the past several decades, the United States has created an elaborate superstructure for consultations with the Japanese. We talk a great deal with each other. Contacts have proliferated between our respective bureaucracies. At the highest level, our political leaders not only know each other but even like each other. Given the importance of our relationship to both countries and to the world, it is essential that we reach some broad understandings on key issues through mutual give and take.

Bilateral Trade

The U.S. trade deficit will have to be reduced. The only question is whether the reduction will be accomplished in a manner that strengthens or weakens the broader U.S.-Japanese relationship. On the U.S. side, it is important that we resist the temptation to legislate ill-considered protectionist measures. While protectionism may offer temporary relief to some producers, it will also reduce opportunities for American consumers to buy high-quality products at reasonable prices; remove the spur of competition from our industry; encourage inflation; invite retaliation; introduce rigidities into the international trading system; and exacerbate tensions among the Western democracies at a time when unity, cohesion, and cooperation are needed.

The United States must deal forthrightly with its huge budget deficit. Market-opening efforts with Japan and others will not bring benefits to the United States unless U.S. businesses do their homework and aggressively work to sell their products in one of the most sophisticated markets in the world. And we need to restore for the long term the sources of our competitiveness in the field of trade.

On Japan's side, it is essential that wider access to its market be promptly extended. It always takes time to translate professions of intent into results. But now is the time for action, particularly with respect to Japan's recent efforts to stimulate domestic demand and spur higher growth. Prompt implementation will provide an acid test of Japan's commitment to diminishing reliance upon export-led growth.

Aid and the Debt Problem

As the U.S. budget deficit has grown, congressional support for foreign aid has diminished. Over the past three years, Congress has cut the international affairs budget by more than 25%. These cuts are unwise and imprudent. They are "penny wise and pound foolish." They offer little immediate budgetary relief while jeopardizing long-term interests. This is *our* problem. We must deal with it. We will, but it may take time.

In the meantime, Japan's aid efforts become all the more critical. The United States welcomes the large prospective increases in Japan's foreign assistance budget. I hope to see Japan's concessionality of loan terms improved even further, along with an increase in the grant component of Japanese aid. I think we may realistically anticipate a doubling of overall Japanese assistance levels within the next few years, and I hope that a disproportionate share of the increases will be devoted to areas other than Asia, which currently absorbs 70% of all Japanese aid. Asia is important, and Japan's assistance programs have contributed to the remarkable growth and stability of that area. But the vitality and resilience of the Pacific Basin permits increased attention to other, less fortunate regions. In particular, expanded efforts are warranted in Central America, where fledgling democracies are struggling to consolidate recent political and economic reforms; in Southern Africa, where the "front-line countries" are vulnerable to economic sanctions from Pretoria; and in the Middle East, where declining economic fortunes in countries like Egypt and Jordan pose challenges to regional stability.

Japan, moreover, is well-positioned to take a larger leadership role in dealing with Third World debt problems. Indebtedness of developing countries is growing. Efforts to reduce the U.S. trade deficit may impinge on the export earnings of these countries, and reductions in the U.S. aid budget hamper the ability of the United States to encourage needed policy reforms. Austerity has eroded the political framework that enabled Third World leaders to accord priority to debt servicing over domestic growth. Japan's role in augmenting its own growth, opening its markets, and expanding capital transfers to less developed countries is crucial.

Japan's plan to make $20 billion of foreign exchange earning available to debtor nations through a combination of untied export credits, increased contributions to multilateral development banks, and loans jointly financed by government and private institutions is particularly timely. The United States shall await details with interest and a certain amount of envy.

Not long ago, the United States marked the fortieth anniversary of the Marshall Plan for European recovery, which I believe Winston Churchill once characterized as one of the most magnanimous acts of enlightened self-interest in the history of diplomacy. It was an act in which Americans can take great pride, as it produced tremendous results for the United States and for Europe over a lengthy period. One would wish that the United States again was in a position to set a comparable ambitious target. Japan, on the other hand, is in a strong position. It has great financial resources, and it has a stake in the resolution of debt problems. This is an area where Japan could take a strong leadership role and, judging from recent announcements, it apparently is preparing to do so. In June 1988, just prior to the Toronto summit, for example, Prime Minister Noboru Takeshita unveiled a $10 billion foreign aid package, thus making Japan the world's largest donor.

Mutual Security

The United States and Japan must also continue to deepen their defense cooperation. In this area, Americans remain deeply ambivalent. Some apparently wish to see a Japan with sufficient military power to counter the Russians yet without so much as to reawaken the fears of neighbors like the Chinese and Koreans. This is a difficult trick to pull off. Undoubtedly, Japan could do more to improve its defenses. One percent of GNP was a very modest ceiling for defense spending. We need have no fear that breaching it will revive Japanese militarism. The United States devotes 7% of its own GNP to defense. The accelerated fulfillment of Japan's mid-range plans for augmented self-defense capabilities is fully justified, and it poses no threat to Japan's neighbors.

Yet Asian nations do have their own concerns about the magnitude of Japan's defense effort. And the Japanese are appropriately sensitive to those concerns, as the United States should be. That means, above all, that the United States should continue to sustain a strong alliance with Japan. We should not encourage Japan to assume overseas military responsibilities; neither Tokyo nor its neighbors desire this. We should remain attentive to Japanese interests as we pursue our own arms control negotiations with the Soviet Union. We should continue to support Japan's historic experiment in attaining economic superpower status while maintaining relatively modest military capabilities. Since Japanese defense expenditures are limited, and interoperability of equipment is critical to close U.S.-Japanese defense coordination, the United States should continue to encourage cost-effective decisions on major defense procurement items such as the FSX fighter.

International Political Issues

Finally, the United States should broaden its consultations with Japan on international political issues. In areas like the Persian Gulf, the United States is stepping up its responsibilities because it is a global superpower with an enduring interest in protecting an extremely valuable international waterway from encroachment by the Soviet Union. This project necessarily entails some added costs and risks for the United States. Others will benefit; indeed, Japan has considerable interests in the Gulf. Japan's Constitution and its politics deprive it of any military role in the Gulf. But its political influence can be brought to bear along with other Western nations to encourage restraint and to promote a resolution of the Iran-Iraq war while perhaps making nonmilitary contributions to Western efforts to protect free navigation there.

Conclusion

An ambitious agenda obviously awaits both Americans and Japanese who are interested in preserving and deepening the cooperation that has served both our nations so well for more than a generation. I am confident that our friendship and cooperation will be sustained. The best means of assuring this alliance will be to take to heart Jean Monnet's wise dictum that, instead of sitting across the table from each other arguing and complaining, we should sit beside one another, place the problem on the other side of the table, and work together to find a mutually acceptable solution and to recognize our shared destinies. That certainly would be in keeping with the spirit in which Mike Mansfield has approached the relationship between Japan and the United States.

Suggestions for Further Reading

Barnett, Robert, *Beyond War: Japan's Concept of Comprehensive National Security* (Elmsford, NY: Pergamon-Brassey, 1984).

Buss, Claude A., ed., *National Security Interests in the Pacific Basin* (Stanford, CA: Hoover Institution, 1985).

"Japan: From Superrich to Superpower," *Time*, 4 July 1988, pp. 28–31.

Japan Defense Agency, *Defense of Japan, 1987* (Tokyo: Japan Times, 1987).

Kihl, Young W. and Lawrence E. Grinter, eds., *Asian-Pacific Security: Emerging Challenges and Responses* (Boulder, CO: Lynne Rienner, 1986).

Morley, James, ed., *Security Interdependence in the Asia Pacific Region* (Lexington, MA: Lexington Books, 1986).

Sigur, Gaston, "Current Reflections on U.S.-Japan Relations," U.S. Department of State, *Current Policy No. 1056* (Washington, D.C.: Government Printing Office, 1988).

Sigur, Gaston and Y. C. Kim, *Japanese and U.S. Policy in Asia* (New York: Praeger, 1982).

Sneider, Richard, *US-Japan Security Relations: A Historical Perspective* (New York: East Asian Institute, Columbia University, 1982).

4

The U.S.-Japanese
Security Relationship:
Retrospect and Prospect

Raymond F. Wylie

After many false starts, the much heralded Age of the Pacific appears to have arrived.[1] Spearheaded by Japan, most of the nations of the western Pacific are setting the global pace in economic growth. With a gross national product (GNP) well over $2 trillion, Japan now ranks second only to the United States and has surpassed it in GNP per capita. Nor are the smaller nations of the region lagging behind. The "four little dragons" (South Korea, Taiwan, Hong Kong, and Singapore) are an example for newly industrializing countries (NICs) everywhere. And China, with its vast human and physical resources, is making significant headway with an ambitious program of "four modernizations" in agriculture, industry, science and technology, and national defense.

To many observers around the world, the nations of the Pacific rim seem to have an "edge" over traditional economic centers such as Western Europe and the United States itself.[2] For Americans a handy benchmark for the arrival of the Age of the Pacific is 1980, when for the first time ever United States trade with the Far East surpassed that with Europe. Since then the gap has continued to widen.

From the perspective of strategic affairs, the rapidly growing importance of the Asia-Pacific region was apparent at the end of World War II. The Pacific War and the subsequent defeat and occupation of Japan placed the United States in the center of the international relations of the region. This development, coupled with the failure of the intervention in China and the unexpected victory of the Chinese Communists, forced Washington to modify its traditional preoccupation with Europe. Despite constant sabre-rattling in Europe in the postwar years, it was the western Pacific where the United States was to engage in direct military conflict. The Korean War proved costly to the United States (and its antagonists), but at least a claim of partial victory could be made. In Vietnam the costs were even greater, but there U.S. losses could not be justified by any compensating gain. On the contrary, Vietnam dealt a severe blow both to U.S. domestic stability and military self-confidence from which the United States has not recovered even today. The Nixon (Guam) Doctrine of 1969 set the stage for a fundamental reappraisal of U.S. security interests in the region and a reformulation of the role of the United States and its fellow protagonists, friend and foe alike.

Not surprising in light of previous attitudes, this reappraisal maintained Washington's focus on the Soviet Union as the greatest potential threat to the stability of the Asia-Pacific region. But it also called for a readjustment in U.S. relations with the other key players in the area— China and Japan. As it happened, forces in both Washington and Beijing were ready for a new course, and by 1978–1979 the two sides had agreed to reopen formal diplomatic relations and to seek common security interests vis-à-vis the growing power of Moscow in the Soviet Far East and elsewhere in Asia.

This turn of events still left the issue of Japan. Since 1951 the U.S.-Japanese alliance has been the cornerstone of Washington's military posture in the western Pacific, and it has served its purpose well. From its Japanese base, the United States was able to project its power into Northeast Asia with great conviction, and Japan, for its part, benefited from the U.S. military shield at very little financial cost. This arrangement proved satisfactory for everyone concerned: Tokyo could devote its energies to stimulating economic recovery at home, while Washington could pursue its strategic objectives in the region with little interference from its nominal ally.

By the late 1970s, however, this arrangement came under closer scrutiny in Washington as a result of Japan's unprecedented "economic miracle" and the United States's faltering performance in sustaining the economic vitality upon which its military prowess ultimately depends. To increasing numbers of Americans it seemed that Japan was getting a "free ride" on defense and security matters at the expense of the beleaguered American taxpayer. To the Japanese, who despite their U.S.-imposed "peace constitution" have the fifth largest military budget in the world as of 1988–1989, the "free ride" thesis had a false ring. It appeared that Americans were merely venting their frustration with their own domestic and foreign problems on the Japanese because Japan was upstaging the United States on the global economic scene.

This sometimes acrimonious debate over defense sharing has introduced another discordant note into the U.S.-Japanese relationship. Like the concurrent controversy over the "level playing field" in the economic and trade sectors, it has led to considerable strains between the two leading members of the "trilateral group" of democratic nations. Yet times of stress and challenge, though often fraught with danger, also afford opportunities for thoughtful reassessment of the past and the setting of a new course for the future.[3] In this sense, the years ahead to the turn of the century will almost certainly constitute a watershed in U.S.-Japanese relations as both sides adjust to changed circumstances that hold both promise and peril. It will be a test of the political acumen and diplomacy of Japanese and Americans alike to articulate a new vision of their global roles that will set the stage for their mutual benefit and continuing friendship for years to come.

The Bilateral Security Relationship

The U.S.-Japanese security relationship is a product of Japan's defeat and occupation by the United States in the aftermath of World War II. It is not a partnership established on the basis of equality; rather, Washington set the terms which Tokyo, with minor modifications, was induced to accept. Over the years since the peace treaty signed in 1951 Tokyo has scrupulously adhered to the spirit and the letter of these original terms while the United States has gradually grown dissatisfied with the limitations it imposed on Japan's military role within the alliance. During the 1980s this dissatisfaction has grown increasingly vocal, culminating in the often acrimonious "free ride" debate of today.

The bilateral security relationship is based on three pillars: (1) the 1947 Japanese Constitution, particularly Article 9; (2) the Treaty of Mutual Security and Cooperation, signed in 1951 (or Mutual Security Treaty); (3) the Mutual Defense Assistance Agreement of 1954. Article 9 of the Constitution (the so-called "peace clause") denied Japan the right to use force in the resolution of international disputes and, in keeping with this principle, prohibited the maintenance of "land, sea, and air forces, as well as other war potential."[4] With Japan thus disarmed and defenseless, something was needed to guarantee its security in the dangerous international currents of the Cold War years. This was the Mutual Security Treaty, which placed Japan under the conventional and nuclear umbrella of the United States. This treaty required Washington to come to Japan's military assistance if any outside power assaulted either Japanese or U.S. personnel on Japanese territory. It did not, it should be noted, place an equal obligation on Japan to render assistance if Americans were attacked anywhere outside Japan. In this sense, then, the alliance is not one of equals based on the principle of mutual assistance. It was and remains a promise by the United States to defend Japan should it be attacked by an outside power; no names were mentioned, but the potential aggressors were presumed to be the Soviet Union and/or Communist China.

The final element in the security relationship was the Mutual Defense Assistance Agreement of 1954, which was negotiated as part of an important reinterpretation of the Constitution dating back to 1950. Under the new reading of Article 9 Japan was to be permitted to rebuild a postwar military capability for purely defensive purposes. The development of the new military was accomplished in stages: the army (National Police Reserve) in 1950; a naval component in 1952; and an air force group in 1954. Finally, also in 1954, laws were enacted to consolidate these separate forces into a new Self-Defense Force (SDF) and to place operational control of the military under a subcabinet Japan Defense Agency (JDA). The JDA was made fully responsible to civilian control encompassing the prime minister, the cabinet, and ultimately the Diet (the national parliament) itself. Under the terms of the Mutual Defense Assistance Agreement, the United States undertook to provide the fledgling Self-Defense Forces with whatever training and equipment, including weapons, were required for the performance of their duties.[5]

The reinterpretation of the Constitution and the reestablishment of the military were not accomplished without a good deal of turmoil in Japanese society. Liberals and progressives of every stripe, including opposition political parties, trade unions, students, and many of the intelligentsia, vociferously opposed these developments, but to no avail. Opposition was most organized and militant in 1960 when the Mutual Security Treaty came up for renewal, leading to widespread demonstrations in Tokyo and throughout the country. With minor modifications calling for greater consultation and the termination of the U.S. role in internal security matters, the revised treaty was pushed through the Diet by Prime Minister Nobusuki Kishi. He thereupon resigned in the interests of restoring social harmony. The crisis soon passed, and to many it seemed that the renewed alliance would continue very much along the lines laid down in the 1950s.[6]

Despite recurring controversies over the U.S. military bases in Japan, the passage of United States nuclear weapons through Japanese territory, and the status of Okinawa, the security relationship remained intact throughout the 1960s. But soon forces were afoot that were to call into question the very basis of the alliance and to inject a note of animosity into continuing negotiations between Washington and Tokyo. Hayato Ikeda, who succeeded Kishi as prime minister in 1960, launched his now-famous "income doubling" economic program in part, at least, to turn the Japanese people away from the contentious security issues of the previous decade. Under Ikeda and his successors, Japan laid the foundations of the "economic miracle" that was to transform Japan and bring it into head-on trade competition with the United States.

The United States, for its part, had plunged into an ultimately disastrous war in Vietnam, leading many Japanese to fear being dragged into this or any other U.S. military adventure in Asia. Even to pro-American Japanese, it seemed that the security alliance had potential costs as well as benefits and that a more skeptical attitude was called for regarding the link with Washington. Japanese skepticism was further fueled by the Nixon Doctrine of 1969, which cautioned America's Asian allies that the United States could no longer shoulder the primary responsibility for their domestic and external security. Henceforth, they would have to devote more of their own manpower and resources to this end, even if this meant sacrifices at home.[7]

In retrospect the stresses in the U.S.-Japanese alliance in the 1960s, while real enough, pale in comparison with the shocks of the 1970s. It was during this decade that the sharp tone characteristic of today's security debate began to creep into the relationship. By and large the initiatives came from the American side, but they were amplified and deepened by developments elsewhere. Between 1971 and 1974, President Richard Nixon, without consulting Tokyo, announced a series of moves that severely affected Japan: a sudden rapprochement with the People's Republic of China; the effective devaluation of the dollar with the subsequent appreciation of the yen; a 10% surcharge on all imports (including Japanese goods); and a temporary reduction in exports of U.S. soybeans to Japan.

The Japanese response was at first bewilderment, then anger; not only were most of these measures harmful to Japan's interests but they were enacted without prior consultation, let alone agreement, with Tokyo. Although Washington later took steps to conciliate Tokyo on a number of these issues, the damage had been done. To many Japanese their American friend and protector was becoming increasingly unpredictable and high-handed. This development suggested that greater caution in dealing with subsequent issues between the two partners was in order. Based on extensive public opinion surveys in Japan in 1982–1983, William Watts identified the "lack of consultation and continuity" of U.S. policy during the Nixon years as part of a "catalogue of ills" that continue to afflict the conduct of U.S.-Japanese relations.[8]

To the "Nixon shocks" was added, in 1973, the "OPEC shock." In the aftermath of the 1973 Arab-Israeli War, the largely Arab Organization of Petroleum Exporting Countries (OPEC) imposed an oil embargo (followed by greatly increased prices) on the United States and its allies, including Japan. The oil embargo, although short-lived, sent shock waves throughout Japan, which was (and still is) highly dependent on the Middle East for its vital supply of petroleum. With the costs of following the United States lead in policy toward Israel so starkly real, Tokyo immediately began to disengage from Washington and sought to rebuild its bridges with the Arab Middle East. This move not unnaturally aroused resentment in the United States, which was further exacerbated by Tokyo's reluctance to support America's position during the Iranian hostage crisis of 1978 and its equivocation when the Soviets invaded Afghanistan the following year.

Although the worst damage to U.S.-Japanese relations occasioned by these disputes was eventually repaired, there was no concealing the bitter residue it left behind. On one hand, to many Americans it appeared that Japan was at best a fair-weather friend who could not be trusted to stand by in times of need. To the Japanese, on the other hand, it did not seem to be in their own national interest to be dragged into U.S. disputes of which they had no part and in which they had no interest. Both Japan and the United States wanted the mutual benefits of their alliance, but both recognized that the alliance could entail considerable costs as well.

Behind these quarrels, and in part disguised by them, lay the overriding development that was to force the security issue fully into the open. This was Tokyo's continuing economic resurgence, which by the end of the 1970s had positioned Japan as the second largest economy in the pro-Western bloc and made it the foremost economic competitor of the United States. Japanese manufactured goods were flooding into the United States and many other global markets, and the first signs of a bilateral trade imbalance in Japan's favor had appeared. Worse still, many of America's own economic indicators were beginning to falter; traditional industries such as steel and automobiles slumped badly in the face of their own inefficiencies and the Japanese trade onslaught.

To many Americans, including those in official positions, the situation with Japan had become particularly difficult by the early 1980s. Not only were the Japanese judged to be uncertain friends on critical security issues but they were financially negligent as well. Thus the "free ride" thesis, which became current in the late 1970s, encapsulated two distinct meanings: Not only did the United States have to pick up most of the cost for Japan's national security, but it also had to "carry" Japan in the performance of the West's security obligations in the Middle East and other global flash points. And all this at a time when, at least in part because of its resort to "unfair" trade practices, Japan was bleeding the U.S. economy white.

The upshot of these ominous developments was a call, largely (but not entirely) on the part of Washington, for Tokyo to rethink its security position and its role within the evolving U.S.-Japanese alliance. During the stresses and strains (and even the "shocks") of the previous decades, the security relationship had largely escaped close scrutiny, at least in part because of the need for unity in the face of a perceived common enemy, namely, the Soviet Union and/or Communist China. But in the changed political circumstances of the post-Vietnam era, and in light of the massive trade imbalance against the United States, Washington's security differences with Tokyo could no longer be ignored. In the words of one foreign observer, the security issue had at long last "come out of the closet."[9]

The "Free Ride" Debate

U.S. critics of Japan's defense effort have focused on three main issues: (1) a lack of a credible strategic doctrine; (2) a reluctance to cooperate with U.S. regional policies; (3) and a failure to assume a "fair share" of defense costs. These dissatisfactions, though serious, should be seen in the context of the overall security picture. The United States and Japan both have a strong geopolitical interest in maintaining a stable balance of power in the Asia-Pacific region; this is especially true regarding Northeast Asia, where Korea remains potentially volatile and subject to outside intervention. In light of this, the U.S.-Japanese alliance provides a significant counterbalance to growing Soviet and Chinese power in the region. Washington and Tokyo are equally cognizant of the deterrent effect of the alliance and have no desire to call its fundamental value into question. Rather, the current controversy revolves around the relative contributions of the two allies in pursuing the common goal of maintaining a stable balance of power in the western Pacific. For both Washington and Tokyo, Japan's potential security role in global regions other than the Far East is a matter of secondary concern and will remain so for the foreseeable future.

American critics have charged that Japan's strategic doctrine lacks a global perspective, underestimates the Soviet threat, and encourages ad hoc, piecemeal responses to critical world issues. The Japanese have responded by reaffirming their commitment to the doctrine of "comprehensive national security," a concept dating at least to 1957 when the Defense Agency issued its *Basic Policy for National Defense*. As the term implies, national security is seen as a complex set of variables of which military power is not necessarily the most important. In its current formulation, "comprehensive security" is based on the proposition that Japan can be secure only if the following nonmilitary objectives are met: domestic tranquillity and economic prosperity; international stability in the East Asian region; an open trading system for raw materials and manufactured goods; and global cooperation through multilateral institutions. At the same time the purely military dimension is not overlooked: Japan's national defense needs are to be provided for primarily by the U.S.-Japanese Mutual Security Treaty and only secondarily by Japan's own Self-Defense Forces.[10] In Tokyo's view, this arrangement provided the original basis of the security relationship with the United States and no pressing need for radical change has yet emerged.

In the Japanese prism neither the Soviet Union nor China poses the kind of military threat, immediate or potential, that has often characterized U.S. strategic doctrine. Attitudes in Japan toward China are highly ambivalent: The Japanese greatly admire Chinese history and culture but are puzzled over China's apparent inability to stabilize and develop economically. Fears of Chinese military aggression do not figure prominently in Japanese opinion, whether among the political elite or in the eyes of the average citizen. The Soviet Union is another matter. The Japanese tend to be suspicious of and to some degree hostile toward the Soviet Union, an attitude that can be traced back to the rivalry between imperial Russia and the rising Japanese empire at the turn of the century. Nor is the Soviet image enhanced by the continuing dispute between the two sides over the Northern Territories, a cluster of small islands the Soviets occupy as part of the postwar disposition of the Kurile Islands in favor of Moscow. Even so, Japanese concerns over the alleged Soviet threat are rather muted in contrast to the vivid hostilities typical of American images of the Soviet Union and its role in international affairs.[11] It therefore follows that to many Japanese, the military buildup envisioned by Washington, at least in its more extreme manifestations, is neither needed nor desired.

With its lack of a firm ideological fix directed against the Soviet Union, "comprehensive security" suggests to Tokyo the importance of viewing regional conflicts on a case-by-case basis; there is no imperative to tie them into the global East-West struggle between Washington and Moscow. For Tokyo the key question is and must always be: How does a given regional issue affect Japan, and what steps can Japan take to protect and/or promote Japanese interests?

Although previous Japanese leaders were slow to respond to United States pressures on security issues, this was not true of Yasuhiro Nakasone, who became prime minister in 1982. Nakasone was personally well disposed toward Washington's entreaties on security matters, but even so, he had to persuade his political colleagues in the Liberal

Democratic party to go along. Fortunately for him, the timing was right. The Japanese ruling elite had taken into account the momentous changes in the international system in the post-Vietnam era. They had recognized, in the words of the influential 1980 *Report on Comprehensive National Security*, that "In considering the question of Japan's security, the most fundamental change in the international situation that took place in the 1970s is the termination of clear American supremacy in both military and economic spheres. . . . As a result, U.S. military power is no longer able to provide its allies and friends with nearly full security."[12] With this thinking in mind, Nakasone, upon assuming power two years later, was in a position to start Japan along the road to a slow and deliberate enhancement of the nation's military capabilities.

Accommodations were made in response to Washington's prodding on the following: better cooperation on important regional issues, such as Afghanistan, sea-lane patrols, and the Persian Gulf; more foreign aid to Third World countries with fewer strings attached; certain aid targeted to countries of special concern to the United States, such as Egypt, Pakistan, and Thailand; transfer of militarily related technologies to the United States; more joint planning and maneuvers between Japanese and U.S. armed forces, and so on. Already, though, U.S. critics are suggesting that there is less to many of these agreements than meets the eye; in the case of technology transfers, for example, it seems that few concrete results have been achieved thus far.[13] Indeed, in the eyes of many frustrated American critics, these various agreements are examples of the "too little, too late" syndrome—and even then granted begrudgingly only under intense U.S. pressure.

In addition to strategic doctrine and regional cooperation, Washington also has found fault with Tokyo regarding the level of spending on the Self-Defense Forces. It is above all the symbolic issue of the 1% of GNP cap (approximate) that Tokyo has placed on defense spending that has become the focus of the current dispute. In a world where the Western democracies are prepared to commit significant proportions of their GNPs to defense (6–7% in the case of the United States), Japan is sometimes said to be getting a "free ride" at the expense of everyone else, especially the American taxpayer.

What is often overlooked is that as Japan's GNP has increased over the years, so has the value of the 1%; in 1988–1989 for example, it amounted to approximately $30 billion, placing Japan in fifth place in the global defense spending race. Also, if Japan's defense-related spending is calculated on the same basis as that of the NATO countries, that is, with pension payments factored in, then Tokyo devotes some 1.7% of GNP to this area.[14] The Self-Defense Forces are by no means negligible: Some 243,000 strong (currently under authorized strength), they are by world standards well educated, well trained, and well equipped. They do of course lack actual combat experience, and it is unlikely that Tokyo would authorize the use of Japanese troops in any conflict outside Japan itself.

Washington has never spelled out exactly how much Japan should be spending on national defense, but obviously many in the United States feel that more than 1% is in order. (One enterprising U.S. Congressman, Stephen Neal, Democrat of North Carolina, put forward the notion in 1981 that Japan should pay Washington a "security tax" of 2% of GNP annually. Not surprisingly, this idea was greeted with derision in Tokyo and failed to attract support in the United States.) This pressure puts even promilitary leaders (such as Nakasone) in a quandary: While the 1% cap is not official policy, and even though it has recently been breached a bit, there is little popular support in Japan for any radical departure from the formula. On the contrary, despite muted support from conservatives and defense-oriented industrial leaders, a sharp increase over 1% would likely occasion stiff opposition. Nor would the Ministry of Finance, which is beleaguered by a persistent budget deficit, be enthusiastic about the idea. This is not to mention the alarm that would be triggered in much of East and Southeast Asia, whose peoples have suffered from a strong Japanese military in the past.

It is perhaps worth noting that the United States is sending mixed signals to Japan, for many Americans themselves are hesitant about encouraging Tokyo along the road to rearmament. On one occasion in 1977, in obvious frustration at U.S. ambivalence on the issue, Nakasone was moved to exclaim to a Washington audience that the United States should decide whether it wants Japan to "get on or get off the bus."[15] This ambivalence in American attitudes continues to the present time. Generally speaking, the most strident calls for Japan to "do its share" in security matters come from Congress, some of whose members have even threatened to "renegotiate" the alliance to Tokyo's detriment if acceptable changes in Japanese policy are not forthcoming. Also, there is a growing alliance of political and business leaders (e.g., Donald Trump, the New York property magnate), along with some military leaders and defense-related intellectuals, who echo the more outspoken voices in Congress. Even so, American attitudes remain ambivalent, for there is a significant body of elite and public opinion that is suspicious of current U.S. strategic policy and, at the same time, of the implications of a renewed Japanese military role in the Asia-Pacific region.[16] Still, in a sense the Japanese strategic genie has been let out of the bottle and will have to be dealt with in terms of the current debate.

There is little doubt that in the years ahead Japanese defense spending will gradually creep upward, although perhaps not quickly enough to satisfy the more strident U.S. critics. Eventually, though, a sharply enhanced military posture will run afoul of the Constitution; to depart any further from the spirit (not to say the word) of Article 9 would do an injustice to Japan's legal system and probably lead to a public outcry. As in the United States, it is not an easy matter to amend the Constitution; a two-thirds majority is needed in both houses of the Diet followed by a simple majority in a national referendum.[17] Given the highly sensitive nature of the issue, it is not likely that most Japanese leaders now and in the immediate future will commit themselves or their party to such a risky venture. No doubt a "clear and present danger" in the form of an imminent Soviet or Chinese threat would speed up the process considerably, but such a scenario does not appear to be likely in the foreseeable future.

Following Nakasone's lead, his successors will now be able to move ahead with the reformulation of Japan's increasing global political role in keeping with the economic power it has achieved. Just what this role will be is at this time unclear, but there can be little doubt that it will eventually bring into question the relationship between Japan's doctrine of comprehensive security and its military alliance with the United States.

Options for the Future

For the United States and Japan alike the closing decade of the century will call for a reconsideration of their changing global roles and an appropriate strategic doctrine and military posture. In the United States, some voices are already calling for a "new grand strategy" that would shift U.S. foreign policy emphasis "from the European theatre to the Far East, where the economic stakes are greater than ever and a shifting balance of power creates new opportunities and new dangers for American security."[18] For its part, the Soviet Union, as indicated in Mikhail Gorbachev's July 1986 speech in Vladivostok, is itself preparing for a more active role in East Asia. This move is not exceptional in light of Russia's geopolitical position, but it provides further confirmation, if such were needed, of the rapidly growing importance of the Asia-Pacific region in the global balance of power. The Chinese are watching these developments very closely as they continue to modernize and diversify their armed forces for the uncertain years ahead. Faced with declining U.S. power in a dynamic regional situation, the Japanese will certainly be forced to consider all of their options for the 1990s and beyond.

In this context the U.S.-Japanese security relationship is unlikely to remain static. Two broad scenarios are possible: (1) a gradual loosening or even dissolution of the alliance as trade and security disputes begin to take their toll and Japan seeks other avenues to guarantee its national security on both a regional and global basis; or, (2) a strengthening of the alliance through greater coordination and perhaps even integration of trade and military relations across the Pacific. It is perhaps inevitable that most specialists on Japan tend to emphasize the second, or benign outcome; but a notable exception is George R. Packard, who has written recently of the "coming crisis" in U.S.-Japanese relations.[19] In either event, it would be prudent for both Japanese and Americans to give careful consideration to both scenarios because, paradoxical though it may seem, the evolving bilateral relationship will likely contain elements of both scenarios.

The actualization of the first scenario could take several very different forms, but all of them would necessitate a drastic change in the U.S.-Japanese alliance as we know it. History is not replete with examples of great powers able to hold their alliances intact during periods of disequilibrium in the prevailing international system. Japan and the United States may indeed succeed in this endeavor, but in light of their current troubled relationship, it would be shortsighted to take for granted that this success is assured. Certainly, many thoughtful Japanese have considered options other than the alliance with the United States.

There is a small but articulate peace-oriented group that would point Japan along the path to pacifism based on renewed emphasis on Article 9 in the Constitution. A token military presence might be maintained along the lines of the present Self Defense Forces, but any further buildup would be eschewed in favor of continued economic development and increased foreign aid programs. Naturally, the alliance with the United States would be allowed to lapse and Japanese participation in global multilateral bodies such as the United Nations would be encouraged. This pacifist option, despite its theoretical attractiveness, can only be considered quixotic in view of the potentially unstable and militarily dense geopolitical circumstances of Northeast Asia.

A less extreme variant of this pacifist scenario would call for a new policy of nonalignment or "positive neutrality," perhaps along the lines of India's current policy. This idea in various forms enjoys support among important opposition parties in Japan, including the Socialists, the Communists, and even the Komeito (Clean Government party). It is also popular with many large unions (e.g., the teachers) and within important sections of the intelligentsia, including the media. Supporters of this view would leave the Constitution intact, sustain a credible self-defense and limited regional military capacity, and terminate, in an orderly fashion, the alliance with the United States. They would also emphasize the maintenance of constructive relationships with the East Asian regional powers (China, the Soviet Union, and the United States) and expanded participation in the political and economic institutions of the global system. Part of this option's attractiveness to many Japanese is its potential for the articulation of a new Japanese global role free from the inhibitions of the U.S. alliance. Despite anticipated U.S. objections, nonalignment (perhaps modified by a pro-Western tilt) must be regarded as a viable long-term option, especially if U.S.-Japanese relations continue to deteriorate into the 1990s.

Finally, on the other extreme, there are fringe groups within Japan that are putting forward what might be called a "neonationalist" view of Japan's future international role. Ian Buruma and others have called attention to the more extreme exponents of this "new nationalism," and their ideas are chilling indeed: elimination of Article 9; termination of the U.S. alliance; massive rearmament (including nuclear weapons); regional "leadership"; a strong global role, and so on, along with a "cleansing" of left-liberals, trade unions, and sundry foreign influences to form a "purified" Japanese society.[20] These extremists are as unlikely as the radical pacifists to win the day. But their views, in a considerably more moderate form, are reflected in certain conservative elements of the Liberal Democratic party (LDP), the government bureaucracy, and the business elite. Indeed, former Prime Minister Nakasone, with his self-consciously symbolic visits to the Yasukuni war martyrs shrine in Tokyo, is quite properly thought of as a member of this more moderate nationalist school of thought.

The realization of this nationalist scenario in its most extreme form would certainly be a tragedy for the Japanese people, who have suffered through it once already. It would alarm all of Japan's regional neighbors, from China and the Soviet Union to North and South Korea, all the way to Southeast Asia. It likely would lead to a serious rupture in Japan's relations with the United States, Western Europe, and other members and friends of the Western alliance everywhere. For all these reasons such a vision is unlikely to be realized in the near future, but history suggests that, especially in a more moderate form, it is not beyond the realm of possibility.

I turn now to the second of the broad scenarios that are possible in the future: a strengthening of the U.S.-Japanese alliance based on a growing commonality of perceived interests in trade and security matters between the two countries and between them and the democratic world more generally. Proponents of this possibility point to the undeniable "convergence" that has brought U.S. and Japanese societies closer together in the postwar years: the "Americanization" of Japanese society during the occupation; the integration of Japan into the Western-oriented global economy; the huge trade and investment stakes that both countries have in each other; the working experience of the security alliance since establishment of the peace treaty in 1951; and even the recent "Japanization" of certain aspects of American society (the ubiquitous spread of Japanese ways of doing things, from management to high fashion). The mania for "internationalization" currently sweeping Japan, despite certain superficialities, can be interpreted as Japan's way of preparing its people for greater participation in the international system.[21]

Will this greater openness on the part of Japan strengthen the alliance with the United States, or will it increasingly direct Japanese interests toward the wider global community? Partly in recognition that the latter may prove to be the case, former U.S. Ambassador to Japan Mike Mansfield and other influential voices in Washington have recently espoused the idea of "free trade" between the two countries.[22] (See his comments in the Introduction to this book.) This notion, although not yet clearly articulated, is based in part on the experience of the European Community and the recently signed free-trade agreement between the United States and Canada. In the case of the U.S.-Canadian agreement which took effect in January 1989, the trade dimensions of the bilateral relationship have been isolated from the more contentious issues pertaining to political integration (toward which the Europeans are striving to move). In this important sense, then, the situation between the United States and Canada is much more applicable to the evolving U.S. relationship with Japan than is the U.S.-European relationship.[23]

It is much too early to know whether talks along these lines will ultimately lead to anything resembling a free (or freer) trade agreement between Japan and the United States. Clearly, though, forward movement in this area would provide a critical underpinning for further advances toward greater integration of U.S. and Japanese efforts in the political/security realm.

Is strategic integration between the United States and Japan feasible? Is it desirable? These are difficult questions and the answers do not come readily. The first is perhaps the easiest to deal with: Strategic integration presumably would bring U.S. and Japanese strategic doctrine (especially with regard to the Soviet global role) into harmony; it would foster a cooperative approach to regional issues; and it would coordinate military deployment (everything from equipment standardization to technology transfers to joint exercises). It would also involve the United States and Japan in more effective alliance-building efforts outside the bilateral relationship. Edward A. Olsen, for example, has suggested that the existing ANZUS pact between the United States, Australia, and New Zealand could, with Japanese participation, be reinvigorated and made more creditable as "JANZUS."[24] Certainly, an integrated U.S.-Japanese security alliance and its concomitant regional offshoots would give the two partners a commanding presence in the Asia-Pacific region. It might even lead to certain much-needed economies on the part of Washington as Tokyo picks up an ever-increasing share of the joint defense bill.

On the other hand, there is a negative side to this scenario. Strategic integration would inevitably lead to a revision of the Japanese Constitution (Article 9) and a renegotiation (and strengthening) of the existing Mutual Security Treaty. It would also reopen the issue of Japan's long-standing nonnuclear policy, which prohibits the manufacture, stockpiling, or transit of nuclear weapons on Japanese territory.[25] These would be highly contentious issues in both countries but especially in Japan, where the passions of the 1960 crisis would be revived in the body politic. Integration would also pull the United States more deeply into the regional affairs of Northeast Asia, which, despite its current tranquillity, is arguably one of the most unstable geopolitical areas in the world. Such a strategy, in light of U.S. experience in Korea and especially Vietnam, should be subject to the closest scrutiny.

Such scrutiny is all the more necessary because of the probable reactions of the other major players in the region to an expanded U.S.-Japanese alliance system. North Korea, for one, would feel considerably more threatened, especially if South Korea expanded its security cooperation with the refurbished alliance. Pyongyang in all likelihood would feel compelled to move even closer to Moscow and/or Beijing, depending on what those powers would be prepared to offer. Not only that, but the already bad relations between Seoul and Pyongyang would deteriorate even further, thus opening up new uncertainties on the peninsula. China would scarcely be pleased. While Beijing's leaders have given cautious support to a U.S. military role in the western Pacific, they are likely to grow apprehensive if that role were to be upgraded substantially in consort with Japan. Nor would the Soviet Union stand idly by. It would move quickly to step up its already considerable military presence in the Soviet Far East and the western Pacific. Indeed, if there ever were a sure-fire formula for stimulating the arms race in this highly unstable region, U.S.-Japanese security integration and its regional ramifications are surely the methods of choice.[26]

A Turning Point in U.S.-Japanese Relations

As we approach the closing decade of the century it becomes ever more apparent that the U.S.-Japanese relationship is at a critical turning point. Neither side could have foreseen in the early postwar years the "coming of age" of Japan along with the maturation and possible decline of the United States. These tremendous changes of the last several decades are certain to be reflected in the military alliance established during and immediately following the U.S. occupation. Which way will Tokyo and Washington move? As we have seen, one possible scenario posits a gradual drift away from the existing security alliance and toward a more independent role for Japan, perhaps along the lines of nonalignment or "positive neutrality." The other scenario envisions a renewal and even strengthening of the alliance leading to some form of free trade and security integration in the years ahead, perhaps by the end of the century.

It would seem to be in the best national interests of both Japan and the United States not to attempt to force the issue at the present time. The East Asian international system is perhaps as stable as it ever has been in the previous two centuries; the major regional players, while cognizant of their respective security interests, have chosen to place their current policy emphasis on issues of economic development rather than military aggrandizement. In the case of Tokyo this set of priorities is of course obvious. Even Beijing, which is highly sensitive on matters of national security, has decided to place the military last in its "four modernizations" in favor of domestic economic growth.

Moscow, which has been engaged in a substantial rearmament program in the Soviet Far East and Northeast Asia, seems to be ready for a reconsideration of its plans. In his important speech at Vladivostok in July 1986, General Secretary Gorbachev stressed his desire to moderate the Soviet position. He called, inter alia, for the reduction of armed forces and conventional arms in Asia, the paring back of navies in the Indian Ocean, and the creation of specific "nuclear-free weapons zones" in the Asia-Pacific region. Further, in a clear overture to Washington, he hailed the United States as a "great Pacific Ocean power" whose active participation was essential in solving the "problem of security and cooperation in the Pacific Ocean zone in a manner satisfactory to all the states in the region."[27] There is little reason to doubt that Gorbachev and his fellow reformers, if they survive the unknowns of the inner-party struggle, intend to direct their energies to rebuilding the domestic Soviet economy. In this they share a common concern with former President Reagan and President George Bush, who have realized, however belatedly, that economic revitalization must take precedent over military growth in the immediate years ahead.

In light of the relative stability in Northeast Asia and the growing economic priorities of all the major actors involved, the time is opportune for the United States to rethink its security commitments in the Asia-Pacific region. The current situation would seem to call for a well-considered reduction rather than an increase in U.S. military deployments in the area. At present, U.S. commitments in the Asia-Pacific theatre are considerable, amounting to some $42 billion in a total defense budget of about $304 billion for fiscal year 1988–1989.[28]

Although former President Jimmy Carter lacked the political will to go through with his original plans (partly as a result of the Afghanistan crisis), he was pointed in the right direction with his proposals in 1978–1979 to reduce the number of United States troops in South Korea (currently about 43,000). This is a proposal that the Bush administration should take up as a matter of the highest priority. Further, the same principle should be extended to other U.S. troop deployments in the region: for example, Japan (47,000), the Philippines (16,000), and the Seventh (Pacific) Fleet (33,000). These phased reductions would mirror similar proposed cutbacks in the U.S. military presence in Western Europe, where economic prosperity and political stability suggest that the Europeans should perhaps assume a greater portion of the security burden. It is preferable for these cutbacks to be implemented as part of a well-considered global strategy; otherwise, they risk being forced through Congress in reaction to a rapidly declining ability on the part of the United States to finance its over-committed military posture inherited from the Cold War years.

These planned reductions, although they would have to be quantified and phased in only after careful deliberation, would be of immediate benefit to Washington's seriously out-of-balance budget. It goes without saying that the Japanese should be consulted every step of the way in working out specific plans for a phased and orderly rollback of U.S. obligations on both a bilateral and regional basis. Tokyo would then be in a position, without U.S. pressure, to map out its own defense requirements in keeping with the strategic doctrine of comprehensive security. If at all possible, Japan's assumption of moderately enhanced security responsibilities should be—and be seen to be—a reasoned response to new national needs rather than a reaction to international pressures from the United States and its allies. This approach would make the process all the more palatable to the growing self-consciousness of the Japanese as they struggle to redefine their global role.

A program of phased reductions in U.S. commitments to the military balance in Japan and East Asia would place the ball squarely in Tokyo's court regarding its own national security needs. It would also encourage Tokyo to give more serious consideration to the security concerns of its powerful neighbors in the Asia-Pacific region—China, the Soviet Union, and the United States itself. (We do not wish to ignore the position of the two Koreas, but they do not have the power-balancing and system-defining potential of the great powers in the region; they are more objects than subjects in the international regional system.) Despite Japan's rapidly increasing role in the wider global scene, the fact remains that its most important security concerns remain rooted in East Asia, and this is likely to be the case for many years to come.

In his bold and innovative speech at Vladivostok, Gorbachev took the initiative in rethinking the emerging security needs of the Pacific rim. He called for a highly inclusive regional meeting, "with the participation of all countries having a relationship with the ocean," to map out a path for the future. Few details were spelled out, but Gorbachev took as his model the Conference on Security and Cooperation in Europe held in Helsinki in 1975.[29] Should Gorbachev's proposals be taken seriously by the United States, Japan, China, and other key players in the region? Moscow is clearly in an accommodating frame of mind when one considers *perestroika* and *glasnost'*, the recent withdrawal from Afghanistan, a possible settlement in Kampuchea, and other signs of change in Soviet domestic and foreign policies. An opportunity like this does not come every day, and it should be seized without hesitation. As James Chace argued, "Clearly the United States will have to probe the seriousness of Gorbachev's proposals. A failure to do so will yield diplomatic momentum to the USSR while ignoring potential openings to fostering security throughout East Asia."[30] Should such a conference eventually be convened, Japan would make an ideal choice for the site in order to encourage active Japanese participation and symbolically mark Tokyo's assumption of a more prominent regional security role.

In conclusion, I would like to reiterate my belief that the United States should not push too hard in its attempt to pressure Japan into a greater military and security role in the Asia-Pacific region and around the world. Like the Japanese themselves, Americans should learn to live with a scaled-back military posture within the present parameters of the bilateral security relationship. They should put their own house in order, attending to economic revitalization at home and planned and prudent reductions in their military commitments abroad, in Europe and the Pacific rim alike. In this context the Japanese are more likely to look to their own security affairs in a more deliberate light while continuing to maintain close ties with the United States. Should opportunities for a more balanced division of responsibilities in security affairs arise, they should be taken; complete security integration, on the other hand, despite its attractiveness to its zealous U.S. proponents, should be approached only with extreme caution and perhaps not at all.

Some Americans fear that without a firm U.S. leadership role in the partnership, there is a danger that Japan will drift from the U.S. alliance into a posture of nonalignment, even if modified by a pro-Western tilt. There is nothing inevitable about this scenario, but it is an eventuality that the United States should be prepared to accept. Japan is today poised to reassert the national independence that is its historical legacy and to play an innovative, economically oriented role on the global scene. The United States, even with the best of intentions, should not try to sustain a security relationship that no longer accords with political realities. It is in the best interests of both nations to move toward a new, perhaps looser alignment freely arrived at rather than to hold on to an alliance based on concerns and needs inherited from the past.

Notes

1. For a historical interpretation of the coming of the Age of the Pacific, see John Curtis Perry, "The New World of the North Pacific: An Emerging Fulcrum in World Affairs," *Speaking of Japan* 7 (February 1987):20–29.

2. Roy Hofheinz and Kent E. Calder, *The Eastasia Edge* (New York: Basic Books, 1982).

3. One is reminded of the Chinese word for "crisis"—*weiji*, a two-character compound meaning in a literal sense "danger" (*wei*) and "opportunity" (*ji*).

4. The Constitution of Japan, 1947. The full text is in the *Kodansha Encyclopedia of Japan*, vol. 2 (Tokyo: Kodansha, 1983), pp. 9–13.

5. A concise account of the SDF is provided by James H. Buck, "Japan's Self-Defense Forces," in Edward A. Olsen and Stephen Jurika, eds., *The Armed Forces in Contemporary Asian Societies* (Boulder, CO: Westview, 1986), pp. 70–86.

6. The struggle over the renewal of the Mutual Security Treaty is recounted in George R. Packard, *Protest in Tokyo: The Security Treaty Crisis of 1960* (Princeton: Princeton University Press, 1967).

7. The Nixon doctrine and other elements of Nixon's strategic thinking at the time are capsulated in *United States Foreign Policy for the 1970s: A New Strategy for Peace*, Report to the Congress by Richard Nixon, President of the United States, 18 February 1970 (Washington, D.C.: Government Printing Office, 1970).

8. William Watts, *The United States and Japan: A Troubled Partnership* (Cambridge, MA: Ballinger, 1984), pp. 91, 95.

9. *Far Eastern Economic Review,* 20 April 1979, as quoted in Taketsugu Tsurutani, *Japanese Policy and East Asian Security* (New York: Praeger, 1981), p. 92.

10. For a summary of the *Report on Comprehensive National Security* (1980), see Robert W. Barnett, *Beyond War: Japan's Concept of Comprehensive National Security* (Washington, D.C.: Pergamon-Brassey's, 1984), pp. 1–6.

11. This issue is discussed in Hiroshi Kimura, "The Love-Hate Relationship with the Polar Bear: Japanese Feelings Towards the Soviet Union," *Japan Quarterly* 28 (January–March 1981):39–44.

12. Barnett, *Beyond War,* p. 1.

13. "Whatever Happened to Defense Technology Transfers?" *JEI Report* (7 August 1987), p. 30A. Currently, a potential dispute is emerging between Congress and the Bush administration over plans to transfer to Japan $7 billion in advanced aircraft technology developed for the F-16 fighter, which will be produced in Japan as the FSX.

14. Malcolm McIntosh, *Japan Re-armed* (New York: St. Martin's, 1986), pp. 41–42.

15. Yasuhiro Nakasone, "Japan Confronts the Future," paper presented at a meeting of the Sino-Soviet Institute, George Washington University, 26 September 1977, as quoted in Edward A. Olsen, *U.S.-Japan Strategic Reciprocity: A Neo-Internationalist View* (Stanford, CA: Hoover Institution Press, 1985), p. 112.

16. Some of these issues are discussed in Richard B. Finn, "Does the United States Want a Big Japan?" *Asian Pacific Community* 19 (Winter 1983):41–51.

17. For a fuller discussion see Wolf Mendl, "The Japanese Constitution and Japan's Security Policy," *Millennium* 7 (Spring 1978):36–51.

18. James Chace, "A New Grand Strategy," *Foreign Policy* 70 (Spring 1988):4.

19. George R. Packard, "The Coming U.S.-Japan Crisis," *Foreign Affairs* 66 (Winter 1987–1988):348–367.

20. Ian Buruma, "A New Japanese Nationalism," *New York Times Magazine,* 12 April 1987.

21. Japanese and Western views on this subject are included in Hiroshi Mannari and Harumi Befu, eds., *The Challenge of Japan's Internationalization* (New York: Kodansha International, 1983).

22. "Baker Says United States Is Ready for Free Trade with Japan," *Toronto Star,* 18 June 1988.

23. For a comprehensive discussion of this issue see Peter J. Wylie and Raymond F. Wylie, "The Free-Trade Issue in Canada's Relations with the United States," in Robert J. Thornton, Thomas Hyclak, and J. Richard Aronson, eds., *Canada at the Crossroads: Essays on Canadian Political Economy* (Greenwich, CT: JAI Publishers, 1988), pp. 81–114.

24. Olsen, *U.S.-Japan Strategic Reciprocity,* p. 136.

25. It should be recalled here that Japan is a signatory to the Non-Proliferation Treaty and that Prime Minister Eisaku Sato won the 1967 Nobel Peace Prize for his Three Nonnuclear Principles.

26. Significantly, Soviet reactions to U.S.-Japanese security integration are studiously ignored by Olsen in his discussion of the "regional implications"

of his proposals. Perhaps he believes the Soviet Union is not a part of the Asia-Pacific region? Olsen, *U.S.-Japan Strategic Reciprocity*, pp. 143–154.

27. The text of Gorbachev's address on 28 July 1986 can be found in *Vital Speeches of the Day* 52 (15 September 1986):706–711.

28. Chace, "A New Grand Strategy," p. 12.

29. Gorbachev, *Vital Speeches*, pp. 706–711.

30. Chace, "A New Grand Strategy," p. 18.

5

Japan and the United States: Dynamics of the Economic Relationship

Saburo Okita

There can be no question that the U.S.-Japanese relationship is of critical importance not only to the two countries immediately involved but also to much of the world. The leaders of both countries agree that the relationship is extremely significant, especially politically and in terms of national security, and that their basically good bilateral relations must be preserved. Even in the midst of tension, there is active cooperation between Japanese and U.S. businesses and increasingly closer cultural ties between our two peoples.

Relations between Japan and the United States have been marked in recent years, however, by frequent friction, particularly in the area of trade. Four areas have been identified as the main causes of the U.S. frustration with Japan: (1) U.S. critics feel that the Japanese market is more closed than the U.S. market; (2) they feel that the U.S. trade deficit with Japan is too large, regardless of the reasons; (3) many Americans have the impression that Japan has not accepted its international responsibilities or taken on a role commensurate with its growing economic strength; and (4) Japan has emerged as a strong competitor for the United States in semiconductors and other high-technology fields.

Although the Japanese government has been making continued efforts to further open its markets, discontent is still strong among the foreign suppliers. The semiconductor dispute has become explosive. The U.S. trade deficit with Japan remains large in spite of the yen's sharp appreciation since early 1985. Japan continues its low-profile posture in global issues, laying itself open to criticism of taking a "free ride."

These factors combined account for the increased irritation with Japan, particularly in the U.S. Congress.

At the same time, Japanese frustration is also growing because the United States seems to be arbitrarily blaming Japan for its economic woes and conveniently ignoring the fact that its huge trade imbalance is mainly due to its own domestic policies. The Japanese argue that the United States's global trade imbalance has been aggravated since the early 1980s by the mounting budget deficit and the combination of excess consumer demand and a low domestic savings rate. While the U.S. global trade deficit increased from $36 billion in 1980 to $170 billion in 1986, its deficit with Japan increased from $12 billion to $58 billion during the same period. Japan's share of the total U.S. trade deficit thus stayed at about one-third throughout this period. In effect, the U.S. trade deficit with Japan has increased roughly in parallel with its global trade imbalance.

Because I believe that the historical context is important to understanding this issue, I would like to present an overview of the U.S.-Japanese relationship, with an emphasis on the dynamics of our economic relations, during the past quarter-century.

History and Economics

In 1960, the Japanese government under Prime Minister Hayato Ikeda devised and announced a plan to double the national income. At the time, I was responsible for this income-doubling plan as director-general of the Economic Planning Agency's Planning Bureau. This plan played an important role in fostering Japan's rapid growth in the 1960s and giving direction to its economic development. In *The Management Challenge: Japanese Views*, a record of the Massachusetts Institute of Technology symposium on Japan's postwar economic performance, Professor Lester C. Thurow wrote of this plan:

> Consider the five elements in the Japanese economic strategy at the beginning of the income-doubling decade: strengthen social overhead capital, push growth industries, promote exports, develop human ability and technology, and secure social stability by mitigating the dual structure of the economy. This list could easily serve as strategic objectives for the American economy by the year 2000.[1]

When the plan was devised, Japan's GNP was approximately 3% of the world total and that of the United States was 30%, meaning that the U.S. economy was ten times as large as that of Japan. Japan was then running a deficit in its trade with the United States. There was no talk of trade friction. Yet, in the 1960s, a number of problems arose. For example, in 1962, while I was still with the Economic Planning Agency, Congressman Hale Boggs from Louisiana (Chairman of the House of Representatives Commerce Committee) came to Japan to talk with Japanese trade officials. At the time, there was already criticism in the United States over the rapid increases in Japanese exports of transistors, sewing machines, binoculars, metal flatware, footwear, pianos, and inexpensive cotton blouses. Referring to these blouses, Congressman Boggs said, "We have a lot of knit plants in my district. But we have these Japanese one-dollar blouses selling now for about a third the price of an American blouse. Workers in my district have strung up the Japanese one-dollar blouses and marched on my house. They are petitioning me, telling me to do something, because there is no way they can compete against those kinds of prices. I'm a free trader, but I can't turn my back on my own people."[2] Sparked by these labor demonstrations against one-dollar Japanese blouses, a bilateral governmental agreement was concluded in 1967 providing for Japanese voluntary export restraints for five years.

Subsequent to this agreement, trouble arose between Japan and the United States over wool and synthetic textiles. This friction was sparked by a promise that presidential candidate Richard Nixon had made to senators from the South—a focus of discontent over textiles—promising to restrict textile imports. The next year, in 1969, while achieving the nuclear-free reversion of Okinawa was a major political goal for Prime Minister Eisaku Sato, Nixon was primarily concerned with keeping his promise to limit Japanese textile exports to the United States. It was in this climate that the Sato-Nixon Summit was held, and thus, regional industrial interests came to have major political ramifications for postwar free-trade arrangements. Textiles, an important industry for both countries but a crucial industry for neither, was suddenly catapulted into prominence as a political issue. Because Japan was not the only country exporting textiles to the United States, Korea, Taiwan, Hong Kong, and the other newly industrializing countries (NICs) also took a strong interest in these bilateral textile negotiations.

The problem over textiles proved to be the first of a long series of trade frictions that plagued Japanese exports. The textile negotiations dragged on for three years until, in January 1972, the Japan–United States Textile Agreement was signed as part of a package including the reversion of Okinawa to Japanese sovereignty. The fallout from these negotiations later resulted in the conclusion of the Multilateral Fiber Agreement (MFA). Although the specific products under contention have changed, trade friction between Japan and the United States continues even today and the prototype established in the textile negotiations—of politicizing the problem and then resolving it with a political agreement negotiated between the two governments—remains unchanged.

These trade frictions have involved Japanese exports as well as Japanese imports. In the 1960s, the United States ran a surplus in its trade with Japan, but by 1971 this trend was reversed to a $3.2 billion deficit. It was about this same time that the term "trade friction" began to be heard. The 1973 oil crisis had a traumatic impact on the Japanese economy; for a time, Japanese exports to the United States slowed and the two countries enjoyed a brief period of calm in their trading relations. Yet as Japan adapted to higher oil prices and its economy got back on its feet, problems developed with steel, color television sets, and other export products. Around November 1979, about the same time that the U.S. Embassy in Teheran was occupied and its staff taken hostage by Iranian radicals, serious problems arose over automobile exports from Japan to the United States. While these problems involved specific trade practices and products, in the 1980s the issue of U.S.-Japanese competition and trade friction in high-technology fields became a concern, particularly with reference to machine tools and semiconductors.

On the Japanese import side, the United States has been sharply critical of Japan and has pressed strongly for an opening of the Japanese market. Among the issues cited here are agricultural products such as beef and oranges, tobacco products, and Nippon Telegraph and Telephone Public Corporation (NTT) procurement. On these items, the United States has claimed that Japan is limiting imports with import quotas, tariff barriers, and nontariff barriers.

In 1969 Professors Hendrik S. Houthakker and Stephen P. Magee, who were then members of the President's Council of Economic Advisors, released a study concluding that the U.S.-Japanese bilateral trade balance would gradually tend to increase U.S. deficits over the long term.[3] At that time, Japanese government officials and economists did not take this report very seriously, but it seems to be a rather prescient forecast in light of subsequent trade developments. At present, despite the many improvements that Japan has made and is making on both exports and imports, a steady stream of trade issues vexes our two countries. Yet it is of paramount importance that we resign ourselves to living with these continuing problems and resolve to find solutions to new problems as they arise so that this economic friction will not be allowed to damage our basic diplomatic relations.

Trade Friction

It would be useful at this point to look at what these economic problems and their political offspring mean for the future of the U.S.-Japanese relationship. Here it is important to make six essential points.

First, the friction, starting with textiles and proceeding to steel and color television sets, was generated as Japan moved from labor-intensive industries to capital- and technology-intensive industries. This is the classical pattern of how friction naturally occurs under free-trade arrangements as later-developing nations seek to catch up. However, the United States has not made the classical response. In the textile case, for example, rather than initiating the necessary positive adjustment policies—that is, rather than shifting away from an industry where it was at a comparative disadvantage and moving toward more capital-intensive and technology-intensive industries—the United States focused on the problem as a political issue and sought a solution in linkage with other bilateral political issues.

By contrast, Japan has sought coordinated reductions in production capacity, supported technical development, and worked under the Temporary Measure Law for the Structural Adjustment of Specific Industries and other temporary legislation to restructure depressed industries that have become less competitive internationally. This difference is largely the result of contrasting cultural patterns that determine how economic policies are formulated in Japan and the United States. These differences show up most vividly in U.S. criticism of Japanese industrial policy. Yet is important to note here that Japanese industrial restructuring does not always take the form of import restrictions but rather is implemented through domestic adjustments; in Japan there is an aversion to political interference in the ever-changing international division of labor that is inevitable with free-market economies.

In 1970, I was asked to testify before the Joint Congressional Economic Committee's subcommittee on external economic policy in order to give my views as an economist on the bilateral textile issue and other economic issues. In line with the major points outlined above, I testified as follows:

Production of labor intensive products, including many items of textile goods, are now rapidly moving to other Asian countries where labor is still abundant and the wage levels are relatively low. In the United States market, for example, Japan's share of these items are declining while the share of the newly industrializing countries is increasing. The same products will start flowing into Japanese domestic markets.

If we introduce voluntary restrictions on textile exports to the U.S. market, then our industry will say, when they face the growing pressure from the newly industrializing countries to import more textile products, that because the United States is imposing voluntary restrictions on our textile exports, why should we not follow the same practice and restrict the imports of textile products into Japan? This will mean that there may be a chain reaction of anti-liberalization all over the world. Those who suffer most will be the poorer countries of the world which are striving to expand their exports of manufactured goods.[4]

Second, after the friction over color television sets, and after the problem was politicized, a bilateral agreement was finally worked out by the two governments. Under the Orderly Marketing Agreement (OMA), Japan was to hold its exports of color television sets to 1.75 million per year for three years starting 1 July 1977. Following the signing of this agreement, most of Japan's large television manufacturers rushed to set up production facilities in the United States. This friction over color television exports seems typical of the kinds of problems that arise when Japan continues to export products instead of switching to direct overseas investment. However, the Japanese justification for its export-minded approach is that Japan, dependent as it is upon overseas sources of foodstuffs, energy, and other raw materials, has to sell its products overseas, and particularly in the United States, if it is to fulfill its international balance-of-payments requirements. While this is a liability for the Japanese economy, the fact that the Japanese people are strongly aware of their economic vulnerability has provided a major support for Japan's consensus-oriented social structures, economic adaptability, and decision-making flexibility. These qualities enabled Japan to weather the two severe oil crises of the 1970s. Since the opening of the country in the late nineteenth century, Japan has earned its way in the international community by exporting, and it will take a long time for the Japanese export mentality to change. In the 1960s and 1970s, Japan's current account was in deficit eleven years and in surplus nine years. It was only in the 1980s that the current account was continuously and massively in the black. This is a new experience for the Japanese, and one that will take some time to get used to in light of the social and historical factors that have shaped the Japanese people.

My third point is illustrated by the automobile issue. With the new era of higher oil prices, there was a definite shift in market demand away from big gas-guzzling cars and toward fuel-efficient compacts. Whereas the U.S. and Japanese automobile markets were once separate and distinct, a definite overlap developed in the small-car segment.

With this development, Washington was divided into two camps—those favoring restrictions and those opposing them, with the result being that the U.S. government expressed its hope that the Japanese government would voluntarily restrict Japanese exports. In effect, the automobile problem was "solved" by having the Japanese side unilaterally impose voluntary export restraints. During May 1981, Japanese Minister of International Trade and Industry Rokusuke Tanaka met with U.S. Trade Representative William Brock and the two agreed that Japan would restrict exports of passenger cars to the United States to 1.68 million vehicles per year. Voluntary export restraints are still in effect today, even though the U.S. auto industry appears to have recovered, but the quota has been raised to 2.3 million vehicles per year.

Harvard University professor Ezra Vogel wrote an article entitled "Pax Nipponica?" in *Foreign Affairs* in which he stated that "Japanese trade surpluses with the United States are not likely to be resolved by changes in the exchange rate or by changes in Japanese macroeconomic policy. The reasons for the Japanese economic success are much deeper."[5] Because little immediate correction is likely, he said, U.S.-Japanese relations may well develop in cartel-like directions with specific quotas and other agreements for specific trade sectors. Such tendencies were obviously evident in textiles, steel, automobiles, and other products. The automobile problem is especially noteworthy in that, unlike previous cases, the voluntary export restraints were not the result of any official bilateral agreement. In trying to discern the direction of the U.S.-Japanese relationship and predict the future of free trade, it is extremely important that we look at whether such unofficial agreements are likely to play an increasingly important role in resolving trade issues and maintaining international economic arrangements and whether this pattern could begin to factor into trade problems among other countries as well.

Fourth, the friction that has developed in semiconductors, computers, telecommunications equipment, machine tools, and other high-technology fields in the 1970s and 1980s is even more serious. As epitomized by computers, these high-technology fields are areas in which the United States has the strongest competitive advantage. However, there is a sense of crisis in the United States that a trade deficit in these fields may signal an end to U.S. leadership in the international economy. As stated in the January 1979 *Task Force Report on U.S.-Japan Trade* the House Subcommittee on Trade,

> Part of the certainty of a recurrent or continuing trade crisis with Japan is due to Japan's industrial policy which has recently targeted or set as a goal Japanese leadership in high technology fields presently dominated

by the United States and constituting our areas of strongest exports: computers, advanced electronics, telecommunications equipment, industrial robots (possibly aircraft, at least at the co-production stage), etc.

These are the high value industries of the future, and it is perfectly logical that Japan should be moving out of older, labor intensive, and less sophisticated industries into these new 21st century fields.

The problem lies (1) in the way that Japan is achieving this transition; and (2) U.S. failure to have a comparable industrial policy in which there is a consensus in American business, labor, and government of where we as a society should be going.

We believe that the Japanese threat in these high technology areas may soon become the most explosive economic issue between our two nations.[6]

However, the Japanese edge lies in processing and production technology for high quality and superior reliability, and Japan still lags far behind the United States in such areas as basic research and new product development. Nor does Japan have the domestic natural resources that the United States has. The only way Japan can survive is to develop the human resources it needs to go into high-technology fields; becoming a high-technology nation is critically important for the Japanese economy. Yet accompanying this imperative, there is a concern in Japan that pursuing this goal might bring Japan into conflict with the countries of North America and Western Europe; therefore, we recognize that the need now is for Japan, the United States, and Europe to promote international cooperation for joint development in high-technology fields at both the governmental and private-sector levels. Crisis in the U.S. and European economies can only mean crisis for free trade as well.

In this regard, questions have been raised about Japan's so-called "industrial targeting policy." Speaking before the House of Representatives Ways and Means Committee Subcommittee on Trade in 1983, Under-Secretary of Commerce Lionel Olmer said that he had studied Japanese market-opening measures over the previous two years and had concluded that Japan is dedicated to averting specific trade friction issues but has yet to deal with such basic issues as government policies to foster specific industries and government-led cartels. Speaking about industrial policy, he said that the Japanese government is involved in arranging both withdrawal from sunset industries and entry into high-technology industries and voiced the criticism that the Japanese government provides attractive financing and preferential taxation treatment, directs the allocation of resources toward promising industries, and even undertakes part of the research and development risks. This speech probably marked the first time that a U.S. government official had spoken out so critically about Japan's industrial targeting policy.[7] If by "industrial targeting policy" one means that the Japanese government concentrates on specific high-technology industries and protects them from imports while providing subsidies and other assistance until they are strong enough to export, I should say that such policies of the past are virtually nonexistent today.

The fifth point relates to the issue of the Japanese market's openness to imports. Japanese industry is highly competitive and very productive in automobiles, electronics, and a host of other fields, but it is still very weak in such areas as agriculture and distribution. It is true that there are still some protectionist measures in place in these fields in which we are weak and productivity is low. Yet the criticism that agriculture is a "sacred cow" in Japan exempt from the rules of free trade is becoming increasingly untenable. In 1977 and 1978, when the issue arose of liberalizing agricultural imports, especially beef and oranges, it was argued that even if these products were liberalized, the additional imports would amount to no more than several hundred million dollars, an almost insignificant amount in terms of the total U.S.-Japanese trade imbalance. Yet because agriculture was seen to represent the closed nature of the Japanese market, it became of symbolic importance for the United States to achieve an increase in Japanese agricultural imports. In January 1978, Japanese Minister for External Economic Affairs Nobuhiko Ushiba and President Carter's Special Representative for Trade Negotiations Robert Strauss agreed that Japan would take measures to expand its agricultural imports, and a joint communiqué was issued summarizing the results of their negotiations.[8] In the spring of 1978, the United States was back, this time demanding the complete deregulation of beef and orange imports. Although Japan felt that agricultural negotiations should really be handled in the multilateral Tokyo Round, they were taken up in bilateral negotiations in light of Japan's major surplus in its trade with the United States and in response to American statements that beef and oranges were symbolic of the openness of the Japanese market and demands that Japan import more of these commodities. These bilateral negotiations were the focus of intense pressure by special-interest groups on both sides of the Pacific and became quite emotional at times. They presented a serious political problem. Today, this agricultural trade friction has spread even to the issue of rice, and there is a widespread feeling in Japan that it is impossible to ignore the international price and productivity differentials involved.

Postwar Japan was arguably the prime beneficiary of the Kennedy Round, since it made it possible for Japan to achieve rapid economic growth in the 1960s. The Tokyo Round was thus initiated in the hope that agreement among the member countries to further lower their tariffs and to lower or dismantle nontariff barriers could lead to a further expansion of international trade. On one sensitive nontariff barrier, a government procurement code was negotiated providing that each of the three major trading powers—Japan, the United States, and the European Community—would seek to ensure that their procurement procedures were open to competitive bidding from the other two areas. Under this code, the three exchanged information on the value of their anticipated government procurements in July 1978. Seeking to ensure that the procurement values were more nearly equal, the United States demanded that procurement by the Nippon Telegraph and Telephone Public Corporation, the largest Japanese purchaser of goods, be more open to competitive tenders. Both Japan and the United States faced domestic controversy with regard to this issue. At the time, Japanese telecommunications people felt they were being sacrificed and complained that pressure from the United States would cut off any chance Japan might have to develop advanced technologies. In turn, smaller U.S. companies were concerned that reciprocal opening would only benefit the big firms and do nothing for them. As global economic relations—and U.S.-Japanese economic relations in particular—have become more tightly interdependent, the conflicts of interests in both countries have become intertwined with trade issues and thereby further complicated the search for solutions.

The government of Japan has acted to lower and dismantle nontariff trade barriers. Every country has its own standards and certification systems drawn up to protect the consumer, to ensure health and sanitation, to preserve the environment, and to promote better product quality—and not devised simply to block imports. Japan has taken the initiative in revising these standards and certification systems when they are seen to impede imports, even though they were not created initially with import-impediment in mind. As part of this effort, the Japanese government resolved in March 1983 to accord foreign-made imported products exactly the same treatment as Japanese-made products for the purposes of product inspections, and there is now no discrimination whatsoever by country of origin. At the same time, it was decided: (1) to ensure transparency in the drafting and amending of standards and certification regulations, (2) to seek to bring Japanese standards and certification procedures more into line with internationally accepted norms, (3) to accept foreign test data whenever possible, and (4) to simplify and streamline import procedures.

While the United States has been pressing for self-certification in this system of standards and certification, the situation in Japan is such that, in the case of a drug with harmful side effects, for example, the product liability is not limited to the manufacturer alone but also extends to the government. Case law suggests that this is so, and there have been cases in which the government officials concerned have been severely castigated in the Diet for not "doing something" about such a company. Whether one believes that this is the way things should be or not, the approaches are decidedly different in Japan and the United States, and these social differences would have to be eliminated before we could fully resolve this source of friction.

In January 1985, negotiations were begun not on specific items but on a market-oriented sector-selective (MOSS) approach taking up a number of areas in which the United States is competitive. The four sectors that were included in these talks were telecommunications, electronics, medical equipment and pharmaceuticals, and timber and forestry products, and an effort was made to address the standards and certification issues, import procedures, trade practices, and distribution issues for each of these four sectors with a view to eliminating the problems all at once.

In March 1985, with the Senate passing a resolution critical of Japan by a vote of 92–0, it became painfully apparent to trade officials on both sides of the Pacific that there were obvious limits to arguing the economic logic of the trade imbalance between Japan and the United States. Following that, a number of additional political efforts were made by both sides. During April 1985, Japan's Advisory Committee for External Economic Issues, which I chaired, submitted a report advocating: (1) further efforts for improved market access, (2) sustained economic growth powered by domestic demand, (3) expanded overseas investment and industrial cooperation, (4) the promotion of a new round of multilateral trade negotiations under GATT, and (5) responses to the developing countries' concerns.[9] In line with this report, the government announced an Action Program for Improved Market Access, which included the reduction or elimination of tariffs on more than 1,800 items, further simplification of import procedures, and other import-promotion measures.

In the early 1980s, the focus of economic friction broadened to encompass not only the markets for goods but also capital markets, distribution systems, and other such services. Behind this push for liberalization in Japan's capital and financial markets was a drive to rectify the dollar's overvaluation as U.S. government officials who had previously contended that the strong dollar was symbolic of a strong America concluded, in the face of massive trade deficits, that currency misalignment was responsible for much of the trade imbalance between Japan and the United States. Averse to market intervention, maintaining that the markets should determine exchange rates, and believing that

Japan should do more to create a climate conducive to allowing exchange markets to reflect economic fundamentals, the United States pressed Japan to liberalize its capital and financial markets. The argument claimed that Japan was artificially holding interest rates down, that capital was thus flowing from Japan to the United States to take advantage of the interest spread that had developed between Japan and the United States, and that this capital flow, by creating a strong demand for the dollar, was driving the dollar up and the yen down and was hence responsible for the trade imbalance as well. Given these demands that Japanese capital and financial markets be liberalized to bring the yen back up on currency exchange markets, the Joint Japan–U.S. Ad-hoc Group on Financial and Capital Market Issues was established in February 1984. Three months later, the Group announced a program for liberalizing Japanese capital and financial markets and for enhancing the yen's role as an international currency.

Following this action, around February the next year, the yen began to appreciate against the dollar. This trend was further accelerated by the G-5 Plaza Accord of September 1985. Since then, the yen has moved from 240 to the dollar to less than 135 to the dollar. Enabling the yen to play a great international role means finding ways for the yen to supplement and complement the dollar as an international currency, and I see the G-5 accord as evidence that the United States has redirected its policy toward cooperative management of the world economy through policy coordination among the major industrialized nations. Macroeconomic policy coordination among the leading industrialized nations will become increasingly important, and it is noteworthy in this regard that the OECD Ministerial Conference of May 1987 called upon Japan to expand domestic demand, West Germany to lower interest rates, and the United States to reduce its fiscal deficit.

Recent and Future Trends

Looking at recent trade trends, Japan recorded a $97 billion current account surplus and a $96.3 billion trade surplus and had a net long-term capital outflow of $136.5 billion in 1987, despite the yen's rapid appreciation against the dollar. Most of these increases were due to the fall in oil prices and the J-curve effect as the yen appreciated. While dollar-denominated exports were up 19.1% over the previous year, yen-denominated exports were down 15.9% and export volume was down 1.2%. Particularly noteworthy here is the fact that there has not only been a drop in the value of exports, with all of the deflationary consequences that entails, but there has even been a decline in export volume. On the import side, imports were down 2.3% in dollar-denominated terms and down 30.6% in yen-denominated terms but up 12.5% in volume terms.

According to U.S. statistics, the U.S. trade deficit with Japan went from $49.7 billion in 1985 to $60 billion in 1987. Yet during the same period, the U.S. global trade deficit went from $148.5 billion in 1985 to $172 billion in 1987; thus, the deficit with Japan continued to account for approximately one third of the total. In bilateral trade between Japan and the United States, even as total U.S. exports were declining from $233.7 billion in 1981 to $217.3 billion in 1986, exports to Japan rose from $21.8 billion in 1981 to $26.9 billion in 1986. Likewise, the ratio of manufactures to Japan's total imports from the United States rose from 45.3% in 1981 to 60.7% in 1986. During the same period, manufacturers' shares of total Japanese imports rose from 24.3% in 1981 to 41.7% in 1986. It would thus appear that there is a very good chance that the impact of currency exchange rate adjustments will result in shrinking both Japan's surplus in its trade with the United States and its overall current account surplus in the future.

In an effort to deal with some of these issues, a seventeen-member Advisory Group on Economic Structural Adjustment for International Harmony was formed in Japan. I was a member of this group. We met every Wednesday morning at the Prime Minister's residence, and out of a total of nineteen meetings, Nakasone attended seventeen of them personally. The result, known as the Maekawa Report of April 1986, was a very important document in postwar Japanese economic history. It recognized the need to change long-cherished and well-established customs and argued that Japan needed to be even more activist in expanding domestic demand, enhancing market access, and investing overseas. As the report noted,

> It is imperative that we recognize that continued large current account imbalances create a critical situation not only for the management of the Japanese economy but also for the harmonious development of the world economy.
>
> The time has thus come for Japan to make a historical transformation in its traditional policies on economic management and the nation's life-style. There can be no further development for Japan without this transformation.[10]

However, even with all the best efforts that it can make to promote imports and spur domestic demand, Japan will continue to record substantial current account surpluses for some years to come. And while currency exchange rate adjustments are important, there is a limit, economically and politically, to what they can achieve. In effect, the success of these efforts hinges upon the ability of both Japan and the United States to break ingrained behavioral patterns. Just as it is forecast that Japan's net overseas assets will top $500 billion by the end of 1990, International Monetary Fund (IMF) projections have the accumulated U.S. debt topping the $800 billion mark that same year. As *The Times* of London recently stated, "The U.S. is a debtor nation with the habits of a creditor nation: Germany and Japan are creditor nations with the habits of debtor nations."[11]

The United States, formerly a major source of development capital, is now a major debtor nation, a black hole draining savings from Japan, Europe, and the rest of the world. If we leave the flow of capital to laissez-faire market mechanisms, the bulk of the capital will be drawn to the United States in search of investment security and high interest rates. Conscious policy measures, including risk insurance and interest subsidies to offset the low-interest and long-term nature of the return, are needed if we are to divert at least some of this capital flow to the developing countries. In so doing, it may be necessary for Japan to formulate its own "Marshall Plan" for the developing countries. The problem here is that the surpluses are entirely in the hands of the private sector. The government of Japan moved to recycle the current account surplus to the developing countries with subscriptions to the Asian Development Bank, the IMF, the World Bank, and the International Development Agency (IDA) with a total 1989 commitment of more than $10 billion, but these efforts should be stepped up. In addition, the government decided on a seven-year plan to double Japanese Official Development Assistance (ODA) by 1992 (with the target year since moved up to 1990), and there is increasing acceptance within Japan of the idea that the government should offer incentives to promote the flow of private-sector savings to the developing countries through regional development banks, the Export Import Bank of Japan, Japan's Overseas Economic Cooperation Fund, and other institutions.

This need was also highlighted by the World Institute for Development Economics Research (WIDER), established in Helsinki under the auspices of the United Nations University, in its April 1986 report entitled "The Potential of the Japanese Surplus for World Economic Development" drawn up by WIDER Director Lal Jayawardena, WIDER Advisor on International Economic Issues and IMF Executive Director Arjun Sengupta, and myself as chairman of the WIDER governing board. To follow up, WIDER released a second research report, "Mobilizing International Surpluses for World Development: A WIDER Plan for a Japanese Initiative," in Tokyo in May 1987.[12] Starting with the forecast that Japan's current account surplus will run $60–80 billion every year for the next five years, this report calls upon Japan to take the initiative in channeling about one-third of that—$25 billion a year or $125 billion over the five-year period—to the developing countries. There was an annual flow of up to $30 billion a year from the developed to the developing countries in the early 1980s. Today, that flow has been reversed, with a $30 billion net outflow from the poor to the rich countries, with all of the devastating impacts that this trend implies for the industrialized countries' exports, and we have fallen into a vicious cycle. The WIDER report argues that initiating a renewed strong flow of funds to the developing countries can stimulate economic growth in these regions, spark an export recovery by the industrialized countries, and thus restore the virtuous cycle of trade.

This issue might not appear to have much relevance to the economic friction between Japan and the United States. But it should be noted that our bilateral problems have arisen within the broader global economic context and that it is impossible to consider the proper responses to the bilateral problems without at the same time examining how we can best respond to the larger issues that confront the world, including, for example, the massive Japanese and West German current account surpluses, the twin fiscal and trade deficits in the United States, the developing countries' mounting cumulative debt burdens, and the deterioration in commodity prices. The economic problems among Japan, the United States, and Europe cannot be solved by bilateral negotiations alone. What is needed are multilateral efforts to revitalize the entire world economy, including the developing countries. If there are doubts on this matter, one only needs to be reminded that one of the major causes of the U.S. trade deficit is that Latin America, long a major market for U.S. exports, has had to cut back sharply on its imports in the face of unmanageable external debts.

By the same token, relations between Japan and the United States will have a major impact upon the future of the Pacific Basin region and the newly industrializing countries (NICs) in particular, as Ambassador Tommy Koh discusses elsewhere in this volume. With the exception of Singapore, the Asian NICs (South Korea, Taiwan, Hong Kong, and Singapore) recorded strong economic growth during 1986. GNP growth rates went from 5.4% in 1985 to 12.2% in 1986 in South Korea, from 5.1% to 10.8% in Taiwan, and from 0.8% to 8.7% in Hong Kong. Because most of the currencies in this region are linked to the dollar, they have depreciated sharply against the yen since September 1985 and these countries have seen their exports become much more competitive. However, given their industrial structures, their trade with Japan continues to be imbalanced because of their need to import semi-finished goods and capital equipment. Any real rectification of their trade imbalances with Japan will have to await changes in their

TABLE 5.1
United States Balance of Payments: 1960–1986 (in millions of dollars)

Year	Merchandise Trade Balance	Net Investment Income	Current Account Balance
1960	4,892	3,379	2,824
1961	5,571	3,754	3,822
1962	4,521	4,294	3,387
1963	5,224	4,596	4,414
1964	6,801	5,040	6,823
1965	4,951	5,349	5,431
1966	3,817	5,047	3,031
1967	3,800	5,273	2,583
1968	635	5,990	611
1969	607	6,043	399
1970	2,603	6,231	2,331
1971	−2,260	7,271	−1,433
1972	−6,416	8,192	−5,795
1973	911	12,153	7,140
1974	−5,505	15,503	1,962
1975	8,903	12,787	18,116
1976	9,483	15,975	4,207
1977	−31,091	17,962	−14,511
1978	−33,947	20,565	−15,427
1979	−27,536	31,172	−991
1980	−25,480	30,386	1,873
1981	−27,978	34,082	6,339
1982	−36,444	28,666	−9,131
1983	−67,080	24,841	−46,604
1984	−112,522	18,752	−106,466
1985	−124,439	25,188	−117,677
1986	−147,708	—	−140,569

Source: Bureau of Economic Analysis, U.S. Department of Commerce

industrial structures, and this goal cannot be accomplished overnight. In contrast to Japan, the United States has recorded trade deficits with the NICs every year since 1980 (see Tables 5.1 and 5.2). While the NICs increased their total global exports approximately $56 billion between 1980 and 1986, about $30 million, or 54% of the total increase, was to the United States.

There have been two major waves of economic development in the Asia-Pacific region since 1960, and a third wave is likely. The first wave was the rapid growth achieved by Japan in the 1960s when Japan enjoyed real economic growth rates in excess of 10% per annum and grew to stand as one of the world's leading economic powers. The second wave was the rapid growth recorded by the Asian NICs in the 1970s. Although the world economy has been somewhat sluggish since

TABLE 5.2
Japan's Merchandise Trade: 1960–1986 (in millions of dollars)

Year	Total Trade Balance	Trade Balance with the United States			Current Account Balance
		Exports	Imports	Balance	
1960	− 436	1,102	1,554	− 452	143
1961	−1,574	1,067	2,096	−1,029	−982
1962	− 721	1,400	1,809	− 409	−48
1963	−1,284	1,507	2,077	− 570	−780
1964	−1,265	1,842	2,336	− 494	−480
1965	283	2,479	2,366	113	932
1966	253	2,969	2,658	311	1,254
1967	−1,221	3,012	3,212	− 200	−190
1968	− 15	4,086	3,527	559	1,048
1969	966	4,958	4,090	868	2,119
1970	437	5,940	5,560	380	1,970
1971	4,307	7,495	4,978	2,517	5,797
1972	5,120	8,848	5,852	2,996	6,624
1973	−1,384	9,449	9,270	179	−136
1974	−6,574	12,799	12,682	177	−4,693
1975	−2,110	11,149	11,608	− 459	−682
1976	2,426	15,690	11,809	3,881	3,680
1977	9,686	19,717	12,396	7,321	10,918
1978	18,200	24,915	14,790	10,125	16,534
1979	−7,640	26,403	20,431	5,972	−8,754
1980	−10,721	31,367	24,408	6,959	−10,746
1981	8,740	38,609	25,297	13,312	4,770
1982	6,900	36,330	24,179	12,151	6,850
1983	20,534	42,829	24,647	18,182	20,779
1984	33,611	59,937	26,862	33,075	35,003
1985	46,099	65,278	25,793	39,485	49,169
1986	82,456	80,456	20,054	51,402	85,845

Source: Japanese Ministry of Finance, except Japanese current account balance, which is from the Bank of Japan.

the beginning of the 1980s, these countries have continued to enjoy fairly high growth rates. And now the third wave is building in China and in the Association of Southeast Asian Nations, which includes Thailand, Malaysia, Singapore, Indonesia, the Philippines, and Brunei. As waves move up in the NICs, the ASEAN countries and China may rightly be expected to become increasingly competitive in labor-intensive industries and to shift to export-oriented economic structures.

However, this process will also cause friction with the countries of North America and Europe, and there are fears that these industrial countries could turn increasingly to protectionism. Accordingly, it is imperative both that the countries involved make the necessary industrial structural adjustments and that an effort be made to expand intraregional trade. These measures would serve to promote the development of stronger economic and trade relations and to fend off the protectionist threat to the free-trading system that has sustained the export-oriented economies of the Pacific. Intraregional trade within Europe accounted for 53%, and trade with the United States only 10%, of total EEC trade in 1985. For the countries of the western Pacific, by contrast, intraregional trade accounted for only 15% and trade with the United States for 40% of the total. There is clearly room for expanding intraregional trade in this area.

Reflecting the increasing interdependence among the countries of the Pacific Basin, the idea of economic cooperation has been a subject of active discussion among scholars, industrialists, and governmental officials. In addition to the academic-oriented Pacific Trade and Development Conference (PAFTAD) and the business-oriented Pacific Basin Economic Council (PBEC), the Pacific Economic Cooperation Conference (PECC) was established in September 1980 building upon a seminar on Pacific Economic Cooperation held at the initiative of Prime Minister Masayoshi Ohira of Japan and Prime Minister Malcolm Fraser of Australia. Concentrating on areas where problems are already evident, PECC has adopted a tripartite structure of scholars, business leaders, and governmental officials to enable it to take a pragmatic and flexible approach. PECC held its fifth General Meeting in Vancouver in November 1986, and the Standing Committee of PECC approved an important statement of Pacific economic cooperation, a basic document defining and directing PECC activities for the future.

Another major highlight of this meeting was that China and Taipei were both accepted as full members. Given the one-China policy pursued by both Beijing and Taipei, this question of Chinese representation is a very delicate issue, as has been shown, for example, in the dispute over participation in the Asian Development Bank's annual meetings. Yet, thanks to the determined efforts of Eric Trigg of Canada and the fact that PECC, while including government officials, is a purely private organization with all members participating as private individuals, it was possible for both Beijing and Taipei to take part in the discussions at the Vancouver meeting. Chinese participation not only presents new possibilities for trade and economic relations within the region, but is also very important for the region's political future. It is imperative that we work to create a climate in which China can play a positive role in the interdependent system of the Asia-Pacific region.

The Soviet Union is another major player that must be taken into account in discussing the outlook for the Asia-Pacific region. Having recognized the urgent imperative of revitalizing its economy, the Soviet

Union under General Secretary Mikhail Gorbachev has become increasingly interested in the fast-growing Asia-Pacific region. Thus, General Secretary Gorbachev's speech in Vladivostok in July of 1986 defined the Soviet Union as a Pacific nation and clearly stated that the Soviet Union intends to take an active part in the region's development.[13] The fact that the Soviet Union attended the Vancouver meeting of the PECC with observer status further indicates its new interest in the Pacific region. In December 1986, I was invited to Moscow by the Academy of Sciences to discuss new Soviet economic and Pacific policies. One of the Soviet experts on Pacific problems told me that, while the Soviet interest in the Pacific has focused mainly on security concerns so far, economic issues should account for 90% of the Soviet concern with the Pacific from now on. Although it is still too early to predict the outcome of this debate within the Soviet Union, it is a development that certainly bears watching.

U.S. economic trends are obviously another important factor for the future of U.S.-Japanese relations. It is inconceivable that the United States should continue this hemorrhaging in its trade balance for the indefinite future, and adjustment policies will have to be implemented sooner or later. This imperative was certainly recognized by Martin Feldstein, the president of the National Bureau of Economic Research (NBER), who expressed his views on correcting the world trade imbalance with these words:

> The United States cannot continue to have annual trade deficits of more than $100 billion financed by an ever-increasing inflow of foreign capital. The U.S. trade deficit will therefore soon shrink and, as it does, the other countries of the world will experience a corresponding reduction in their trade surpluses. Indeed, within the next decade, the United States will shift from trade deficit to trade surplus.[14]

For the United States to go from its current trade deficit of more than $170 billion to a trade surplus in the range of several tens of billions of dollars will have a major deflationary impact on the world economy. It will thus be imperative that Japan and Europe make even greater efforts to stimulate their domestic economies and to recycle part of their surpluses to the developing countries to offset this consequence and to contribute to the growth of the world economy at large.

Conclusion

The U.S.-Japanese relationship is not only closely related to domestic policy issues within Japan and the United States but is also closely connected to world economic development, particularly economic trends in the Pacific region. Given that Japan and the United States together account for nearly 40% of world GNP, it is to be hoped that both countries will turn away from negatively criticizing each other's policies, which only makes the tension between the two countries worse, and will turn to the more constructive role of promoting cooperation in the best interests of world economic growth and development. Relations between Japan and the United States have become increasingly close in the more than forty years since the end of World War II—so close that Ambassador Mike Mansfield could quite rightly title his recent book *No Country More Important: Trials in a Maturing U.S.-Japanese Relationship.*[15] I hope our passing trials will not lead us to lose sight of the overriding importance of this relationship and our shared destinies.

Notes

1. Lester C. Thurow, ed., *The Management Challenge: Japanese Views* (Cambridge, MA: MIT Press, 1985), p. 216.

2. Personal notes of the author.

3. Hendrik S. Houthakker and Stephen P. Magee, "Income and Price Elasticities in World Trade," *The Review of Economics and Statistics* 51 (May 1969):121–122.

4. Hearings on 29–30 September and 1 October 1970 before the U.S. Congress, Subcommittee on Foreign Economic Policy of the Joint Economic Committee, Part 5, *United States Foreign Trade: The Internal and External Adjustment Mechanisms* (Washington, D.C.: Government Printing Office, 1970), p. 967.

5. Ezra Vogel, "Pax Nipponica?" *Foreign Affairs* 64 (Spring 1986):764.

6. U.S. Congress, House Committee on Ways and Means, Subcommittee on Trade, *Task Force Report on U.S.-Japan Trade* (Washington, D.C.: Government Printing Office, 1979), pp. 50–51.

7. Hearings on 10 March and 26–27 April 1983 before the U.S. Congress, House Committee on Ways and Means, Subcommittee on Trade (Washington, D.C.: Government Printing Office, 1983), pp. 215–241.

8. The complete text of this communiqué of 13 January 1979 can be found in U.S. Congress, House Committee on Ways and Means, Subcommittee on Trade, *Task Force Report on U.S.-Japan Trade*, Appendix D, pp. 70–72.

9. The texts (in Japanese and English) of the report of 9 April 1985 and the Action Program of 30 July 1985 are contained in *Action Program for Improved Market Access* (Tokyo: Gyosei, 1986).

10. Haruo Maekawa et al., "The Report of the Advisory Group on Economic Structural Adjustment for International Harmony, Submitted to the Prime Minister, Mr. Yasuhiro Nakasone, 7 April 1986," as reproduced in Jon K.T.

Choy, ed., *Japan: Exploring New Paths* (Washington, D.C.: Japan Economic Institute, 1988), p. 9.

11. David Hale, "How the World Will Pay for America's Built-In Debt," *The Times* (London), 5 December 1986.

12. These reports are part of the working paper series inaugurated in 1986 and published by the World Institute for Development Economics Research (WIDER), United Nations University in Helsinki.

13. An English text of Gorbachev's speech of 29 July 1986 is in "Gorbachev Accents Soviet Role in Asia," *Current Digest of the Soviet Press* 38 (27 August 1986):1–8, 32.

14. Martin Feldstein, "Correcting the Trade Deficit," *Foreign Affairs* 65 (Spring 1987):795.

15. Mike Mansfield, *No Country More Important: Trials in a Maturing Japan-U.S. Relationship* (Tokyo: Simul Press, 1984).

6

Rhetoric and Reality in Bilateral Trade

Akio Morita

Ambassador Mike Mansfield has often made the point that the most important bilateral relationship in the world is the one between the United States and Japan. For many years he also has been declaring that the twenty-first century will be the Age of the Pacific, and that a harmonious relationship between the United States and Japan will be the key to the prosperity of the coming new era. I believe that these statements are profoundly true.

But an imbalance in trade between our two countries, an imbalance which is growing annually, is now putting a strain on this vital relationship. Some have begun to talk of a "trade war." In two countries whose destinies are so interlinked, particularly among such close friends, it is simply terrible that we should use a word like "war." We should recognize and be grateful for the fact that our problems are not yet so badly politicized that we cannot sit down and talk rationally about them.

The United States and Japan: An Essential Relationship

It is necessary to remind ourselves just how closely Japan and the United States are interlinked. Japan cannot feed itself. It is a nation of 125 million people living in a space slightly smaller than the state of Montana. Japan must import $18 billion worth of agricultural products every year. One-third of this amount comes from the United States. Japan imports more agricultural products from the United States than from any other country. In fact, 20% of all agricultural products exported by the United States goes to Japan, followed by 9% to Holland and

6% to Canada. Japan takes more than three-fourths of all the beef the United States exports, and half of the pork and citrus fruits. More than half of the Japanese soft drink market belongs to Coca Cola. Seventy percent of the razor blades sold in Japan are made by Schick. More than 60% of the top 200 of America's Fortune 500 companies have business ties with Japan. The United States exports more to Japan than to West Germany, France, and Italy combined.

As Japan is dependent on the United States, so is the United States dependent on Japan. One-third of the total exports from Japan to the United States is closely related to U.S. industrial activity. Some $2.2 billion, for example, represents exports to the United States by U.S. industries located in Japan. Another $6.6 billion represents products made in Japan by Japanese industries and shipped to the United States to be sold under the brand names of U.S. manufacturers. Another $8.2 billion represents parts and components to be assembled into U.S. products and sold by U.S. manufacturers. The balance of $4.3 billion includes products not produced in the United States, such as videotape recorders and 35mm cameras. In addition, trade with Japan has created roughly 650,000 jobs in the United States. Of these, approximately 240,000 Americans now work directly for Japanese companies in the United States, and these companies together have invested more than $25 billion in the U.S. economy. From this it can be seen that the manufacturing industries of the United States and Japan are related as your right hand is to your left. Someone coined the word "Amerippon"—for America-Nippon ("Nippon" being the Japanese country name in Japanese)—to illustrate this relationship.

Our two nations have a broad and wide-ranging relationship that goes beyond industry and commerce, including the responsibility they share to maintain global peace and stability, as discussed elsewhere in this book by Michael Armacost and Raymond Wylie. Japan, although often criticized for getting a "free ride" in the global peacekeeping efforts, has the fifth largest defense budget in the world and the second largest among America's nonnuclear allies.

The Japanese Liberal Democratic party has been in power for the forty years that have passed since World War II and has maintained a majority in the Diet. Thus, Japan's leadership has remained relatively stable in comparison to that of the United States, and its government policies have been genuinely consistent. This stability is very significant in light of the situations in the Middle East and Latin America. The economic and social stability of Japan in the postwar period has contributed much to the security of the Pacific area and thus, I believe, to world peace.

Japan's location just outside the rim of the Asian continent, which is mostly covered by Communist countries except for half of the Korean Peninsula, means more than the need for a defense budget large enough to build fighter planes and battleships. Japan has been playing a peacekeeping role in Asia somewhat like the "Great Wall" because of its strategic and geopolitical location.

Even in such a close and binding relationship, a trade imbalance of almost $60 billion is unacceptable. Japan is not blameless in this regard. As Ambassador Mansfield noted in his Introduction to this book, Japanese efforts to address these problems have often been called "too little, too late." The Japanese approach has been to address only each specific U.S. complaint as it comes up. There has been little effort to stand back, to look at the issues in a larger context, and then work to solve the underlying problem. Although our two nations are clearly interdependent, there is no long-term vision as to how the United States and Japan should relate to each other. No one has stopped to ask, "Where are we going?" Now we have reached a point where the accumulated U.S. frustration with Japan is about to explode.

Problems in the Relationship

I feel that the Americans are a very proud people. Indeed, they have a great deal to be proud of. But when they feel that they are at a disadvantage, this pride causes them to look for someone else to blame. They wonder, "How could America, a Colossus among nations, be responsible for a situation in which its industry is losing its competitive edge, in which its currency is losing its value, and in which the United States has suddenly become the world's largest debtor nation?" The United States is locked into a "big nation" self-image, and this image is out of date.

The Japanese have a different self-image, but one that is equally out of date. The Japanese persist in thinking of themselves as a poor, dependent nation. This self-image obviously is no longer accurate, for Japan is now the world's largest creditor nation and a world leader in a host of technical areas.

The fact that both Japan and the United States are clinging to outmoded self-images makes it more difficult to see what their true relationship is and perhaps more important, what it should be. The United States is now being forced to take account of its new position in the world because of what is happening to the U. S. dollar. Americans used to be able to buy whatever they wanted with dollars. They never had to earn another country's currency to pay for goods they imported. Now the huge United States deficit is being financed by funds from other nations in the form of capital flow and loans—including a large share from Japan. This gives U.S. citizens the false impression that they can continue living as they have in the past.

Japan's experience has been quite different. Having always had to buy most of its raw materials, energy supplies, and much of its food from abroad, Japan had to export its products in order to earn dollars because no trading partner would accept our yen. We had to export, because our lives depended upon it. It was the dollar that taught us to export. The dollar forced not only Japan, but also other countries that needed this key currency, to become export-oriented. As a result, the United States is buying $60 billion worth of exports from Japan, $16 billion from West Germany, $14 billion from Korea, and $21 billion from Taiwan.

Now, some people in the United States (including some in political office) are saying that the trade imbalance is Japan's fault and are proposing retaliatory measures. The fact that the United States also maintains quotas on steel, textiles, machine tools, and other products is seldom mentioned. But I feel certain that such retaliatory measures are not the solution to our problems. Indeed, sanctimony and self-righteousness, as Mansfield himself points out in his Introduction to this book, rarely result in sound policy.

My company's business is to supply electronic products to the world market. We discovered that our products were being well received in the United States. Our policy is to make products where the market is. In 1970, we decided to build a factory to produce television sets in San Diego. At the time, it took 360 yen to buy one dollar, so operating costs in the United States were much higher than in Japan. Nevertheless, we were confident that our judgment was a correct one in the long run. We invested our money, transferred our technology, and trained our people in California. Now our plant in San Diego is exporting television sets back to Japan. In this way our San Diego plant is contributing to improvement of the bilateral trade imbalance by reducing exports from Japan and increasing exports from the United States.

Some people think that this is a curious situation. One of my American friends recently said to me, "Akio, I bought an American TV rather than a Japanese TV because we have a terrible trade deficit. I found out later that the American brand set I had bought was made in Taiwan, and the SONY set that I decided I wouldn't buy was made in the U.S." I had to tell my American friend that this situation was not strange at all. What we were seeing was the difference between a company that had enough faith to invest in itself and a company that had no faith in itself at all.

I am afraid that U.S. industry has lost faith in itself and hollowed out and that the trade imbalance will not be corrected until that faith is regained. The Japanese automobile industry, in particular, is investing heavily in new plants in the United States and creating thousands of new jobs. The United States automobile industry, in contrast, is investing in the Japanese automobile industry—not in order to obtain a foothold in the Japanese market, but instead to buy engines and even complete automobiles to be sold in the United States market under their own brand names.

Several years ago, I helped General Motors to acquire a one-third interest in the Japanese automobile manufacturer Isuzu because I thought this would help sell GM cars in the Japanese market. Instead, GM started to import components and completed cars from Isuzu. Lee Iacocca, the head of Chrysler, criticized the trade imbalance while he himself aggressively imported from Japan. It is a terrible irony that those engines and automobiles are then accounted as Japanese exports to the United States, tipping the trade balance further in the direction of Japan. For Americans to brand Japan as "unfair" strikes me as very unfair itself.

I see very encouraging signs that Americans are now realizing that the trade imbalance cannot be solved by erecting a protectionary wall around themselves. Such protectionist measures would only serve to restrict trade and introduce the threat of worldwide recession. Neither will the trade problem be solved by the manipulation of the yen-dollar exchange rate, because if U.S. industry does not generate products to sell, the attractiveness of their price will not matter. No, the only solution is for U.S. industry to regain its competitive edge.

One way for the United States to do this would be for it to once again become genuinely interested in productivity. Let me provide just one example of a contrast between our two countries in this regard. There are more than 500,000 lawyers in the United States, and I understand that every year more than 39,000 individuals pass the bar examinations, so the number of lawyers continues to grow. In Japan we have approximately 17,000 lawyers, and the number grows only by about 300 persons a year. While the United States has been busy creating lawyers, Japan has been busier creating engineering students. Many of the best students in the United States do not study engineering but become lawyers or MBAs. This is not a productive enterprise.

To make matters worse, much of this managerial talent now is being distracted by a game of mergers and acquisitions where people spend their time designing take-over moves and building empires. In the greatest attraction of U.S. business, the money game, profits are made not by manufacturing and selling goods but by guessing whether the dollar will rise or fall against, say, the Deutsche mark in the next ten minutes. This also is not a constructive enterprise. The money game is exciting, no doubt, but the swings it causes in the value of the world's currency make it impossible for a responsible industry to make any rational plans to invest for the future. It is necessary to go back to fundamentals to see what constitutes real value.

Such short-term money making by mergers and acquisitions might destroy the unity of people in a company. I have learned that a business organization's real asset is its people—their goodwill, their enthusiasm, and their creativity. How can you expect your people to be motivated to work when they are traded like merchandise? In Japan, management works very hard to treat employees like partners and colleagues. We have a responsibility to do so.

In addition, I believe that any business in any part of the world will be successful only if three elements are present. One of these is creative technology in the form of invention and innovation. The second is creativity in product planning and production. The final element is creative marketing. Without all three, a business will not succeed. I write here from personal experience.

A nation's economy is only as strong as its manufacturing base, and this base is chipped away by every mindless merger and by every decision to shift production to a newly developed country only to save on labor. The world's economy depends on the United States dollar, and the dollar must be strong, based on a strong American industry. The United States must get back to business!

Money is a measuring stick. When the floating system started in 1973, we thought this system would work as a handicap balancing each country's competitiveness. We can enjoy playing golf even with professional players if we are given the appropriate handicap. High handicap players and single handicap players can compete because of this system. Handicaps are assigned according to each player's skill. Now suppose a third party comes in while you are playing golf and tells you to change the handicaps with every hole without evaluating the golfing techniques of the players. You would soon lose your interest in playing the game. You might laugh at this particular analogy, because what I have described never happens on the golf course, but this is exactly what is happening in international business.

Hopeful Signs

There are signs that the United States is waking up to the fact that international trade is the engine that drives the world economy. One example is the interest that Japanese and U.S. businesspeople have shown in investing in each other's countries. This year I cochaired the meeting of the Japan–Western United States Association (JWA), which acts as a forum for discussion on investment operations and many other business relations. Since this forum started twenty years ago as the Japan California Association (JCA), interest has focused mainly on Japan's friendship with California. When I took the chairmanship two years ago, I proposed to our United States counterpart to expand our activities to all western United States and to rename the association so that the participation of interested parties from throughout this entire region would be possible.

Let us begin to work together, not in an atmosphere of blame and suspicion, but in an atmosphere of constructive cooperation. I am writing here not as a Japanese businessman, but as an international businessman.

There is an emerging need for an organic partnership, with joint business enterprises and a pooling of technical expertise and financial resources. This partnership should be administered by an informal complex of overlapping leaders from academia, business, and politics.

A prototype of such a gathering was spearheaded by President Carter and Prime Minister Ohira, who created the first so-called "Wisemen's Group," which is formally named the Japan–United States Economic Relations Group. The second group was established by President Reagan and Prime Minister Nakasone—the United States–Japan Advisory Commission. The aim of this commission was to come up with joint recommendations for the two nations. In 1981 I was a member of the Wisemen's Group, which was comprised of four representatives from the United States and four from Japan. Led by our friend Ambassador Robert Ingersoll and the late Ambassador Nobuhiko Ushiba, we proposed, among other things, an immediate and effective measure to help expand U.S. exports—that the United States sell Alaskan oil to Japan. The dollars earned from these exports could then be used to purchase oil from Mexico, and in this way, the United States would reduce the accumulating foreign debt of Mexico. We believe this measure would work both ways, for it would reduce Japan's dangerous dependence on the Middle East for 70% of its oil (as compared to only 3% for the United States) and help the United States reduce its serious debt problem. Unfortunately, this approach was not given serious consideration by the United States Congress. I wonder why not.

The answer, of course, lies in part in the politics involved. I have a very strong belief in democracy—both for Japan and for the United States. But the biggest problem in a democratic system is that politicians tend to be domestically oriented. They see things from the sometimes narrow perspective of their particular constituents because it is necessary to be elected in order to be a politician. If problems arise, the easiest thing to do is to blame others and then get headlines in the newspapers. This happens in Washington and it happens in Tokyo. It is the fate of any democratic system.

Many people in both countries know that changes are needed, but it is obviously difficult to make these changes. Perhaps a coalition of experienced businesspeople, who could draw on the expertise of the academic world and the consensus-building capabilities of our best politicians, could make very useful contributions. Government leaders and businesspeople in both countries must realize that the world has only one economy.

Conclusion

I believe that the future of our world trading system depends upon increasing, not stemming, trade. Right now Japan is digging its own grave in this regard. If the trade imbalance does not change, then the reaction from abroad will be to demand greater and greater restrictions on Japanese exports. We must get to the root causes of these problems and not just react to them superficially. U.S. industrial competitiveness must be restored.

The trade, financial, and cultural ties between Japan and the United States are complex, and the important relationship between our two countries may be uncomfortable from time to time. Nevertheless, the right prescription is not confrontation and protection, but rather cooperation as we realize that our destinies are shared.

Suggestions for Further Reading

Abegglen, James, and George Stalk, Jr., *Kaisha, The Japanese Corporation* (New York: Basic Books, 1985).

Destler, I. M., and Hideo Sato, *Coping with U.S.-Japanese Economic Conflicts* (Lexington, MA: Lexington Books, 1982).

Japan-U.S. Businessmen's Conference, *Understanding the Industrial Policies and Practices of Japan and the United States: A Business Perspective* (Tokyo and Washington, D.C.: The Japan-U.S. Businessmen's Conference, 1984).

McGraw, Thomas K., ed., *America Versus Japan* (Boston: Harvard Business School Press, 1986).

Morita, Akio, *Made in Japan: Akio Morita and SONY* (New York: Dutton, 1986).

Prestowitz, Clyde, *Trading Places: How We Allowed Japan to Take the Lead* (New York: Basic Books, 1988).

Pugel, Thomas, and Robert Hawkins, eds., *Fragile Interdependence* (Lexington, MA: Lexington Books, 1986).

"SONY's Challenge," *Business Week*, 1 June 1987, pp. 64–69.

United States–Japan Advisory Commission, *Challenges and Opportunities in United States–Japan Relations: A Report Submitted to the President of the United States and the Prime Minister of Japan* (Washington, D.C.: Government Printing Office, 1984).

7

Japan, the United States, and Economic Development in the Asia-Pacific Region

Dennis J. O'Donnell

If an economic era is defined by who plays the role of the creditor, then the mid-1980s witnessed a transition from Pax Americana to Pax Nipponica.[1] This reversal of the relative Japanese and U.S. financial positions alters the fundamental relationship between the United States and Japan and, by extension, the economic environment for the rest of the Asia-Pacific region. This dramatic change is best illustrated by balance-of-payments figures for the United States and Japan over the period 1975 to 1986, as shown in Table 7.1. The Japanese trade surplus resulted in a 1986 net overseas asset position for Japan of $180.4 billion. During the same year, the U.S. trade deficit with Japan amounted to $55 billion.[2] As Nigel Holloway has stated, "the world must help Japan recycle its wealth as efficiently as possible and find ways to make it attractive for Japanese institutions to invest in capital-starved countries. Unfortunately, these are not always the poorest. The U.S. looks like being the biggest debtor nation for the foreseeable future."[3] This dramatic reversal where Japan is now the creditor—the surplus-generating economic powerhouse—and the United States is the debtor—the deficit-ridden nation—creates an extremely unpredictable set of economic and political forces between these two nations. The countries of the Asia-Pacific region face a risky, difficult, and turbulent economic environment over the next twenty years that ultimately depends upon the actions of the United States and Japan. To paraphrase Peter Drucker, we are now facing a world where the economy has already changed from the prevailing dominance of the United States in the post–World War II period. The effects of Britain's replacement by the United States

TABLE 7.1

U.S.-Japanese Total Merchandise Trade, 1975–1986 (in millions of dollars)

Year	Total Japanese Mercandise Trade			Total U.S. Merchandise Trade		
	Exports	Imports	Balance	Exports	Imports	Balance
1975	55,753	57,863	−2,110	107,088	98,185	8,903
1976	67,225	64,799	2,426	114,745	124,228	−9,483
1977	80,495	70,809	9,686	120,816	151,907	−31,091
1978	97,543	79,343	18,200	142,054	176,001	−33,947
1979	103,032	110,672	−7,640	184,473	212,009	−27,536
1980	129,807	140,528	−10,721	224,269	249,750	−25,481
1981	152,030	143,290	8,740	237,085	265,063	−27,978
1982	138,831	131,931	6,900	211,198	247,642	−36,444
1983	146,927	126,393	20,534	200,745	262,757	−62,013
1984	170,114	136,503	33,611	217,888	325,726	−107,838
1985	175,638	129,539	46,099	213,146	345,276	−132,130
1986	209,151	126,408	82,743	217,304	369,961	−152,657

Source: Japan Institute for Social and Economic Affairs, *Japan 1988: An International Comparison* (Tokyo: Japan Institute, 1988), pp. 36–38.

were profound; should we expect any less as Japan replaces the United States?[4]

It is my contention in this chapter that the relationship between the United States and Japan will control the destiny and development of the Asia-Pacific region over the next twenty years. If Japan invests in Asia wisely through aid and direct capital flows that augment local development as well as serve long-term Japanese interests and efficiency, future trade-based growth in the region will be enhanced. This type of progress, combined with the further opening of Japan's domestic markets and the development of a mature postindustrial economy, would do much to ensure that Japan would contribute to the well-being of the Asia-Pacific region. If the United States avoids protectionism, manages to continue the reordering of its economic system, encouraging real capital investment and rapid technological change, and functions effectively in world markets with the realigned dollar, the basis for its nonsustainable deficits will be eroded. The destabilization and potential worldwide recession caused by distortions in the United States global role must be avoided if internal development of the Asia-Pacific region is to proceed in an orderly fashion.

In contrast, if Japan turns to nationalistic investment strategies, fails to open its internal markets, and reacts fearfully to the uncertainties of the dollar-yen relationship, the future will be bleak. If the United

States fails to correct its deficit problems, fails to engage in rational real capital formation linked to worldwide comparative advantage, and yields to protectionism, the future will be equally bleak. And if either side blames the other for domestic difficulties, the environment for Third World development will deteriorate to an even greater degree.

In this new era of a changed world economy, Japan and the United States are both uncertain in their roles. The quality of their relationship will determine whether lesser nations in the Asia-Pacific region are carried along on a path of improvement, based on the earlier examples provided by Japan and the Asian NICs in the postwar era, or toward painful stagnation or decline.

Drucker identified three fundamental changes that have occurred in the fabric of the world economy: (1) the primary products economy has become separated from the industrial economy; (2) in the industrial economy itself, production has become uncoupled from employment; and (3) capital movements rather than trade in goods and services have become the driving force of the world economy. Trade in goods and services has not quite come uncoupled but the link has become loose and, even worse, unpredictable.[5] Moreover, the past century, and especially the period since 1945, has seen, in the words of Richard Rosecrance, the rise of the "trading state." In Rosecrance's view, the trading state, whose power emanates from its ability to engage in trade and does not derive from its military or territorial power, has become the dominant form of political economic organization in the world.[6] Japan is clearly the dominant example, although West Germany is also a prototype of this phenomenon.

Asia Caught Between Unpredictable Superpowers

In the old regime, characterized by Great Britain and the United States, success was based not only on the economic development process but also on having extensive geopolitical and military involvements. Yet, as in the case of the United States in the post–World War II period, a legacy of power based on military and geopolitical influence can gradually become disproportionate in relation to a country's economic power. Thus, in the current world political economy, where trade for trade's sake determines the attainment of creditor status and the ability to set the tone for the economic future, the United States finds itself in an uncomfortable position. Its efforts to formulate clear directions for its international economic policies may well be confused by its legacy of geopolitical responsibilities and military commitments. For the Asia-Pacific region, this confusion on the part of the United States presents a risky situation fraught with many problems.

The remarkable emergence of Japan as the major creditor nation in the world leaves it equally in a state of uncertainty. Its single-minded pursuit of economic and trade development has been accomplished with a minimum of political and military involvements. This achievement makes Japan the archetypical trading state. However, the world will not expect or allow the continuation of such a simple role once power has been transferred. Will Japan remain single minded? As *The Economist* has recently observed, "A country that has become top manufacturer and top banker in forty surprising years is bound eventually to mold its era instead of sitting idly on its money."[7] In noting that the Japanese are bound eventually to find something political as well as economic to do with their money, *The Economist* posed a major question: What does the Japanese experience mean now that Japan is on top?

This question has two clear dimensions. The first aspect arises for those countries eager to follow in Japan's footsteps. Does the Japanese experience create a "demonstration effect" for other nations of Asia and the Pacific? The second aspect arises for those countries affected by Japan and centers on the role Japan will play now that it is a developed creditor nation able to set the tone for economic development in the Asia-Pacific region for the next twenty years. The United States is today among those nations asking the question, "How will Japan play its hand and use its trump cards now that it has control of the game?"

As the nations of Asia and the Pacific try to negotiate a continued path toward export-oriented industrialization, this situation may be much like the dilemma faced by someone tied between a racehorse (Japan) and an elephant (the United States). If relations between the two are peaceful, clearly the person stuck in the middle will go wherever the two beasts choose to go, be it forward or backward, because by doing so one remains intact. If the two beasts fight, or choose to run in opposite directions, the person in the middle will certainly be crushed or torn asunder. The present unpredictable state of both the United States and Japan will have powerful effects throughout the world. But their economic relationship will have profound effects within the Asia-Pacific region and will clearly cause anxiety until the end of the twentieth century.

New Meaning to the Debate over NICs

Many economic analysts have expressed hope that the recent experience of the newly industrializing countries (NICs) in Asia is indicative of the future. They suggest that the development of industrialization and the expansion of trade will create a new world of economic prosperity in Asia that could conceivably spread to the remote corners of the less developed world.[8] If they are correct, then the NICs serve as proof that the Japanese model is transferable and that it demonstrates a path to development that other nations may follow.

Other economists have begun to fear that continued growth based on Japan and the NICs' experience is unlikely to occur.[9] This set of economists has focused on the problems inherent in a world dominated by the United States deficits, both domestic and in the balance-of-payments, and the consequent crisis of the dollar. In addition, these economists fear that the industrialization of less developed countries (LDCs) in the late 1980s and 1990s may occur in a world not of open economies, but of closing economies where economic growth has largely stagnated. These analysts have also raised serious questions as to whether the lessons we have learned from Japan's industrialization, and from the early experiences of the newly industrializing countries in Asia, will remain valid in a world where the U.S.-Japanese relationship has been fundamentally altered. They are concerned that the era of U.S. economic preeminence from the end of World War II to 1974 was a unique, nonrepeatable phenomenon. Finally, they ask disturbing questions about the prospects of LDCs in a world where growth has stagnated, where technology has advanced, and where the openness of markets that prevailed in the postwar era has come to an end.

At root, these economists are questioning whether we might be generalizing the experience of the NICs too much. They point out that Singapore and Hong Kong are unique city-states with little general applicability; they further argue that both Taiwan and South Korea are examples of nations with special historical and geopolitical relationships to the United States and Japan that are not applicable to other nations that might follow in the development process.

Until the mid-1980s, this debate appeared to be academic and largely unfocused. There was a pronounced gulf between the opposing schools of thought, and the subtleties of the argument were often lost. To many, it appeared that the theoretical and empirical arguments of the economists who heralded the progress of the NICs and spoke of new technology and entrepreneurialism easily overcame the picayune and dismal projections of their colleagues working from Marxist ideological bases or positing unpopular limits to growth models. However, the recent experiences of 1986–1987 have certainly changed the relative positions of the two camps and improved the clarity of the issues.

Dramatic Changes 1986–1987

This shift in the debate was set off by research conducted at the Institute of International Economics by Stephen Marris and published in October 1985 as *Deficits and the Dollar: The World Economy at Risk*. Marris developed several disturbing scenarios, one of which contemplated a continuation of balance-of-payments and internal deficits for the United States along with deepening stagnation of the world economy marked by balance-of-payments and external debt crises. Marris defined this scenario as the "hard landing."[10] Events moved rapidly, and by August 1987 Marris was compelled by the speed and nature of those events to reassess the issue. In a pamphlet entitled *Deficits and the Dollar Revisited*, he concluded that the hard landing had in part occurred:

> There were two key features of the hard landing predicted in *Deficits and the Dollar*. The first was that the dollar would fall very sharply, and in the end too far. The second was that, as confidence ebbed, strong upward pressures on U.S. interest rates would lead to a recession in the United States. This recession, combined with the weak dollar, would have a very negative impact on growth both in Europe and Japan and in the indebted developing countries and, hence, would spread throughout the entire world economy.[11]

The specter of rising interest rates, a declining dollar, and future inflation brought panic into the hearts of both U.S. and foreign investors, as evidenced in the October 1987 stock market crash in the United States. The crash reverberated throughout the world but, as indicated in Table 7.2, was reflected most dramatically in stock markets in the Asia-Pacific region.[12]

In the wake of the hard landing of the U.S. dollar, Japan finally yielded to the inevitability of an appreciation of the yen. Japan will face a significant decline in its ability to export based on an undervalued currency. This scenario may not look so bleak, however, in light of the fact that the powerful yen will now enable Japan to buy real and financial assets on the world market and to make prudent investments throughout Asia.

This potential optimistic outcome must be viewed cautiously, given the fact that a vast majority of Japan's net foreign assets are denominated in dollars. Those dollars not only have declining value but are exposed to significant further devaluation in the form of foreign exchange risk. The dollar would also depreciate if inflation in the United States were to accelerate. In addition, many options available to the Japanese are

TABLE 7.2

Changes in Stock Market Indices Worldwide Following the October 19, 1987 U.S. Stock Market Crash

Year	New York	London	Tokyo	Hong Kong	Singapore	Sydney	Taipei	Bangkok
20 October	1,841.01	1,439.20	21,910.08	3,362.39	5,614.00	1,549.50	3,491.94	377.13
Year high	2,722.42	1,926.20	26,646.00	3,949.73	8,628.34	2,305.90	4,673.14	423.03
Year ago	1,811.02	1,277.60	16,523.37	2,227.76	5,526.75	1,361.30	999.31	160.46
5 years ago	1,013.80	626.10	7,371.65	886.65	4,079.11	524.60	na	110.12
Negative percentage change due to the U.S. Stock Market crash	0.323759	0.252829	0.177734	0.148705	0.349353	0.328028	0.252549	0.10850

Source: Compiled from data in Philip Bowring, "The End of the Ride," Far Eastern Economic Review (29 October 1987), p. 87.

like two-edged swords; for example, the decline in Japanese exports can be mitigated in the short run by reductions in profit margins. In the long run, the Japanese must come to terms with the changing character of comparative advantage and technological change throughout the rest of the world without the protection of an undervalued currency. Japan's ability to invest successfully in the rest of the world may be a much more risky proposition than was their ability to invest in Japan over the past forty years. In addition, enormous pressure currently exists for the Japanese to open their economy, much as the Americans did in the postwar period when the United States was the major creditor nation. At that time, the United States provided markets for industrializing and developing Asia; Japan will soon be expected to do the same.

The part of the hard landing that did not occur is in fact detrimental to the current system of flexible exchange rates and world monetary order. Under the hard landing scenario, a rapidly falling dollar would correct the trade imbalance between the United States and Japan. The fact that this correction has not occurred[13] has led to the realization that flexible exchange rates pegged to the dollar, in a world where the majority of the financial assets are dollar denominated, are not self-correcting for the real trade balance. As a result, countries are now asking for fixed exchange rate bands and the creation of a reserve system based on the yen, European currency, and the dollar. This idea, if implemented, would represent a monumental change in the structure of world monetary arrangements and would create significant pressures on the Japanese economy.[14]

The Japanese/NICs
Demonstration Effect Debate

The Japanese postwar economic miracle and the more recent economic development of the NICs are impressive. However, their "demonstration effect" on the future economic well-being of nations not similarly situated may be in doubt in light of the economic changes that took place from 1985 to 1987.

The conventional view of the economic performance of Japan and the NICs argues that these countries adopted "right policies." These nations adopted realistic exchange rates, provided incentives for exports, and above all managed to get factor prices right so that their economies could expand in line with their comparative advantage. These nations relied on market forces and integration into the world economy, which yielded results superior to those that might be expected from protectionist policies and dissociation from the world economy. They adopted export-oriented industrialization policies rather than import-substitution industrialization policies. The import policies of these countries were liberalized so that they could import raw materials. Moreover, they minimized growth in consumption, thereby discouraging final goods imports and encouraging domestic savings. In these and other ways, Japan and the NICs represent the neoclassical laissez-faire model of economic development.

Indications that not everyone interpreted the NICs' experience in this way began to appear in the early 1980s. Hubert Schmitz gave a useful summary of this opposing view:

> The emergence of the NICs is seen as a response to a set of international circumstances which at one and the same time produced relatively favorable access to the markets of advanced countries, dramatically increased access to international finance and increased relocation of production by transnational corporations to the periphery. These factors are seen as having conditioned the emergence of the NICs but not as having determined which countries would seize the opportunities. The view is that this was determined partly by location and geopolitical significance; partly by the existence of a strong (repressive) internationally reliable regime; and partly by the existence of a technological infrastructure resulting from earlier import substitution policies. Finally, state control over industrial development is held to be extensive and decisive in bringing about the dynamic growth.[15]

If one looks at Japan, Taiwan, and South Korea, one can see a definite pattern. That pattern consists of early import-substituting industrialization, particularly in the case of Japan and South Korea. It also shows the development of educational and communication infrastructures, as well as the creation of a strong state bureaucracy with considerable influence in the overall economy. As these strong internal controls were established, domestic markets were largely controlled by competition. In Taiwan and South Korea, the dominant economic structure was, in fact, an embryonic form of the Japanese model. Since Taiwan and South Korea were both ruled by Japan, from 1895 and 1910, respectively, until the end of World War II, the apparent power of the Japanese model is probably linked to this unique historical experience. Hong Kong and Singapore, in contrast, were highly influenced by foreign capital investments and movements. Their ability to engage in industrial production was directly dependent upon the overall volume and growth of international trade in the Asia-Pacific region and not on domestic resources or markets.

The question that then arises centers on whether the Japanese model can be applied to Asian countries not similarly situated—either as city-states, or, in the case of South Korea and Taiwan, as nations with prior significant import-substituting industrialization and significant development of educational and communication infrastructures linked to Japanese control. Certainly none of these NICs has undergone an independent modernization/transformation similar to that of Japan during the Meiji Restoration in the latter part of the nineteenth century. In addition, Japan, South Korea, and Taiwan were very favorably treated by the United States due to their geopolitical importance during the post-1945 Cold War era. If the United States changes its economic policy in the new postindustrial era, as suggested by Rosecrance, then no newly industrializing nations will be so favorably treated. This argument tends to emphasize the importance of cyclical and historical factors in the growth of Japan and the NICs. Will the same cyclical and historical factors recur in the future for countries with differing historical backgrounds and differing world economic conditions? The outlook is uncertain.

This critique of the neoclassical interpretation of the economic development experience of Japan and the NICs has been associated with the Institute of Development Studies at the University of Sussex in England. Even though the Institute's theorists strain to give a Marxist interpretation to Asian development, they raise important questions. These questions include the following: (1) What is the future of export-led industrialization if it depends on expanding U.S., Japanese, and European import markets? (2) What is the future for industrial exports in low-wage countries, given new developments in the technology of production? (3) Was Japanese and NIC development in part due to U.S. geopolitical decisions that were wisely exploited, but not likely to be repeated? (4) Does the era of Pax Nipponica call for a different development strategy for the LDCs of the Asia-Pacific region?

The Late 1980s and Early 1990s:
Slow Growth and Protectionism

What is the future of export-led industrialization if it depends on expanding U.S., Japanese, and European import markets? In the next ten years, the United States and Japan will be responding to events that occurred in the 1970s and early 1980s. The international patterns that supported the export-led development of the NICs in the 1980s are already starting to change, and this prospect bodes ill for the smaller Asian nations hoping to follow in the footsteps of these leaders.

The United States already represents a declining share of the export market for Hong Kong, Taiwan, and South Korea owing to dollar devaluation and slow U.S. demand growth. The ASEAN nations have also experienced declining or stagnant export demand since 1983 because of the same factors. If the United States corrects its federal budget deficit through deflationary policies, the problems of penetrating U.S. markets will be magnified. The assumption that the U.S. export market is available indefinitely is no longer safe. The closing of the U.S. market is further complicated by the realization that much inter-Asian trade is ultimately dependent on U.S. re-export markets. The outsourcing of Japanese production to the NICs and other Asian nations depends on U.S. markets as much as on the revaluation of the yen and rising Japanese production costs.

The fact that the U.S. trade deficit is not responding to dollar devaluation further adds to the potential shrinkage of the U.S. market. Continuing U.S. trade deficits will lead to further accumulation of dollars abroad and downward pressure on the yen/dollar rate, and this trend will induce recessionary pressures in Japan and the United States.[16] This process emphasizes the interdependence of the Japanese and U.S. economies. To illustrate the economic linkages between the rest of the world, the Asia-Pacific region, and the United States in the late 1980s, Stephen Marris has emphasized a series of crucial issues. He finds that since 1985 the most striking development outside the United States has been the slowdown in growth in Japan and Europe due to the drop in oil prices. The conventional wisdom saw falling oil prices in Japan and Europe as a condition for economic growth. What these growth forecasts missed was the decline in demand for exports to oil-producing nations that Japan and Europe would experience, which was also a result of falling oil prices. From 1984 to 1987, imports from oil producers fell by 45% in volume terms with devastating consequences for Europe and Japan. At the same time, world commodity prices fell, reducing the purchasing power of non-oil-exporting countries by more than $50 billion, which led to additional reductions of import demand. To compound this problem, the U.S. export market deteriorated for Japan and Europe and is continuing to do so as the dollar weakens and U.S. growth rates remain low. Marris concluded that the cumulative effect of these three shocks on world import demand from Japan and Europe would amount to more than 5 percent of the total GNP for Japan and Europe in the "hard landing" scenario that is currently under way.[17]

Since the European markets, suffering double-digit inflation, have remained stagnant since the late 1970s, Japan has been touted as the likely successor to the United States as the new export market of the future. However, as Marris made clear, despite Japan's vast accumulations of foreign assets, its domestic economy is stagnant. In fact, the Japan Economic Research Center noted that the increase in domestic demand over the past ten years in Japan has been considerably below the natural rate of growth. This slow economic growth caused a rise in the current account surplus in the 1980s. The major cause of stagnation was the negative growth of public fixed capital formation, with decreased housing demand and a low rate of increase in consumption demand relative to income.[18]

Calls from world exporters for access to Japanese markets are loud and continuous. But the ability to penetrate Japanese markets will depend on more than just a reduction of trade barriers and a rejuvenation of the economy. It will depend on a change in Japanese society at the household level. Many have observed the persistently low rates of consumption in Japan relative to income growth. Times of slow income growth tend to bring about an even higher resistance to imports. Higher per capita consumption in Japan would require a change in savings behavior that has developed and persisted over many decades within a relatively short period of time. This change, given the aging of the Japanese population and current increases in retirement savings rates, is unlikely.[19] In addition, consumption growth in Japan depends on long-term changes in life-style and land-use patterns. Therefore, growth would likely have to follow a huge construction boom in new housing and public infrastructure as well as abandonment of the agricultural production of "Sunday farmers," which would together bring about an enormous distortion of land prices and the cost of food. For these things to happen, substantial changes in Japanese culture would be required. The presence of wealth and foreign products at prices cheaper than Japanese equivalents might slowly cause U.S.-style consumption change. But the change will probably occur only after the current export-led objectives of the rest of the Asia-Pacific region have long been obsolete.

The Japan Economic Research Center contends that in the future "a rise in the propensity to consume and the active execution of public investment policies will be able to prevent a let up in demand."[20] Some hope for these changes can be found in the 1986 Maekawa Report and the 1987 Fourth Comprehensive National Development Plan (or the Yonzenso Plan). In the case of the Maekawa Report, the importance of Japan's large international trade imbalance is dramatically stated as follows:

It is necessary to view a continuation of Japan's large imbalance in the current trade account as a crisis condition not only in managing our own economy but also in cooperative development of the world economy. Today, Japan has entered a period in which historic changes must be made in its economic policies as well as in the lives of the people. Without such changes, there can be no progress for Japan.[21]

The Maekawa Report emphasized the following priorities: (1) increasing domestic demand, (2) improving foreign access to Japanese markets and promoting importation of manufactured products. The Yonzenso program commits $8 trillion between 1986 and the year 2000 to upgrade Japanese public infrastructure. This commitment aims to reduce regional imbalances inside Japan and to overcome the "hollow development" issues (which were part of the recent political debate over the succession to the prime ministry spurred by economist Kiichi Miyazawa).[22] The Maekawa Report received very poor reviews from the Japanese press, much skepticism from the body politic, and criticism from the professional management elite. The primary problem was its failure to set goals, identify means, and indicate timetables.[23] The Yonzenso plan faces severe constraints if the federal Japanese budget is to be balanced as a macroeconomic stimulus. A history in Japan of slow progress on public works when national budgets are tight further complicates matters.[24] In addition, no guarantees of foreign importer participation are included, so the potential of the Yonzenso plan to enlarge Japan's import market is initially indirect at best.

The intent of the Maekawa and Yonzenso approaches are positive, but at this point expectations for a rapid turnaround of Japanese domestic demand growth are unchanged given the fundamental issues involved. If U.S., Japanese, and European markets are stagnant—and, in the case of Japan, inflexible, owing to cultural factors—then export-led growth must depend on reduced protectionism in the advanced nations and/or continued market penetration capabilities stemming from low wages. Yet recent evidence suggests that protectionism is on the rise in the developed nations.

Japan and the United States appear to have roughly equivalent levels of protection when all factors are considered relative to the industrial products of the developing world.[25] Recent World Bank estimates indicate that nontariff barriers (NTBs) are becoming the dominant form of protection. These NTBs include voluntary export restrictions, quotas, preferential government purchasing policies, local content requirements and subsidies, and orderly marketing arrangements. Through tariff escalation, where tariffs are raised on manufactured goods relative to raw materials, the ability to internalize value added through exports is hindered in the developing countries. The World Bank reported that in 1986 31% of the developing countries' exports of manufactured goods were affected by NTBs compared with 18% of industrial countries' manufactured exports. Europe's tariff and nontariff barriers to the manufactured goods of developing countries matches the U.S. and Japanese performance, leaving no advanced country available for export growth by LCDs in the late 1980s and early 1990s. This situation contrasts dramatically with the free-trade environment of the 1960s and 1970s.

For Japan, South Korea, and Taiwan, economic growth was encouraged by U.S. market availability, capital inflows, dollar infusions following import substitution, and state-managed economic plans based on the Japanese model. Today the United States is a slow-growing debtor; no Asian wars are on the horizon for the United States; and the remaining nations are diverse in historical experience. Because Japan is unlikely to be the next open industrial export market, and the United States is preempted economically and geopolitically from its postwar role, the immediate future for the emerging nations of Asia and the Pacific appears bleak. They appear unlikely to benefit from the same primary sources that gave impetus to the growth of Japan and the other NICs, either in accordance with the neoclassical model or the revisionist interpretation characterized by the Institute of Development Studies. Thus, the future of export-led industrialization is as weak as the stagnant and recession-prone U.S. and European economies (the "two elephants"). The racehorse, Japan, is at the gate, while its jockey contemplates his winnings from the previous race. The devaluation of the dollar and the revaluation of the yen and other Asian currencies appears unable to correct the U.S. trade deficit or stimulate economic growth in the United States. In fact, it seems only to raise worldwide fears of U.S. inflation accompanied by a recession and a further decline in world export markets.[26]

The Late 1980s and Early 1990s:
The End of the Cheap Labor Advantage?

What is the future for industrial exports in low-wage countries, given new developments in the technology of production? This question arises from the second change identified by Drucker, namely, that production has become separated from employment. In addition, doubt raised by recent changes in the technology of production may dampen the basis for continued foreign capital investments in low wage peripheral Asian nations.

Drucker stated the case very clearly: "Increased manufacturing production in developed countries has actually come to mean decreasing blue-collar employment. As a consequence, labor costs are becoming less and less important as a 'comparative cost' and as a factor in competition."[27] This development is due to the response of the U.S.

market to the international competition based on low wages in the 1970s and 1980s. The U.S. response has been dramatic: For example, Ford has been increasing productivity at 6% per year since 1981 and now turns out 10% more output with 47% fewer workers. U.S. Bureau of Labor Statistics indicate that due to increasing U.S. output in manufacturing and lagging wages since 1983, U.S. unit labor costs are now below those of many other industrial nations, including Japan. The decline in the dollar will not only close the U.S. market considerably but may also make the United States an active competitor in manufacturing export markets in the 1990s. In 1985 the market shares of the United States (20%), Japan (16%), and West Germany (18%) comprised 54% of world manufactured exports, and all of these nations are intent on expanding these shares.[28] The devaluation of the dollar and the realignment of the yen and mark will create competition among these nations linked more closely to comparative advantage than to exchange rate distortions.

What does dollar realignment mean to the LDCs and even the NICs of the Asia-Pacific region? It could mean little if low wages in South Korea, Malaysia, Thailand, and other Asian nations continue to yield a competitive edge in the marketplace. However, trends in technology and the calculus of the profitability of foreign capital investment by the United States and Japan may indicate an erosion of low-wage advantages in production costs.

The erosion of low-wage advantages in the LDCs is part and parcel of the response of capital investment strategies to these low-wage advantages themselves. When the United States is faced with low wage–based competition, part of the response has been a slow growth in U.S. wages. But the main response has been capital investment, production management, and research and development strategies to offset that advantage. One example of this process can be found in the manufacture of semiconductors. With the manual production technology of the 1970s, Hong Kong production costs were 33% of those in the United States; with the semi-automatic technology of the early 1980s, these costs rose to 63% of U.S. costs. With automated assembly lines installed in 1983, production costs in Hong Kong were only 8% lower than those in the United States.[29]

Peter Drucker sees the rising importance of non-wage competition in manufacturing as a factor in the historical closing of the door for LDC development. As he stated:

In the rapid industrialization of the nineteenth century, one country, Japan, developed by exporting raw materials, mainly silk and tea, at steadily rising prices. Another, Germany, developed by leap-frogging into the "high-tech" industries of its time, mainly electricity, chemicals and optics. A third, the United States, did both. Both routes are blocked for today's rapidly industrializing countries—the first because of the deterioration of the terms of trade for primary products, the second because it requires an infrastructure of knowledge and education far beyond the reach of a poor country (although South Korea is reaching for it). Competition based on lower labor costs seemed to be the only alternative; *is this also going to be blocked?*[30]

Drucker's question cannot yet be answered with certainty, but technology and foreign capital investment by the United States and Japan over the next ten years may indicate that the answer is "yes."

In a careful assessment of the diffusion of new production technology and the development of new linkages between final markets and production, Raphael Kaplinsky took much the same view as Drucker and concluded that competition based on lower labor costs will be blocked.[31] The driving force in blocking continued LDC development appears to be U.S.-Japanese competition in production technology.

Citing a broad range of sources, Kaplinsky drew the following conclusions regarding the markets of the Asia-Pacific region: (1) The reduction of scale economies in the mass production industries are likely to take production closer to the final market and undermine the logic of building "world plants" and shipping parts around the world, and (2) trade reversal may be occurring, whereby the assembly of electronic circuits, for example, is again being done in the developed countries. For example, very-large scale integration has allowed Japanese TV firms to withdraw from South Korea and return to Japan. New technology of this type will reduce significantly the rate at which production is subcontracted to the Third World. Finally, Kaplinsky also concluded that forms of optimized assembly and "zero inventory" (Kanban) systems, as well as computer-aided design and computer-aided manufacture, will make for a more efficient link between suppliers, assemblers, and final markets. These complex systems will give a disadvantage to LDCs in competing as peripheral suppliers as well as in benefiting from foreign capital investments.[32] Kaplinsky cautions against overextension of these arguments. However, it should be noted that he wrote his ideas before Marris described his "hard landing" theory and before the massive realignment of the dollar and yen took place.

A recent U.S. study reported in the *Far Eastern Economic Review* found that 54% of large and medium-sized companies were more likely to build new plants in the United States than abroad because of declining costs.[33] If the U.S. market is growing slowly, and if low-wage advantages are removed through technical change, then export-oriented industrialization is facing a limited future in the LDCs and even in the NICs in the Asia-Pacific region.

U.S. and Japanese Capital Investment in Asia

Was Japanese and NIC development in part due to U.S. geopolitical decisions that were wisely exploited, but not likely to be repeated? The diffusion of new technology and net capital formation has been an essential part of the development experience of the NICs. Both views of the development success of the NICs point to the important role of foreign capital investment at the margin as the key source of these valuable inputs. In the case of the United States, the questions raised by Drucker, the analysis of Kaplinsky, and the profitability of U.S. corporations all indicate that foreign outsourcing will not be as desirable—and with the devaluation of the dollar, much less feasible— in the future. In the case of Japan, a considerable source of Asian foreign investment has been linked to the outsourcing of intermediate production ultimately dependent on final sales in the U.S. market. Not only is the U.S. market shrinking; in addition, the avoidance of U.S. protectionism and technological imperatives suggest investment in the United States as a key Japanese strategy. The declining dollar adds considerable weight to the argument for investment in U.S. productive capacity. In 1986 Japan invested $10.2 billion in the United States, prompted by the lower value of the dollar, stable U.S. wages, production costs lower than in Japan, and the ability to export back to Japan.[34] Japan's strategy of making capital investments in the United States that produce products for reexport to Japan and lead to an improvement in the U.S. trade balance with Japan wins kudos in Washington and now makes increasing economic sense.

There is no doubt that Japan has the experience and the assets to continue the transfer of production out of Japan to lower-cost Asian economies to counteract yen revaluation. But this strategy depends on a Japanese willingness to accept exposure to the risk of U.S. and European recession. The potential for reexport to Japan depends on the internal growth of the Japanese domestic market and the willingness of the Japanese work force to endure considerable restructuring toward services in the postindustrial transformation of Japan. If the United States and Great Britain are examples by which to judge, this process is painful, recessionary, and politically very difficult. If the changing character of technology makes investment in the LDCs of Asia unjustifiable on economic grounds, then we must hypothesize that Japan will be willing to invest abroad for geopolitical and aid-related motives, much as the United States did in the postwar period. Yet if Rosecrance is correct that Japan is the epitome of the "trading state" and that Japan's sense of historical isolation will remain valid for the future, then it is unlikely that Japan will assume this role.

The other sources of U.S. nontrade-related investment and economic impact in the Asia-Pacific region since 1945 were the postwar recovery efforts, the Korean War, and the Vietnam War. It seems highly improbable that the United States will repeat any of these activities, taking into consideration current levels of foreign aid and the well-documented failure of U.S. objectives in the two wars. The recent handling of the Philippines, the continuing policy of noninvolvement in Southeast Asia, and the political links of the United States to the People's Republic of China all suggest that this period is one of long-term U.S. restraint in the region. The constitutional limits on the Japanese military, the continuing impact of World War II, and political reality all suggest that Japan will not step into the role of policeman in the Asia-Pacific region—a role played by the United States for the past forty years.

A Return to Basics:
Domestic Development

Does the era of Pax Nipponica call for a different development strategy for the LDCs of the Asia-Pacific region? If we return to the preconditions for the extraordinary export-led development of Japan and the NICs in the past forty years, we can see that import-substituting industrialization, internal division of labor, development of agriculture, creation of educational and communication infrastructure, political stability, and the building of public goods such as transportation and health facilities were essential.

Pax Nipponica is a period dominated by a wealth center in the form of Japan that is guided by economic incentives and a United States whose role may well be as a competitive actor in the world industrial markets because of its lower production costs and the devaluation of the dollar. The export markets for the LDCs of Asia and the Pacific will be marginal factors where success in internal development leads to competitive advantages; they will not find markets that result from world currency distortions and open, rapidly growing markets in developed nations.

Essential to the success of the Asia-Pacific LDCs will be success in their own internal and intersectoral trade markets. This process will begin with a primary relationship between the agricultural sector and the import-substituting industrial sector. There is considerable evidence that successful agricultural development has occurred in the region—

in Thailand and the People's Republic of China, for example. This lowering of food costs has wiped out U.S. agricultural export markets, as well as stabilized aggregate food supplies in the region, and has also provided a classical stimulus to urban industrial development.[35]

The conclusion that more inward-oriented policies will characterize the Asia-Pacific region's development strategies for the remainder of this century does not imply repudiation of the past. It is simply a recognition that success breeds certain responses—in this case, changes leading to devaluation of the dollar, innovations in technology (thereby removing advantages in world trade from low-wage competition), and a recognition that long-term expenditures for noneconomic reasons will distort the competitive position of a nation, even one as seemingly powerful as the postwar United States.

There is no doubt that considerable gains in regional efficiency can be reaped from local efforts to lower tariff barriers and to develop means of coordinating economic policies in the Pacific region, as discussed by Saburo Okita in this volume. It is increasingly recognized that efforts to accomplish these objectives will succeed only to the degree that individual nations lay the foundations for internal development and move toward effective international cooperation.[36]

The Importance of the
U.S.-Japanese Relationship

Japan must invest wisely through aid and direct capital flows in the local economic development of LDCs in Asia, including the People's Republic of China, in order to lay the foundation for multisector domestic development in these nations. The removal of low-wage advantages and the character of technological change will minimize export-led growth for the LDCs in the 1990s, thus enhancing the importance of Japanese investment and aid to capital and infrastructure development in the region. This approach would also enhance long-term export markets for Japan.

The United States must reorder its economic system to encourage real capital investment, rapid technological change, and effective marketing using the realigned dollar in order to eliminate balance-of-payments deficits and use real growth to eliminate domestic deficits. This combination would make for a stable United States operating under the rigors of comparative advantage and a realistically valued dollar and create an economic environment in which the countries of the Asia-Pacific region could prosper.

The United States must avoid protectionism and Japan must develop open, broad-based import markets; in this scenario, the realignment of the yen/dollar relationship should reduce the trade imbalance.

U.S. and Japanese balanced trade, Japanese capital investment in Asia, and open U.S. markets would greatly stabilize the domestic development environment for the Asia-Pacific region. The United States and Japan must recognize that the fortunes of this region are in their hands and that a prudent and mutually respectful eye to the future will benefit all to the detriment of none.

Notes

1. Ezra Vogel, "Pax Nipponica?" *Foreign Affairs* 64 (Spring 1986):752–767.

2. Japan Institute for Social and Economic Affairs, *Japan 1988: An International Comparison* (Tokyo: Japan Institute, 1988), pp. 36–38.

3. Nigel Holloway, "The Land of Soaring Assets," *Far Eastern Economic Review* (3 December 1987):59–60.

4. Peter F. Drucker, "The Changed World Economy," *Foreign Affairs* 64 (Spring 1986):758–791.

5. Ibid., p. 766.

6. Richard Rosecrance, *The Rise of the Trading State* (New York: Basic Books, 1986).

7. "Where Will Wealth Propel Japan?" *The Economist* (17 October 1986):19.

8. Bella Balassa and John Williamson, *Adjusting to Success: Balance of Payments Policy in the East Asian NICs* (Washington, D.C.: Institute for International Economics, 1987); C. Fred Bergsten and William R. Cline, *The United States–Japan Economic Problem* (Washington, D.C.: Institute for International Economics, 1985).

9. Raphael Kaplinsky, "The International Context for Industrialization in the Coming Decade," *The Journal of Development Studies* 21 (October 1984):75–96; Stephen Marris, *Deficits and the Dollar: The World Economy at Risk* (Washington, D.C.: Institute for International Economics, 1985); and Herbert Schmitz, "Industrialization Strategies in Less Developed Countries: Some Lessons of Historical Experience," *The Journal of Development Studies* 21 (October 1984):1–21.

10. Marris, *Deficits and the Dollar*, pp. 138–143.

11. Stephen Marris, *Deficits and the Dollar Revisited* (Washington, D.C.: Institute for International Economics, 1987), p. 7.

12. Philip Bowring, "The End of the Ride," *Far Eastern Economic Review* (29 October 1987):87.

13. Marris, *Deficits and the Dollar Revisited*, p. 7; and Paul R. Krugman and Richard E. Baldwin, "The Persistence of the U.S. Trade Deficit," in William C. Brainard and George L. Perry, eds., *Brookings Papers on Economic Activity* (Washington, D.C.: Brookings, 1987).

14. John Williamson and Marcus H. Miller, *Targets and Indicators: A Blueprint for the International Coordination of Economic Policy* (Washington D.C.: Institute for International Economics, 1987).

15. Schmitz, "Industrialization Strategies in Less Developed Countries," p. 9.

16. Marris, *Deficits and the Dollar Revisited*, p. 13.

17. Ibid., pp. 18–19.

18. Hisao Kanamori, *The Industrial Structure in the Year 2000: Are the Propositions Made in the "Maekawa Report" Feasible?* (Tokyo: The Japan Economic Research Center, 1987), p. 11.

19. A. W. Burks, *Japan—A Postindustrial Power* (Boulder, CO: Westview, 1984), pp. 164–178.

20. Kanamori, *The Industrial Structure in the Year 2000*, p. 11.

21. Kozo Yamamiura, "Shedding the Shackles of Success: Saving Less for Japan's Future," in Kenneth B. Pyle, ed., *The Trade Crisis: How Will Japan Respond?* (Seattle: The Society for Japanese Studies, 1987), p. 35.

22. Charles Smith, "Paying for Past Neglect," *Far Eastern Economic Review* (16 June 1988):49.

23. Yamamiura, "Shedding the Shackles of Success," pp. 35–38.

24. See Vincent Reinhardt, "Macroeconomics Influences on the U.S.-Japan Trade Imbalance," *Federal Reserve Bank of New York Quarterly Review* (Spring 1986):11, which indicates that slow income growth in Japan accounted for about 40% of the U.S.-Japanese trade imbalance from 1980–1985.

25. Bergsten and Cline, *The United States–Japan Economic Problem*, pp. 58, 61, and 78.

26. Marris, *Deficits and the Dollar Revisited*, pp. 11–13.

27. Drucker, "The Changed World Economy," p. 775.

28. Kaplinsky, "The International Context," pp. 79–80.

29. Ibid., p. 81.

30. Drucker, "The Changed World Economy," p. 781.

31. Kaplinsky, "The International Context," p. 84.

32. Ibid., pp. 79–84.

33. Nayan Chanda, "Recession Seems the Only U.S. Option Left," *Far Eastern Economic Review* (26 November 1987):100.

34. Ibid.

35. Drucker, "The Changed World Economy," p. 775; *Asian 1985 Yearbook* (Hong Kong: Far Eastern Economic Review, 1985); and Rostam M. Kavoussi, "International Trade and Economic Development: The Recent Experience of Developed Countries," *The Journal of Developing Areas* 19 (April 1985):379–392.

36. B. S. Felmingham, "The Market Integration of Large and Small Economies: Australia, the U.S., and Japan," *Journal of Macroeconomics* (Summer 1984):335–351; W. Chan Kim and Adrian E. Tochoegl, "The Regional Balance of Industrialization of the Asian Pacific Area," *The Journal of Developing Areas* 20 (January 1986):173–183.

8

A View from East
and Southeast Asia

Tommy T.B. Koh

On many occasions Ambassador Mike Mansfield has described the U.S.-Japanese relationship as the most important bilateral relationship in the world. With respect, I would disagree with him only very slightly. That is, I regard the U.S.-Soviet relationship as the most important bilateral relationship in the world, and the U.S.-Japanese relationship as the second most important. The relationships among these giants clearly affect most of the rest of the world, especially the peoples of East and Southeast Asia.

Present State of U.S.-Japanese Relations

What is the present state of this U.S.-Japanese relationship that affects so much of the world? On the political side, the U.S.-Japanese relationship is strong and stable. The two governments share, to a large extent, a common world view. Former Prime Minister Yasuhiro Nakasone and Prime Minister Noboru Takeshita were very supportive of President Reagan's foreign and security policies, and it appears as though the same will hold true for President George Bush. Moreover, there was a close personal and constructive relationship between the Japanese prime ministers and former President Reagan, and Japan has responded positively to U.S. requests that it devote a larger share of its resources to self-defense and to the defense of the sea-lanes around the islands of Japan.

The excellent political relationship between the United States and Japan stands in stark contrast to the state of their economic relationship, however. Many would characterize the present state of U.S.-Japanese economic relations as a serious crisis.[1] Although members of the U.S.

Senate sometimes have difficulty reaching a consensus, they do agree, however, on the opinion that Japan is an unfair trading partner. In a rare show of unanimity, the Senate adopted a resolution in March 1987 by a vote of 93–0 urging the Reagan administration to retaliate against Japan on the issue of semiconductors. On the day on which Nakasone arrived in Washington, the House of Representatives adopted the Gephardt Amendment, a protectionist measure primarily targeted at Japan.

What Are the Causes
of the Current Economic Crisis?

The current crisis in U.S.-Japanese economic relations has at least three causes. The first cause is the size of the U.S. trade deficit with Japan. During 1987 the United States suffered a trade deficit totalling $172 billion. A little over one-third of this amount, or $60 billion, was with Japan. The second cause is the widespread perception in the United States that Japan is not a fair trading partner and has not reciprocated the openness of the U.S. market. This view is held not only by members of Congress but also by the administration and the private sector. U.S. companies, seeking to break into the Japanese market, confront a formidable array of obstacles: tariffs, quotas, product standards, bureaucratic regulations and procedures, government procurement policies, industrial targeting, and the oligopolic behavior of the *keiretsu* conglomerates. The term *keiretsu* refers to a system of social organization under which some firms buy only from other firms in their family group and discriminate against all outsiders. The resentment against Japan is felt by almost every sector of U.S. business and industry. Some recent examples of Japanese protectionism that have evoked much anger in Congress involve rice, telecommunications, supercomputers, the Kansai Airport, and the financial market in Tokyo.

The third cause is the prevailing view in the United States that Japan is not carrying its share of the burden of supporting the world economy. U.S. leaders have often pointed out that the United States is absorbing approximately 60% of the manufactured exports of the developing countries, while Japan is only absorbing less than 10%. The Japanese economy is currently growing at an annual rate of about 2%. The feeling in the United States is that the Japanese economy should be stimulated by domestic demand to grow by an additional two percentage points per year. As James A. Baker, former U.S. Secretary of the Treasury and now Secretary of State, said to the Japan Society in New York on 15 April 1987, "A growing Japan is a precious world asset; a stagnant Japan helps no one."[2]

What Should Japan Do
to Defuse This Conflict?

In order to defuse this conflict Japan should do three things. First, Japan should open up its market to the import of goods and services from around the world. Second, the Japanese should stimulate their own economy to grow at a faster clip. Third, the Japanese government should implement the recommendations of the Advisory Group on Economic Structural Adjustment for International Harmony headed by Haruo Maekawa.

In its first report, the Maekawa Commission said, "The time has come for Japan to make a historical transformation in its traditional policies on economic management and the nation's lifestyle. There can be no further development for Japan without this transformation."[3] The report recommended that Japan should trim its huge trade surplus by stimulating its economy, buying more imports, phasing out inefficient domestic industries, reducing working hours, and changing its tax system laws in order to cut income tax and discourage savings.

In its second report, the Maekawa Commission proposed a number of specific steps that could be undertaken to achieve the stated goals. The proposed steps included spurring housing construction, stimulating Japan's domestic economy, easing import restrictions, allowing foreign companies to participate in Japanese construction projects, and cutting the workweek to less than forty hours.

The recommendations of the Maekawa Commission, it should be noted, are not yet government policy. Indeed, most of the recommendations are opposed by strong vested interests in Japan. It is, however, essential for Japan to undertake these structural reforms for two reasons: (1) because it is an international moral obligation, and (2) because it is in the interests of the Japanese themselves. Peter Drucker wrote that

Japanese consumers pay 30% to 50% more than any westerner does for clothing, cars or cameras, and more for services, whether checking account, railroad fares or postage. And they pay twice as much for food. Competitive pressure on Japan's internal prices may be the only way to revive a sluggish domestic economy that has been generating far too few jobs.[4]

What Should the United States Do
to Defuse This Conflict?

To be fair, however, one has to acknowledge that not all the faults lie with the Japanese. The United States is certainly not blameless.

The large trade and current account deficits that the United States has suffered in recent years are not due primarily to market barriers in Japan but to the large federal budget deficit in the United States. Martin Feldstein, the former chairman of President Reagan's Council of Economic Advisors, has stated that "the primary reason for the deteriorating trade imbalance is the 70% rise of the dollar that occurred between 1980 and the spring of 1985. This unprecedented increase in the exchange value of the dollar dramatically increased the price of American products relative to foreign products, causing the volume of U.S. exports to stagnate or decline while merchandise imports increased by nearly 50%."[5]

The United States must undertake six measures in order to defuse its economic conflict with Japan:

1. It should do whatever is necessary to reduce its tremendous federal budget deficit. The deficit is a serious problem that harms the United States both at home and abroad in countless numbers of ways.

2. Americans must spend less and save more. In 1986 they saved only 3.8% of their disposable incomes.

3. U.S. industries must improve the quality of their products. For example, instead of bemoaning foreign competition, Detroit should try to produce better automobiles. Americans buy foreign-made cars not because they lack patriotism, but because they believe that the imports are superior to domestic products.

4. Companies in the United States must be more skilled in exporting their products in foreign markets. Let me revert to the automobile as an example. Lee Iacocca, the head of the Chrysler Corporation, said that he would not be content until the day when Detroit is shipping automobiles to Japan. One needs to ask, how can Detroit aspire to ship automobiles to Japan when none of the manufacturers make cars with right-hand drive?

5. The United States must improve its competitiveness, as discussed in Chapter 6 by Akio Morita. This means raising the productivity of the U.S. economy, raising the standard of education in U.S. schools, devoting a larger percentage of the GNP to civilian research and development, and improving labor-management relations.

6. Finally, the United States must resist the mounting domestic pressure for protectionism.

The Importance of the U.S.-Japanese
Relationship to East and Southeast Asia

The present good relationship between the United States and Japan in the political and security fields is a force for peace in East and Southeast Asia. Nothing must be done by the United States to make Japan feel that it can no longer rely upon the U.S. security umbrella. If this security relationship should break down, Japan would be forced to develop its own military muscle including, perhaps, the acquisition of nuclear weapons. This development would raise alarm in many parts of East and Southeast Asia, especially in countries that were the victims of Japanese military aggression in the 1930s and 1940s.[6] Recognizing the sensitivities of Japan's neighbors, the United States should also act prudently in exerting pressure on Japan to increase its defense expenditures. As U.S. Senator Bill Bradley said recently, "No country is more important to our economic future than Japan. You want Japan to assume more foreign policy responsibility in the world, but in partnership with the U.S. The key is to get them to assume more responsibility without getting them to rearm."[7]

The economic relationship between the United States and Japan is of paramount importance to the countries of East and Southeast Asia for several reasons. The U.S. and Japanese economies are the two largest dynamos driving the world economy. Their combined GNP is equivalent to 38% of the world GNP. The two-way trade between the United States and Japan last year was about $900 billion, and the capital flow between the two countries in 1986 was about $500 billion. The countries of East and Southeast Asia therefore have a vested interest in the continued health of these two economies, and in preventing the current trade frictions from getting out of hand.

The United States should continue to exert pressure on Japan to open up its market to imports of goods and services—not only from the United States but from all countries. The United States should not, however, close its market to Japanese imports. The United States is not the only victim of Japanese protectionism. The countries of Southeast Asia confront the same hurdles in their attempts to break into the Japanese market. But unlike the United States, they do not have the leverage to pry open the Japanese market. The existing economic relationship between Japan and the countries in the Association of Southeast Asian Nations (ASEAN) is fundamentally an inequitable one.[8] The ASEAN countries include Indonesia, Malaysia, the Philippines, Singapore, and Thailand. Almost all of these countries suffer from a perennial trade deficit with Japan. Japan's imports from the ASEAN countries consist mainly of raw materials and commodities. In return, Japan dominates the markets of the ASEAN countries, supplying them with goods ranging from machinery, equipment, and automobiles to electronics and other consumer goods. Japan also enjoys a substantial presence in the service sector of the ASEAN economies. These countries have been largely unsuccessful in persuading Japan to open up its market to the imports of their manufactured goods and agricultural products. Many Japanese companies have subsidiaries in the ASEAN countries. But unlike the subsidiaries of Western multinational corporations, which export part of their production back to their own countries, the Japanese subsidiaries in the ASEAN countries export their production principally to North America and Europe. Little or none of the production of the Japanese subsidiaries in the ASEAN countries is exported back to Japan.

The United States should not close its market to Japanese imports for two reasons—one economic and the other political. First, the measures aimed at Japan are likely to hurt the countries in East and Southeast Asia even more than Japan. Although the barriers to trade would be targeted at Japan, they would also keep out the exports of the rest of the Pacific. The countries of East and Southeast Asia export between 10 and 30% of their total exports to Japan. If Japan were forced to reduce its exports to the United States, it in turn would reduce its imports from the countries of East and Southeast Asia.

There is also a geopolitical reason for not closing the U.S. market to Japanese imports. In his address to a joint meeting of the U.S. Congress, Prime Minister of Singapore Lee Kuan Yew said:

> A Japan squeezed in such a protectionist trap has few attractive options. After thrashing around looking for market extensions in Latin America, Africa, and West Asia, Japan will turn back to her two major options: closer economic links with the Soviet Union, or closer ties with China. She could try to do both and reconcile or postpone the conflicts inherent in such a policy. In the end, she has to choose one of these two. Either choice conjures up disquieting consequences for the rest of Asia, and for the world.[9]

Japan's Role in the World

Japan's current international role is unique in world history. Never before has a nation with so much economic muscle eschewed the option of developing a military capacity commensurate with its economic strength. The world should reward Japan for its abstinence. This is one of the reasons that has led me to accept Japan's ambition to be a semipermanent member of the UN Security Council. If we do not accept Japan's ambition we will, in effect, be saying that we cannot accept Japan as a great power unless it also becomes a great military power.

Japan must, however, accept its international moral obligations, of which there are several. First, Japan has a moral obligation to stimulate its own domestic economy to grow at a faster pace in order to help drive the world economy. Second, Japan has a moral obligation to open up its market to the imports of goods and services. Third, Japan has a moral obligation to help the less fortunate peoples of the world. In this respect, we can welcome the announcement by Takeshita during the economic summit in Toronto that Japan would increase its total economic aid to $10 billion. Moreover, in consultation with the United States, Japan is stepping up its aid to countries of strategic importance, such as the Philippines, Pakistan, Egypt, and to sub-Saharan Africa. Japan is now the largest donor of aid to the Philippines. This policy should be continued and expanded.

Fourth, Japan should play a bigger role in the multilateral development agencies. Japan is already the second largest shareholder in both the World Bank and the Asian Development Bank and is playing an increasingly important role in the International Development Agency (IDA). For example, Japan recently agreed to contribute an 18.7% share of the eighth replenishment of $11.5 billion and to make an additional contribution of $450 million. Taking the two together, Japan's share in the total is 21%. This step is especially important because 45 to 50% of the IDA's eighth replenishment will be devoted to the low-income countries of sub-Saharan Africa.

The fifth moral obligation for Japan is that it should play a more active role in transferring technology to the developing countries. This process is already underway. The dramatic increase in the value of the yen forced many Japanese companies to transfer their manufacturing processes to the developing countries of East and Southeast Asia. For example, in 1986 Japan became the largest foreign investor in Singapore. We have three requests to make of Japan, however. The first request is for the Japanese companies in our region to export some of their production back to Japan. The second is for Japan to increase the quality of its investment in the East and Southeast Asian countries. In Singapore, for example, the average value added per worker of the Japanese companies was the lowest of all the foreign companies, which means that the level of technology is low, mostly assembly line work, and involves little research and development. The third request is for the Japanese companies to employ more local personnel in the middle and top management of their overseas subsidiaries. At present the top and middle management posts in Japanese overseas ventures are invariably held by Japanese and not local personnel. This practice prevails even in spite of the fact that some of the Japanese overseas ventures have already been established for more than ten years.

Sixth, I believe that Japan should play a more active and creative role in world diplomacy and in international negotiations on scientific, social, cultural, and humanitarian questions. Such a trend is already evident. Japan has tried to play, for example, a helpful role in ending the Iraq-Iran War. The Japanese government also offered to mediate a Vietnamese withdrawal from Kampuchea. At the United Nations, Japan (which contributes nearly 11% of the UN's annual budget, second only to the United States) has taken the lead in proposing the establishment of a group of experts to examine ways to improve management and the budget process. Former Prime Minister Takeo Fukuda has tried to galvanize world consensus and mobilize collective action on important issues relating to population and development. These are all positive signs.

Conclusion

In his speech to the Japan Society, James Baker said, "We have reached a watershed in U.S.-Japan relations. We have reached a period when change is essential if good relations and economic growth are to continue. How well we proceed from here will be a difficult and critical test—a test of our mutual friendship and of our dual leadership."[10] As a Southeast Asian, I wish to say that the countries in East and Southeast Asia have a great deal at stake in the success or failure of the management of the U.S.-Japanese relationship. The United States and Japan have the two largest economies in the world. The current imbalances between the two economies are economically unsustainable and politically dangerous and must be corrected. The correction must, however, be done in such a manner as not to plunge the world economy into a recession or dismantle the world's trading system. The world economy needs leadership. That leadership must be provided by the United States and Japan, preferably working in tandem. However, what is at stake is not merely the future of the international trading system or the prospects of the world economy. What is ultimately at stake is the peace and security of the world.

Notes

1. See George Packard, "The Coming U.S.-Japan Crisis," *Foreign Affairs* 66 (Winter 1987/88):348–367; James Abegglen, "Japan and the United States: Too

Close a Relationship?" *Tokyo Business Today* (February 1986):6; and Nagayo Homma, "Beyond Bashing," *Japan Review of International Affairs* 1 (Fall/Winter 1987):154–169.

2. James A. Baker, "U.S.-Japan Economic Relations: Adapting to Changing Realities," *Japan Society Newsletter* (June 1987):6.

3. Haruo Maekawa et al., "The Report of the Advisory Group on Economic Structural Adjustment for International Harmony, Submitted to the Prime Minister, Mr. Yasuhiro Nakasone, 7 April 1986," as reproduced in Jon K.T. Choy, ed., *Japan: Exploring New Paths* (Washington, D.C.: Japan Economic Institute, 1988), p. 9.

4. Peter Drucker, "The Changed World Economy," *Foreign Affairs* 64 (Spring 1986):758–791.

5. Martin Feldstein, "Correcting the Trade Deficit," *Foreign Affairs* 65 (Spring 1987):796.

6. Masashi Nishihara, *East Asian Security and the Trilateral Countries* (New York: New York University Press, 1985); and Sheldon W. Simon, *The ASEAN States and Regional Security* (Stanford: Hoover Institution, 1982).

7. Bill Bradley, as cited in "Japan: From Superrich to Superpower," *Time* (4 July 1988):29.

8. Among many other sources, see Donald Crane, *The ASEAN States: Coping with Dependence* (New York: Praeger, 1983); Lawrence B. Krause, *U.S. Economic Policy Toward the Association of Southeast Asian Nations: Meeting the Japanese Challenge* (Washington, D.C.: Brookings Institution, 1982); Michael Skully, *ASEAN Financial Cooperation* (New York: St. Martin's Press, 1985); and Marjorie L. Suriyamongkol, *Politics of ASEAN Economic Cooperation* (New York: Oxford University Press, 1988).

9. Lee Kuan Yew, as cited in U.S. Congress, *Congressional Quarterly*, 9 October 1985 (Washington, D.C.: Government Printing Office, 1985), p. H8513.

10. James A. Baker, "U.S.-Japan Economic Relations," p. 13.

9

The Theory and Practice of Public Education in Japan and the United States

William K. Cummings

When the chiefs of state of the United States and Japan met in Tokyo during November 1983, at a time when both governments were deeply worried about dangerous deficits and balance-of-trade problems, they devoted more than half of their private conversations to each other's educational systems. President Ronald Reagan was especially interested in the way the Japanese learned mathematics and science and proposed that the two nations enter into a joint study of each other's systems. Prime Minister Yasuhiro Nakasone readily agreed, for he was on the verge of launching a major review of his nation's educational system with the intent of stimulating more diversity and creativity somewhat along the lines of the U.S. system.

At the official level, the United States and Japan subsequently carried out a joint study that has since been published and widely circulated. Perhaps even more important for the long-term relationship between the two countries is the mounting tide of public interest in the respective educational systems expressed in both the United States and Japan. This trend is especially evident in the United States, where education, for perhaps the first time in its history, has become a major news story. Recent surveys by the Gallup network reveal that less than half of American students know that Tokyo is the capital of Japan, while eight of every ten Japanese students can place Washington as the capital of the United States. The new U.S. interest in education is matched by the long-standing priority on education so characteristic of most Japanese homes and businesses.

It is now appreciated in both the United States and Japan that public education has a critical bearing on the stature of modern societies and on the nature of the relationship between their two countries. The quality of education in any society today will determine its destiny twenty years down the road. Today's students will create tomorrow's ideas for advancing science and industry and will make the decisions that determine the quality of life in postindustrial society. Also, education is important simply because of the enormous resources it commands; it is perhaps the single largest modern industry. In the United States, education absorbs about 8% of the GNP, employing some 4 million individuals, or 6% of the labor force, in positions ranging from administration and teaching to plant maintenance, and providing services to some 50 million children and students. And behind most schoolchildren are loving and concerned parents who pitch in at school fairs, help their children with assignments, and express joy or anxiety when report cards come home. Since education is the biggest business, commanding more resources than any other sector of U.S. society, it is only natural that we should be concerned that it be effective.

Although the United States devotes enormous funds and human energy to education, many experts, including members of the Presidential Commission that prepared *A Nation at Risk: The Imperative for Educational Reform*, now worry that their 1983 warning about the nation being overtaken by foreign competitors has not been effective. They point out that large segments of the U.S. labor force are illiterate and that this incapacity leads to mistakes and inefficiency that threaten the competitiveness of the U.S. economy, especially relative to Japan and the newly industrializing societies, which place a high priority on human resources. These experts worry that something may be wrong with the theory of education in the United States.

Education also commands vast resources in Japan. However, whereas in the United States educational expenditures as a proportion of the GNP have been essentially stable for nearly twenty years, in Japan the proportion has steadily expanded over this same period. This gradual increase in expenditures has enabled Japan to continue to recruit the teaching power necessary to put into practice its comparatively simple educational theory. In contrast, the United States, while evolving an increasingly complex theory, has failed to muster the resources necessary for its implementation. Therein lies the crisis of U.S. public education.

Common Principles of Public Education

Nations normally support public education for the following minimal purposes:

1. To convey an understanding of the principles shared in common by members of society. John Dewey, discussing the American experience, for example, said "Democracy has to be reborn anew every generation and education is the midwife."[1]
2. To provide basic skills of literacy and numeracy to all citizens out of a conviction that these skills will lead to a fuller life, a more efficient economy, and a stronger society.
3. To provide opportunities for the secondary and advanced education of citizens in accordance with individual abilities and public need.

In this era of high technology and global competition, we might ask if these three objectives are sufficient; but even if they are, my concern is that the United States is not meeting them very well. The U.S. system was especially well-regarded through the mid-1960s, but since then it has faltered both in terms of performance and international reputation. A surprising number of those who pass through the public school system fail to achieve basic literacy or numeracy. There have been disturbing declines in academic achievement and increases in juvenile delinquency. The system has not been able to make great progress in addressing issues of racial inequality, especially at the higher educational level. And the United States is failing to motivate a sufficient number of young Americans into critical fields of science and technology.

Many economists now argue that the competitive softness of the United States compared to Japan in high-technology markets can be related to the shortage of trained U.S. scientists and engineers. While the Japanese population is half that of the United States, for example, Japan's institutions of higher education train a larger number of engineers and nearly as many scientists.

The contemporary Japanese educational system serves its society and its people quite effectively. Japan's young people (relative to those in the United States) are more literate, numerate, well-behaved and respectful of law and order, and move more smoothly into the labor force, where they work with impressive energy and intelligence. As the Japanese like to say, the only natural resource they have are their people, and it is obvious that their educational system is effectively adding value to this resource.

In Japan and the United States, formal education is mainly publicly financed and controlled and hence is amenable to improvement through sound public policy. A review of these two systems may suggest new approaches worthy of consideration by both Japanese and U.S. policy-makers. We need in particular to look at the simpler, and hence easier to realize, Japanese theory, for there may be wisdom in it that we could draw on to solve the American dilemma of the growing gap between theory and practice.

Educational Theory and Practice
in the United States

In analyzing public education, it is useful to distinguish between what a system aims to achieve and what it actually accomplishes. The contemporary American dilemma involves the large gap between educational aspirations and achievement, between theory and practice. Given the long and complicated evolution of the U.S. educational system, not all of us will agree on what exactly this theory is. I believe that five major ideas guide U.S. public education: decentralized control, cognitive achievement and civic culture as the curricular goals, equality of opportunity *cum* equality of results, individualized instruction, and quality.

The various groups who came to found colonies in the New World each had their respective purposes when, following the American Revolution, they sat down to devise a new form of government, they agreed that the federal government would have a limited role in local affairs, including education. Thus, a decentralized system of control and finance was established for U.S. education. This plan was intended to make schools responsive to local needs. It has proven productive of many fertile approaches toward realizing better education, although, as we will observe shortly, because of difficulties in securing resources, these approaches often have suffered in implementation.

The founders clearly wanted to restrict the role of the federal government in education in order to ensure the right of individual communities to advance their distinctive values through the institutions of family, church, and school. But, at the same time, they asserted the principle of separation of church and state. When schools were supported by individual donations there were no conflicts, but as schools came to be funded from public sources, the principle of separation of church and state led to a second distinctive feature: the elimination of religious and moral objectives from the curriculum. Over time, education about American values in the public schools became narrowed to the conveyance of civic values. Few public school systems are so limited in this regard as that of the United States. One has to question whether education can be complete without instruction in correct behavior, the importance of respect for others, and a critical albeit respectful examination of enduring values.

While there were wide differences in the religious and social values of the early American communities, most early Americans believed that their young people should learn to read and write. Out of this faith emerged the movement to found common schools. By the middle of the nineteenth century, such schools were widely established, and by the turn of the twentieth century sufficient schools had been established to offer virtually every young person an opportunity for education. In the provision of educational opportunity, the United States moved ahead of all other countries, except possibly Germany and Japan.

During the twentieth century this doctrine of equal opportunity was widely articulated, and it gained an especially strong foothold during the Great Depression. Minorities were afforded "separate but equal" opportunity until 1954, when the Supreme Court ruled that separate could not be equal.[2] While all should be offered the opportunity to pursue education, for much of U.S. history it was up to the individual to take advantage of that opportunity. But in the years since the Supreme Court ruling, U.S. educators have even questioned whether equal opportunity is sufficient; some have proposed that public education should assume responsibility for motivating those who enter schools to achieve equal results.

One of the most distinctive themes in the American dream is the belief that education should respond to individual needs. The Pilgrims and other religious groups that settled in New England stressed basic education to enable the individual to directly interpret God's will. In Virginia, Thomas Jefferson urged popular education so that citizens could choose leaders wisely. So from an early stage, there developed a notion that learning enhanced the individual's enjoyment of life. Building on this tradition, other American pedagogues have stressed life adjustment, learning at one's own pace, and learning what is personally relevant. At the primary level, the concept of individualized instruction has received expression in such experiments as open classrooms and programs for the gifted and talented as well as in programs for those with learning disabilities or cultural disadvantages. At the secondary level, individualized programs of instruction are made possible by the comprehensive high school and its generous offering of electives. A typical high school accommodates students interested in both academic and vocational studies, and within each of these tracks there are numerous combinations of subjects and subject quality levels.

It is interesting that both Ernest Boyer and John Goodlad in their critiques of U.S. high schools speak disparagingly of this freedom and warn of the associated risks. Many students elect frivolous combinations that do not add up to an education, while the economic burden of providing such a diverse program is often staggering.[3] In a similar vein, Eric Ashby, internationally renowned expert on higher education, titled his book on U.S. higher education *Any Person, Any Study*.[4] Our higher educational institutions offer a wider range of majors to a greater cross-section of the population than any other system in the world. Beyond the basic four-year university program is a wide array of graduate and adult educational programs as well as fine research programs. The higher tertiary institutions in the United States, some of which are known as multiversities, are perhaps the most effective component in the national system.

A final theme in U.S. education is quality or excellence. At the same time that our educational system tries to do everything, it aspires to a high standard of accomplishment. It is particularly with respect to this last concern that the American conscience is currently troubled. Recent international studies of science and mathematics achievement indicate that the U.S. average is at or near the bottom relative to other advanced societies. In these studies, our best students are no more accomplished than the average students of some other societies, including Japan.

Problems in American Practice

We are concerned about our academic softness. But what is the problem and what can be done about it? Educational reformers currently are focusing on three issues. The first of these involves lack of standards. Because of the loose admission standards at the tertiary level and the absence of exit exams at the secondary level, high school students tend to study whatever they like, often choosing the easiest courses, and are not challenged to achieve specific objectives. The reformers advocate increasing requirements at the secondary level and stiffening tertiary admissions criteria. The second issue involves the need for improved teacher status and training. The low status of teachers has resulted in the hiring of too many poorly trained and/or poor quality recruits. The usual solutions focus on salary increases, merit pay, and competency testing. The third issue focuses on the need for more effective schools. Many schools seem to be administrative units without a heart. The reformers advocate a commitment to educational goals, clarity of purpose, and improved communication among all members of school faculties and administrations.

It is important to acknowledge that behind these problems lies an even more fundamental issue: Our schools are too ambitious, given the resources they are able to command. Perhaps, in the language of manufacturing, the United States has developed an inefficient educational technology. We have created a customized technology that assumes uneven pupil inputs, sets up parallel educational experiences for each, and aspires to transform each into a unique quality product. An analogy in manufacturing would be to make Rolls-Royces, Maserattis, and Corvettes—that is, customized products—while relying on scarce public funds. A customized product requires a high ratio of workers per product—hence we are always trying to push down the student/teacher ratio. Customized work also requires highly trained and experienced workers, sound diagnostic procedures, and a wealth of materials adjusted to different needs. Our schools and school systems try to procure all of these essential resources, but increasingly they run up against obstacles.

The major obstacle to customized production is expense. Customized education requires a minimum of $5,000 to $10,000 per student, and while some communities are willing to pay the price, many cannot. Lacking local resources, they turn to the state and federal levels of government for assistance. Throughout the 1960s, the level of federal support increased, but since then it has leveled off and even declined. Most states have been unable to fill the gap. Overall, public funds for education have leveled off, resulting in a decline in educational expenditures as a proportion of GNP. The shortage of funds also impacts teacher recruitment. Once U.S. schools could depend on a reserve of talented women who were reluctant to seek "male" jobs. But in the wake of women's liberation, capable women today readily pursue careers in law, engineering, business, and other professions rather than making teaching their first choice.

Looking ahead, we may face an even grimmer picture. As David Tyack indicated, we could be in for another decade of "hard times."[5] If anything, the financial problems are likely to intensify as the state and federal governments experience the pinch of accumulating deficits and seek to restrain expenditures. Two well-publicized examples are California's Proposition 13 and Massachusetts' Proposition 2½, both of which reflected growing voter uneasiness with spiraling state expenditures. So while ambition expands and technology becomes more complicated, demanding better trained teachers and higher teacher/student and staff/student ratios, funds are down. Clearly something is wrong. The United States has created the dilemma of having set bold goals for public education that are difficult to achieve with limited funds. Can the Japanese experience help Americans in dealing with this dilemma?

Japanese Theory

Public education has a shorter but more orderly history in Japan than in the United States. Prior to the founding of the modern Japanese state, Japan was divided into distinctive political units with long-standing rivalries and rather distinctive cultures. Several of the more peripheral leaders, fearful of imminent colonization by the ambitious West, decided to join together and create a new centralized political arrangement in order to build national strength and avert foreign domination. What ensued was the extraordinary Meiji Restoration of 1868.

Following their military triumph, the Meiji leaders quickly turned to reorganize national institutions. The vigor of their initiatives was astounding—the abolition of feudalism, the establishment of new factories, and the creation of a central bureaucracy. Educational reform also played a key role. The new leadership proclaimed the need for Japan to seek knowledge from throughout the world. The Meiji leaders were determined to use education as a means of building national solidarity, developing a technically competent labor force, and identifying and educating the future elite. Every family, whether samurai or commoner, was instructed to send their children to school. Within fifteen years, enrollment ratios at the primary level surpassed those in the United Kingdom and possibly even the United States. The system has steadily expanded and developed since then. These goals have been pursued with surprising consistency down to the present. The only major shift was following World War II when the United States insisted on a broadening of the already substantial level of opportunity at the secondary and tertiary levels.

While the goals of the new government were ambitious, resources were limited. So from the very beginning, the government established what might be called mass-production education. The public education system would make Model T's or Toyotas, not Rolls-Royces. Some of the characteristics of that system are still in evidence today. One of these is the assumption that all students are identical and should be treated in an identical manner.

Another is a uniform curriculum with virtually no electives until secondary level tracking. Thus, all students gain a solid grounding in mathematics and science, and all receive a common exposure to moral education. At the secondary level all take foreign languages. Although the curriculum is uniform, it is also surprisingly rich. Like a Toyota, it comes with lots of accessories—good music and art education, gymnastics, swimming, and home economics. Still another characteristic is that of a uniform finance and personnel policy, in keeping with national resources. Due to equalizing regulations, per-student expenditures in Japanese public schools are remarkably similar between and within major regions. In the Meiji period, student/teacher ratios were in excess of 50/1. Today the overall ratio is down to 30/1, but in particular classes the ratio is more likely to be 40/1, as teachers often share a class so they can have time for lesson preparation. While Japanese teachers face more students than American teachers in any given class, they have fewer contact hours per week and have more time to prepare.

Concerning the critical area of classroom management, observational studies suggest relatively uniform pedagogy and pace across classrooms of the same grade level in different schools. Underlying this uniformity in classroom management is a set of assumptions that seems to pervade all areas of Japanese education. One of these is spirit over matter. Learning is based on effort rather than "ability"; thus, in judo as in public schools, the young student is taught that mind rather than natural skill wins the match. Another is that intellectual and personal achievement depends on building a strong foundation combining moral education and mastery of the basics before moving on to higher levels. There is also the assumption that practice makes perfect, and so repetition at school and home is combined with group drills in the classroom. Finally, there is a belief in the importance of harmonious and supportive human relations for fostering learning. This principle leads to a preference for small groups and small schools over large ones and careful selection of the members of these groups. Once the groups are established, close relations are stressed, and the same class is often kept intact over the years. Stress is placed on cooperation rather than competition. There is no ability grouping, and at the high school level there is no overt tracking.

Summing up, it can be said that the Japanese theory is characterized by centralized organization of education, which brings about uniformity in major resources and procedures. The stress on holistic education with effort, a resource all can muster, is the key to learning. Finally, the group is viewed as the focus of learning rather than the individual.

Practice in Japan

Japanese theory stresses a no-frills approach. School goals are simple, so the administrative requirements are predictable and limited to supplying the buildings, texts, and teachers. At the school level, it is up to principals and teachers to do everything from recordkeeping to counseling to organizing extracurricular activities. The standardization of the Japanese system and the high student/teacher ratios make it a comparatively inexpensive system to run.

Naturally, there have been changes in this system over time. Curriculum offerings were relatively simple in the Meiji period, but gradually have become fuller. Today the curriculum is surprisingly rich. At the primary level, along with the standard "three R's," the curriculum includes systematic instruction in music, art, physical education, and both domestic and industrial arts. At the secondary level, a full program of mathematics and science courses for all students as well as the mandatory study of English for six years and at least three years of a second foreign language are required.

Throughout the 1960s, less of the GNP was expended on education in Japan than in the United States. But the Japanese leaders were concerned about improving quality, and they recognized the importance of education for a technological society and the difficulties of recruiting teachers in a tight labor market. Thus, throughout the 1970s, they steadily increased unit costs. Indeed, in the mid-1970s they promoted a 50% increase in teacher salaries. Today Japanese public education absorbs a greater proportion of GNP than the U.S. system and Japanese teachers make as much as other professionals with a similar level of training.

The Japanese system also has its problems. One is the problem of excessive uniformity, which does not allow for individual creativity. In addition, Japanese children find themselves under considerable pressure to succeed in the classroom. Moreover, in recent years, a motivational problem has emerged as inequalities become more evident. Japanese leaders also are concerned with the lack of internationalism among their young people: While Japanese youth may know many facts about other countries, they have little empathy with other cultures, have difficulty in mastering foreign languages, and express little interest in working overseas—where increasing proportions of Japanese capital will be invested. But by and large, practice is consistent with theory.

Japan's current economic advantage vis-à-vis the United States may derive from the educational system's ability to impart the skills for reading and writing and the will to work to virtually all students. Thus, Japan is said to have the best bottom half of the population of all of the advanced industrial societies. It is this segment that participates in quality-control circles, providing management with plant-level insights on ways to increase productivity, and that is prepared to put in the long hours necessary to bring about the high volume of production characteristic of Japan when its international sales are prospering.

Japan's economic and political future rests in its ability to develop new qualities of leadership and intellectual creativity in the top half of its population. The top half, over the past decades, has been able to build and operate a powerful domestic industrial economy, drawing largely on proven technologies developed outside of Japan. The new challenges include the development of new technologies and organizational forms as well as sensitive negotiation with international partners, especially the United States. The current reforms in Japanese education, especially at the higher educational levels, are directed toward creating this capability in the future.

The "Yes-But" Problem

Ten years ago I was probably one of the few Americans who had anything favorable to say about Japanese education. Over the past year or so, there have been many others. Yet, most of these accounts, at least those that appear in print, combine a quality of wonder and enthusiasm for what the Japanese do with a concluding punchline that the Japanese way is not for us. James Fallows, for example, after acknowledging the impressive achievements of Japanese high school students in science and mathematics in a lead article for *The Atlantic*, concluded, "You would not want your kids to go to a Japanese secondary school."[6] John Cogan, after a year at a Hiroshima teacher education school, similarly concluded that the "first tendency of Japanese education is to change students from happy, carefree children into serious, fatigued, and—too frequently—emotionally disturbed adolescents."[7] Even more caustic are the observations of Roy Andrew Miller, a comparative linguist:

[Japanese] society resolutely refuses to let fiscal consideration stand in its way when education is at issue, any more than it is willing to consider for a moment the appalling physical and mental costs that the whole system extracts from those tiny, sad-faced, listless boys and girls who may be observed every morning fighting for their own places on overcrowded commuter trains and subways, their tiny backs weighted down with backpacks overflowing with dictionaries, pocket calculators, and notebooks. A society so willing to sacrifice its own children's health and happiness to "getting ahead" is quite obviously not going to quibble about anything so minor as money.[8]

Based on these statements, it is obvious that many Americans are reluctant to appreciate the practices of other countries. It was not always like this. As Daniel Boorstein argued in *The National Experience*, America's industrial might was built through exploiting European ideas.[9] Similarly, Japan and East Asia have profited from American ideas.

Perhaps it is time for us to recover our old curiosity and open our eyes to approaches used elsewhere. What is it that holds us back?

One problem may be that our national pride is pricked. Since World War II Americans have become accustomed to thinking of their country as Number One, and as doing everything better than anybody else. Americans, as Akio Morita writes in his contribution to this book, are locked into a big nation psychology. We do not like to be challenged, and we are prone to dismiss any challenge as something that surely will be short-lived—after all, what happened to the Soviet space advantage in the 1960s, the OPEC oil cartel in the 1970s, or even the Japanese edge today in semiconductors? We believe that we can beat them if we try, simply by digging deeper into our endless reserve of ingenuity. Such an attitude of stubborn self-sufficiency is not what made this nation great.

The problem may also be that the intellectual approach we use for examining foreign cultures stands in the way of really learning about them. In our domestic affairs we are a practical people, but in our international affairs we tend to be surprisingly naive. We have tended to focus on the cultural uniqueness of foreign countries, on their distinctiveness from ourselves. Edward Said, in his study of "Orientalism," noted that we tend to stress the weak side of foreign cultures, to patronize them, and to stress their quaintness.[10] This view of other societies leads to poor analyses of foreign practices and often to the conclusion that the different practices of foreign countries derive from their distinctive values. Because their values are different from ours, we think that there is nothing for us to learn. It is important for us to recognize this limitation before we can develop a methodology for appreciating foreign achievements.

In studying foreign cultures I would make two suggestions. First, since we will never be able to fully understand a foreign culture on its own terms, we have to be satisfied with it on our own terms. Exploring foreign cultures helps us to better understand our own. In other words, the foreign culture becomes a mirror that allows us to ask how foreign countries solve problems that are important to us and to consider whether their solutions make sense in our American setting. Pascale and Athos, in their study of excellence, for example, found that the personnel policies of leading U.S. firms such as Polaroid and IBM were similar to those of leading Japanese firms.[11] There are similar patterns in the field of education. Second, we need to make clearer distinctions when looking at foreign achievements. For example, we can make a useful distinction between educational theory and educational practice. Many commentators dismiss Japanese education because they sense the Japanese are trying to achieve something different from what Americans are trying to achieve; but in so doing, they refuse to even broach the question of which theory is best. While the values or theories of Japanese and U.S. education may differ, certain aspects of educational practice still may be transferable.

Are There Cross-National Lessons for the United States?

A number of studies suggest that there may be lessons to be learned, including the recent report of the U.S. Department of Education. Secretary of Education William Bennett, in his conclusion to the report, listed twelve principles that emerged from the analysis and then observed that these may

> be encouraging to Americans who even without benefit of detailed knowledge of Japanese education had adduced these or similar points from research, from experience, from history, from reason, or from common sense. The essential lesson for us to glean from examination of Japanese education, after all, besides the intrinsic rewards of enhanced knowledge and understanding, is that much of what seems to work well for Japan in the field of education closely resembles what works best in the United States—and most likely elsewhere. Good education is good education.[12]

Based on the Department of Education study, several aspects of the Japanese theory of education could profitably be examined by Americans. At least three issues merit attention: the aims of public education with consideration of more moral education and less individualized attention; greater attention to student motivation, especially in the earliest years of schooling; and approaches to education for minorities. Concerning practice, a number of areas deserve consideration: promotion of uniform standards; enrichment and upgrading of curricula; simplification of instruction; increase in the time spent in school and time spent on tasks; and realization of equitable finance. Cultivation of an academic climate, involvement of students in both learning and teaching, promotion of more orderly school and classroom environments, stress on performance over aptitude, and provision of realistic evaluations of student performance also could help improve U.S. schools. Finally, educational practice might be improved by exploring the integration of teachers, administration, and community around the achievement of educational goals; limiting the size of schools; evaluating and curtailing the excesses of extracurricular activities; strengthening the curriculum and pedagogy in mathematics and sciences; improving teacher status and career opportunities; and systematizing transition from school to work.

The Japanese system obviously has some strengths, and other Asian governments have evidenced strong interest in Japanese education. The educational systems of Korea and Taiwan, for example, have been influenced by Japan. Recently, Malaysia initiated a Look East policy and Singapore established a Learn from Japan program. China is sending large numbers of students and experts to Japan to study the Japanese way. Common to these countries is a largely Confucian cultural heritage, a strong work ethic, and strong industrial systems that enable their respective economies to achieve favorable trade balances with the United States. With the new interest in Japanese education, these countries are participating in an expansion of Japanese cultural influence. Their new interest in Japan might also mean a corresponding decline in U.S. influence. Thus, the expansion of Japanese cultural influence is part of the growing friction in the relationship between Japan and the United States. These global trends should not be ignored.

Lessons for Japan

The Japanese have never been embarrassed to look in the mirror. Their current prime minister's Council on Educational Reform has made several observations with regard to U.S. education.[13] At the school level, the council is interested in the practices of individualization of instruction, communication and research skills, diversified school climate, and global education in the United States. But Japan's greatest concern seems to be with higher education and research, and currently it is expressing much interest in American procedures for university admissions as well as in the measures the United States has taken to strengthen graduate education and the university research system.

The United States should take heed of these Japanese concerns, for while its own support for university research and development is wavering, the Japanese university-based research and development efforts are increasing. During 1987, despite budget restraints, Japan's university-based R&D expenditures increased 8%—and overall R&D expenditures increased 11%. Spending in this area has increased at an outstanding rate over the past twenty years in Japan and now constitute a larger proportion of GNP than in the United States. Japanese researchers are meeting the United States head-on in many areas of basic and applied research—computers, fiber optics, telecommunications, and biotechnology (capitalizing on the fact that the AZT compound was discovered by a Japanese researcher). If Japan puts even more resources into this effort, as discussed by Leonard H. Lynn elsewhere in this book, the United States can anticipate formidable competition.

This prospect also offers exciting opportunities for cooperation. The doors to Japan's universities and research institutes are opening wider and wider to foreign participation, both because Japan needs brain labor and because its leaders genuinely want to repay the international scientific community for the debt they incurred over the past century. The United States can only gain by entering this cooperative endeavor. To do so will require the United States to train a new generation of researchers who have a positive disposition toward Japan and are willing to take the trouble to acquire the necessary language skills.

Conclusion

Looking ahead to the twenty-first century, we need to recognize the new world and shared destinies awaiting us. One reality we may face in the years ahead is an absolute limit on the amounts that governments and the public are prepared to spend on education. The Japanese and U.S. systems spend equivalent amounts for every student they graduate from public education, yet it would appear that Japan gets more for its money, at least as judged in terms of motivation, intellectual competence, and a positive orientation to science and technology. In the future the United States will be faced with a more capable array of competitors. The going will not be so easy.

The U.S. educational system has long been regarded as especially successful in training its top 10% to exceptional levels of dedication and excellence. But beyond that, the U.S. labor force is plagued by poor training, lack of motivation, even alienation. Our Asian competitors, on the other hand, have not been noted for their success in stimulating excellence at the top. Their systems are more capable of reaching those at the middle and bottom of society. They bring a greater proportion of the labor force through the educational system with the required traits of competence and effort.

The ideal educational system of the twenty-first century would combine the best in U.S. and Japanese education—Japan's ability to build a strong base that is intelligent and work-oriented, and the United States's ability to lead the exceptional few to outstanding heights of creativity in science, business, government, and the arts. Such a synthesis can only be achieved through an appreciation of the strengths of other systems and through viewing the world not merely as a competitive arena but also as a setting for cooperation and collaboration in building more efficient and effective social institutions. To achieve this goal, both Japanese and U.S. educators must be willing to learn from each other.

Notes

1. John Dewey is quoted in Merle Curti, *The Social Ideas of American Educators* (Totowa, NJ: Littlefield, Adams, 1966), p. 499.

2. This landmark ruling is "Brown v. Board of Education," *U.S. Supreme Court Reports* 347 (1954):483–496.

3. Ernest L. Boyer, *High School: A Report of the Carnegie Foundation for the Advancement of Teaching* (New York: Harper and Row, 1983). Also see J. I. Goodlad, *A Place Called School* (New York: McGraw-Hill, 1984).

4. Eric Ashby, *Any Person, Any Study: An Essay on Higher Education in the United States* (Ann Arbor: Books on Demand, University Microfilms International).

5. David Tyack et al., *Public Schools in Hard Times: The Great Depression and Recent Years* (Cambridge: Harvard University Press, 1984).

6. James Fallows, "Gradgrind's Hairs: Despite What the U.S. Department of Education Says, You Would Not Want Your Kids to Go to a Japanese Secondary School," *The Atlantic* (March 1987):16–24.

7. John J. Cogan and Donald O. Schneider, eds., *Perspectives on Japan: A Guide for Teachers* (Washington, D.C.: National Council for the Social Studies, 1983).

8. Roy Andrew Miller, "The 'Wasted Years' in Japan's Educational System," *Christian Science Monitor* (16 March 1987).

9. Daniel J. Boorstein, *The Americans, 3: The National Experience* (New York: Random House, 1965).

10. Edward W. Said, *Orientalism* (New York: Random House, 1978).

11. Richard T. Pascale and Anthony G. Athos, *The Art of Japanese Management: Applications for American Executives* (New York: Warner Books, 1982).

12. Robert Leestma, William J. Bennett et al., *Japanese Education Today* (Washington, D.C.: Office of Educational Research and Improvement, Department of Education, 1987).

13. *Educational Reform in the United States* (Tokyo: Prime Minister's Council on Educational Reform, 1987).

10

Conflict and Cooperation in U.S.-Japanese Science and Technology

Leonard H. Lynn

The 1980s have seen a number of widely publicized technology conflicts between Japan and the United States. In mid-1987 it was disclosed that Toshiba Machine Company, a member of the Toshiba group, had violated an agreement with the United States and other NATO countries by selling sensitive technology to the Soviet Union. A few months earlier, the U.S. secretaries of commerce and defense had intervened to prevent Fujitsu from buying control of Fairchild Semiconductor Corporation. The organizers of some U.S. technical meetings have discussed excluding Japanese and other foreign re- searchers from attending, and in July 1987 a conference on high temperature superconductivity actually did so. And one of the most dramatic episodes in postwar U.S.-Japanese relations involved a sting operation by the FBI in which Japanese executives from Hitachi and Mitsubishi Electric illegally bought IBM secrets.

Some of these conflicts have been exacerbated by a degree of mutual paranoia between the United States and Japan, and there is a danger of this paranoia getting out of control. Nine U.S. Congressmen chose to smash a Toshiba radio at a press conference to show their contempt for Toshiba Machine's parent company, even though an independent auditor concluded that Toshiba management had known nothing about the export to the Soviet Union.[1] Japanese television repeatedly showed pictures of the Congressmen's actions. It was not difficult for the Japanese to wonder why Japanese control over Fairchild posed any new security problems for the United States, as Fairchild had previously been under the control of a French-owned company. And many Japanese regarded

TABLE 10.1
U.S. and Japanese Shares of Total National Expenditures for R&D by Five Major OECD Countries (in percentages)

Year	U.S.	Japan	W. Ger.	France	U.K.	Total (in billions of constant 1982 U.S. Dollars)
1965	69.1	7.1	7.8	6.7	9.3	86.0
1970	61.8	12.3	9.8	7.0	9.0	100.9
1975	56.1	15.6	11.1	7.6	9.6	106.8
1980	55.2	17.4	11.5	7.4	8.5	132.5
1981	54.5	18.2	11.0	7.7	8.7	140.6
1982	54.4	18.8	10.8	8.0	8.1	145.9
1983	54.7	19.5	10.5	7.8	7.5	153.3
1984	55.3	19.9	10.0	7.7	7.1	163.6
1985	55.1	20.6	10.2	7.4	6.8	175.1

Notes: The total is based on dollar amounts calculated for each country based on OECD purchasing power exchange rates and U.S. Department of Commerce GNP implicit price deflators. These are added to produce a total for the five countries in constant 1982 dollars. Data for the U.K. were not available for 1965 (the datum presented is for 1964), 1970 (the datum presented is an interpolation of 1964 and 1975), 1982 (the datum presented is an interpolation of 1981 and 1983), and 1984 (the datum presented is a interpolation of 1983 and 1985).

Source: National Science Foundation, *International Science and Technology Data Update*, 1987, p. 2.

the FBI sting as part of a somewhat underhanded effort to put the Japanese computer industry in its place.

On the other hand, a network of collaborative activities and interests have rapidly developed between the U.S. and Japanese research and development communities. While these instances of cooperation (and the development of powerful interests with a stake in further increasing such cooperation) have been less dramatic and thus less noticed than the clashes, they may well prove to be much more important for the shared destinies of the two countries.

The Changing Technological Relationship Between the United States and Japan

Table 10.1 suggests one reason for the growing tendency of Americans to view the Japanese technological "challenge" with alarm. In the postwar world the United States has never before faced serious competition in R&D spending from any country except the Soviet Union. The table shows that after controlling for purchasing power and fluctuations in exchange rates, the U.S. share of investment in new technology in 1965 was more than double that of the other four major noncommunist developers of new technology combined. The United

Kingdom was the strongest competitor to the United States in 1965, but the competition was not very strong. The United Kingdom's spending only amounted to just over one-seventh of U.S. spending. As one might expect, given the decline of U.S. economic preeminence, the U.S. share of total spending on R&D dropped substantially in the late 1960s and early 1970s. By 1970 Japan had emerged as the second largest spending nation. Interestingly, the relative U.S. position has remained constant since the 1970s while that of the European countries has declined. The combined share of the European countries dropped from 28.3% in 1975 to 24.4% in 1985. Over the same years the Japanese share rose from 15.6% to 20.6%. In 1985 Japan spent nearly 40% as much as the United States on R&D, and not much less than the three European countries combined. Given that Japan has only about half the population of the United States, this is quite a respectable total. Indeed, Japan now spends more on R&D than the Soviet Union and spends a larger percentage of GNP in this area than the United States. And while both the Soviet Union and the United States spend a substantial share of their R&D budgets on defense-related technology, most of Japan's spending is more directly geared to providing economic benefits.

Given the level of its R&D spending in recent years, it is not surprising that Japan has emerged as a technological superpower. One indication of how far Japan has come was provided in a 1986 *Fortune* magazine article.[2] After asking experts from around the world to assess the relative strength of the United States, Japan, Western Europe, and the Soviet Union in four of the most important areas of new technology (computers, life sciences, advanced materials, and optoelectronics), the author of the article concluded that Japan ranked a strong second to the United States in computer technology and was well ahead of Western Europe and the Soviet Union. In some subfields, such as in the development of gallium arsenide, Japan was seen as being ahead of the United States. Japan was also second only to the United States in the life sciences and advanced materials. In optoelectronics, Japan was seen as holding a clear lead.[3] A 1987 Defense Science Board report said that in virtually every area of semiconductor production the United States has lost or is losing its technological lead to Japan. While the U.S. space program has faltered in the wake of the *Challenger* shuttle disaster, the Japanese have continued to progress in this area and are becoming increasingly independent of U.S. technology. According to one report the Japanese government plans to spend $40 billion or more in commercializing space by the year 2000. In August 1987, Japan launched a 1,200 lb. engineering test satellite in which the second and third stages were based on Japanese technology. By early 1992 the Japanese National Space Development Agency hopes to have tested

TABLE 10.2
Technology Trade Between the United States and Japan

Year	Japanese Technology Imports from the United States		Japanese Technology Exports to the United States	
	Payments (million yen)	% of Total Japanese Tech. Imports	Payments (million yen)	% of Total Japanese Tech. Exports
1974	101,700	63.6	4,400	7.7
1975	106,700	63.1	6,900	10.4
1976	114,600	64.6	7,900	9.5
1977	118,300	62.1	9,000	9.6
1978	123,100	64.1	13,100	10.7
1979	153,600	63.7	19,200	14.4
1980	153,800	64.2	22,100	13.8
1981	171,800	66.2	32,600	18.6
1982	187,000	66.2	35,600	19.3
1983	191,100	68.4	53,600	22.2
1984	193,000	68.6	65,900	23.7

Source: Statistics Bureau, Prime Minister, Report on the Survey of Research and Development (Tokyo: Nippon Tokei Kyokai, various years).

a Japanese first-stage launch vehicle. Meanwhile, Japan is proceeding with plans to launch a space shuttle in 1995 and would reportedly like to have a manned space station and space factory by 2010.[4]

Japan's fast rising technological strength was also reflected in the fact that, in 1986, residents of Japan received nearly one-fifth of all U.S. patents. Perhaps even more startling to Americans is that the firm that received the most U.S. patents was not General Electric or IBM, but Japan's Hitachi. General Electric was second, but Toshiba finished third.[5]

Table 10.2 suggests some other aspects of the changing relationship between the United States and Japan. It provides, first of all, one clear measure of how dependent Japan has been on the United States as a source of technology. In any given year between 1974 and 1984, roughly two-thirds of Japan's payments for technology imports went to the United States. Interestingly, this ratio slowly *increased* over that decade—presumably because as the overall level of Japanese technology increased, fewer European technologies were of value to Japan. The table also shows that the United States has become increasingly important as a market for Japanese technology (and conversely, it also shows the increasing value of Japanese technology for the United States). Less than one-tenth of Japanese receipts for technology came from the United States in 1974. In more recent years this proportion has approached one-fourth. As the level of Japanese technology has increased, there has been a transition from primarily selling simple technologies to newly industrializing or less developed countries to selling more advanced technologies to the United States. Finally, the table shows clearly how technology trade between the two countries has been moving closer to a position of equity. In 1974 the Japanese received 4,400 million yen from the United States for technology. This figure was just a little more than 4% of the 101,700 million yen the Japanese paid Americans for technology. A decade later, the Japanese paid 193,000 million yen for U.S. technology, but received 65,900 million yen for the sale of Japanese technology to the United States, a sales to purchase ratio of 34%. Nor does this ratio give a fair statement of the *current* relative status of technology in the two countries, as payments are still being made for contracts that were made some years ago, and far more of these payments go to the United States than to Japan.

In the earlier stages of U.S.-Japanese technical dealings, U.S. firms were primarily interested in receiving extra payments for technology they had already developed for use at home. Later there was a stronger interest in using technology to gain market access to Japan, but there was still little interest in acquiring technology from Japan. About a decade ago this situation started to reverse in some basic industries, such as steel. Indeed, by 1980 many of the major U.S. steelmakers were eagerly seeking comprehensive technological assistance from the Japanese.[6] Other older industries followed. Even in industries where the United States continues to maintain a technological lead, there has been a sharp awakening to the idea that it is dangerous to ignore developments in Japan.[7]

Given U.S. inexperience in dealing with its allies on a near equal footing in science and technology, Japanese inexperience as a technological superpower, U.S. defensiveness in the face of an array of challenges to U.S. self-confidence, the Japanese desire for recognition (and impatience with stereotypes related to creativity and fair play), and the pervasive economic and strategic importance of technology, it is not surprising that we are seeing the emergence of considerable friction centering on technology between the two countries.

Government-to-Government Relations:
The Pressure for "Equal Access"

The U.S. and Japanese governments have long had formal relations in technology. Just weeks after the end of World War II, a commission was created to allow U.S. and Japanese medical scientists to investigate the biological effects of the atomic bombings of Japan. In 1958 the two countries concluded a treaty under Eisenhower's Atoms for Peace program. As a result of this agreement Japan became a major participant in many U.S. nuclear R&D programs. In the early and mid-1960s, bilateral agreements were signed between Japan and the United States for cooperation in research in basic science, medicine, and natural resources. Other agreements followed in the 1970s and 1980s for research on the environment, space, and energy.[8]

Until fairly recently, much of the emphasis of these agreements was on giving the Japanese access to U.S. technology, often in exchange for substantial payments by the Japanese. The Japanese government, according to Justin Bloom, invested upwards of $150 million in U.S. nuclear programs.[9] In 1979 the United States and Japan entered into a major ten-year agreement on energy technology with heavy Japanese financing. This agreement was supplemented the following year by the U.S.-Japan Cooperation Agreement in Non-energy Fields, which provided a general structure or "umbrella" for U.S.-Japanese joint activities in technology.[10]

In the 1980s there has been a rather sudden emergence of respect for Japanese technology in the United States, and this trend has been accompanied by a much greater U.S. interest in getting access not just to Japanese research money, but to Japanese technology itself. Japan has long been criticized for taking a "free ride" at the expense of U.S. technology, but now the complaint is less that the Japanese do not contribute money than that they do not contribute technology. U.S. officials have increasingly demanded that the Japanese give U.S. researchers access to Japanese technology that is equal to that enjoyed by Japanese researchers in the United States. Unfortunately, it is not clear what "equal access" means or how one would measure the degree to which it has been attained.

An indicator of equality of access that some have used is the number of U.S. researchers working in Japan compared to the number of Japanese researchers working in the United States. In 1986 it was widely reported that while there were more than 300 Japanese scientists working in the United States at the National Institutes of Health (NIH) (about 250 of them with U.S. government support), there were only three National Institutes of Health researchers working in Japan. Nor is the imbalance restricted to medical researchers. An official of the U.S. National Research Council estimated that there were about 7,000 Japanese scientists and researchers working in the United States compared with only 500 U.S. scientists working in Japan.[11]

What are the causes of this "imbalance," and what should be done to correct it? NIH officials stressed that the Japanese researchers were selected based on merit and were making important contributions to their programs. In short, they saw nothing wrong with the large number of Japanese researchers being hosted. Most U.S. scientists would probably sympathize with this feeling. Increased communications with colleagues around the world is likely to speed the advance of science, and few scientists would like to see such communications restricted. The real problem of balance, then, might be that there are not enough U.S. researchers in Japan.

But why are there not more U.S. researchers in Japan? Is it because Japanese government and industrial research laboratories do not allow them in, or is it because not many U.S. researchers want to work in Japan? If the former, the answer may simply be judicious "Japan bashing" by the U.S. government and by industry. But what if the problem is that U.S. researchers do not want to go to Japan? Perhaps the overall quality of research in the United States is higher than that in Japan, so it is only natural that there is an imbalance. Japanese scientists might have more to gain professionally by coming to the United States than U.S. scientists would have to gain by going to Japan. If this is the heart of the problem, the best action might be to allow the imbalance to work itself out as the level of Japanese science and technology rises. Given the current successes of the Japanese R&D community, however, it would seem that the imbalance is far too great to be accounted for by this factor. Perhaps the central problem is that there are too few U.S. researchers willing to adapt to Japanese living conditions or to learn how to speak Japanese, and without the language there is little point in working in Japan. In this case the solution would seem to be to provide special housing or intensive language programs for U.S. researchers interested in working in Japan.

The United States has not made much of an effort to identify what the problem is. Rather, in 1986 and 1987, it simply increased the pressure on the Japanese to do something to ensure "equal access." A statute passed by the U.S. Congress in 1986 authorized U.S. federal laboratories to keep out Japanese researchers if U.S. researchers were not allowed comparable access. In 1987, the White House Economics Policy Council reportedly considered demanding that Japan pay the costs for U.S. scientists to learn Japanese so that they would have greater access to Japanese science and technology. Although this demand was not actually made, U.S. officials were determined to put strong pressure on the Japanese.[12]

This situation came to a head in January 1988, when Prime Minister Noboru Takeshita made his first official visit in that capacity to the United States. One of the items given priority in his discussions with President Ronald Reagan concerned negotiations toward a renewal of the 1980 "umbrella" agreement (which was supposed to have been renewed several months earlier). The Japanese agreed to accept 300 foreign researchers in fiscal 1988 through fellowships to be offered by the Ministry of International Trade and Industry, the Ministry of Education, and the Science and Technology Agency. They also agreed in principle to promote joint research in nine areas, including superconductors, biotechnology, information technology, and the development of databases, and to transfer some thirty government-sponsored R&D projects to a new organization that would allow better access to foreign researchers.[13] Disagreements remained, however, and the treaty could not be signed until later in the year. In any case it appeared unlikely that more than fifty or so of the promised 300 researchers could be found to go to Japan in 1988.

The pressure to internationalize the Japanese R&D system came not only from foreign critics but also from some Japanese leaders who see internationalization as a means of giving new strength to basic research. Throughout the 1980s a stream of announcements of new programs and new initiatives came out of Tokyo. In a 1985 report, the Prime Minister's Council for Science and Technology designated "internationalization" as one of the two major pillars of Japanese science and technology policy (the other was basic research). The report specifically recommended that the government encourage the employment and admission of foreign researchers in universities and national research institutions.[14] A law passed in 1986 included sections making it possible for foreigners to be appointed to research positions at national institutes and to some management positions in research departments. The new law also made it easier for foreigners to get access to patents developed as a result of collaborative research.[15]

The various Japanese government agencies with large research budgets also initiated their own internationalization programs. The ministry with the largest R&D budget, the Ministry of Education, plans to invite about 100 foreign researchers with new doctorates to come to Japan beginning in 1988. Under this program, researchers from the United States, Germany, France, and other countries will do research work in Japan for one year.[16] In addition, the Science and Technology Agency (STA) established the Frontier Research Program in 1986 to promote both basic research and international cooperation. The program is administered by the STA's Institute of Physical and Chemical Research (commonly called "Riken" in both English and Japanese). One of the first two major areas of study, the biology of regulatory processes in organisms, will examine such topics as the aging process. This project will comprise four teams made up of five or six members each. The other initial topic, new functional materials, will be studied by three teams. A third topic, brain research, is slated to begin later. About one-third of the research staff is to be invited from overseas. One of the program's advisers is a foreigner, as are the heads of three of its seven laboratories (although these laboratory heads are not currently based in Japan).[17]

In 1985 the Ministry of International Trade and Industry (MITI) announced plans to inaugurate an international high-technology institute in Tsukuba Science City. This institute, planned to open in 1990, is to be a graduate school that emphasizes both research and training. It is to have 100 faculty and 500 students, of whom more than half are to be non-Japanese. MITI has also said it will hire foreign scientists to work in the laboratories of its Agency for Industrial Science and Technology. In addition, MITI and the Ministry of Post and Telecommunications have jointly set up a major new program of collaborative research on industrial technology, the Japan Key Technology Center. The center is to supply risk capital for research and development on basic industrial technologies. In establishing the center, the Japanese government gave another nod to foreign concerns about access by setting up the Japan Trust Fund as a mechanism to invite foreign researchers to work at private and governmental Japanese laboratories. Although at the end of 1985 the fund had only enough money to invite one researcher, plans call for it to eventually invite 100 per year.[18]

"Equal Access" and the Private Sector

The role of government in Japanese industry, trade, and technology has received widespread attention in the United States, but many authorities conclude that this role is far less important than is commonly assumed.[19] Japanese government financial involvement in R&D has long been relatively low compared to other advanced countries, and in recent years it has continued to decline relative to private spending. In 1985 less than one-fifth of Japanese R&D funding came from the government, compared to 47% in the United States.[20]

Because of this difference in government roles it is important to avoid an excessive focus on government programs in assessing conflict and cooperation in technology between the United States and Japan. Access to Japanese technology by foreigners has increased dramatically in the 1980s as a result of activities by private U.S. and European firms. A recent report in the *Wall Street Journal* suggested some of the reasons for these activities. According to the report, Proctor & Gamble's new Liquid Tide drew on technologies developed not only in the United States but also in Japan and Belgium. Sulfactants, or cleaning agents, for the new detergent were developed in Japan, where people wash their clothes in cold water. For the new sulfactants to work well, however, new water-softening ingredients were needed. These were developed in Belgium, where this particular technology was more advanced because the average mineral content of water in Europe is very high.[21]

In brief, different countries have developed strengths in different technologies as a result of differing conditions. As a result, firms find they can increase their international competitiveness by having R&D capabilities in different countries. There are other advantages as well: Having research facilities in a host country makes it easier for a firm to adapt its products to the host country's markets; it also improves a firm's ability to monitor the technological activities of competitors in the host country.[22]

Procter & Gamble is only one of many foreign firms to have set up research facilities in Japan since 1985. Merck, the pharmaceutical company, built a laboratory there, and Dupont opened a 16-billion-yen central research laboratory with a staff of 180, joining Monsanto in Yokohama. In late 1987 IBM Japan was spending 150 billion yen (over $1 billion) on a software development center in Chiba prefecture near Tokyo, and only two years earlier had consolidated four of its research labs (with 1,500 researchers) into a new laboratory near Tokyo. Kodak is building a 10-billion-yen laboratory near Tokyo. Ciba-Geigy (the Swiss pharmaceutical and chemical company) established a research laboratory in Japan with some 130 Japanese and foreign scientists. Some foreign firms are opening research facilities in Tsukuba Science City, near many of the Japanese government research laboratories. LSI Logic, PLC, and Imperial Chemical Industries opened laboratories there in 1987, and Upjohn completed one in April 1988. In all, some eighteen foreign-affiliated laboratories are planned in Tsukuba.[23]

Japanese firms have also been active in globalizing their research efforts. Kyocera Corporation (a producer of ceramic electronic parts and a wide range of other products), Otsuka Pharmaceuticals, and others have already established research facilities in the United States, and the results of a survey indicated that nearly 100 other Japanese firms intend to do likewise. Some of those that had established facilities in the United States by the end of 1987 were Isuzu Motors, Kao Corporation (a producer of soap, detergent, other home products, and industrial chemicals), Mazda, Nippon Denso (a producer of auto parts), Nippon Telegraph and Telephone, Shin-Etsu Chemical Corporation, and Sumitomo Electric Industries.[24]

Aside from this, a number of Japanese firms, including Furukawa Electric, Honda, Matsushita, Sumitomo Electric, and NEC, have been hiring American and other foreign researchers for their laboratories in

Japan. This, too, is a very recent development. A survey of private Japanese firms with R&D budgets of one billion yen or more by MITI's Agency for Industrial Science and Technology found that these firms employed a total of only sixteen foreign researchers in 1977. This number increased to a still modest eighty-nine researchers in 1982, but since then the increase has been dramatic (although comparable statistics are not available to fully document the increase). Several of these companies were going overseas for some of their recruiting. Fujitsu, for example, started a recruiting program that aimed at hiring more than ten foreign researchers by the spring of 1988.[25]

In 1985 the U.S. National Science Foundation (NSF) carried out a survey of Japanese company laboratories with more than thirty researchers. Nearly half the firms said they were ready to host foreign researchers (or might be in the near future). Most of these firms were ready to back up their words by agreeing to allow the NSF to publish information about them, including the name of a contact person. In some cases they offered to help subsidize the stay of foreign researchers. NSF has proposed a program called the Japan Initiative, which would subsidize Japanese language study by U.S. scientists and engineers and help them to find positions in private Japanese R&D laboratories.

The growing degree of interaction between U.S. and Japanese R&D systems has also included joint research activities by a number of Japanese and U.S. firms in a variety of industries: SONY and Advanced Micro Devices, Inc., have agreed to work together on the development of process technologies; Toshiba and LSI Logic agreed to jointly develop gate arrays; three Japanese airframe makers and Boeing were collaborating on the development of a new generation of commercial aircraft, although this project now seems to be dormant; Hitachi and General Motors agreed to conduct joint R&D in automobile parts, computers, semiconductors, and other electronic parts and new materials; Fanuc and General Electric are to develop factory automation technologies; and Toshiba and Cummins are to develop ceramic parts for diesel engines.

Japanese Research Cartels and U.S. Firms

Access to a nation's R&D system involves more than just allowing individual researchers to work in government laboratories or even internationalizing firms. U.S. firms have long been concerned about the research consortia established by their Japanese rivals and subsidized by MITI and other government agencies.[26] They have complained both because they had difficulty gaining access to patents generated in these programs and because their Japanese subsidiaries were not allowed to join them. Some changes have occurred on both fronts, although complaints about the substance of the changes are still being made. In 1982, for example, MITI established procedures to license Japanese government–controlled patents to foreigners. The procedures did not provide very ready access, however, and even a firm as powerful as IBM was not able to arrange an agreement giving it access to government-controlled computer patents until 1985. This was the first agreement in which MITI concluded an inclusive patent contract with a private foreign-affiliated firm.

On another front—that of membership in the research consortia—there are signs that the Japanese are responding to pressures to allow foreign participation. Here too, however, there have been numerous complaints about the extent of access granted and suspicions that the Japanese are using this device more to gain even further access to U.S. technology than to offer access to their own technology. The result has been that several research consortia have announced their willingness to accept foreign members, but so far the response has seemed unenthusiastic. In 1987 MITI announced the formation of an International Superconductivity Technology Center to exploit this rapidly developing technology. Fifty Japanese companies quickly joined the center, but as of this writing, U.S. firms had not yet taken part. MITI officials say they tried to get foreign firms to join but were unsuccessful. Some foreign officials complained that they did not know they were welcome to join, but by early 1988 the center was advertising in the *Wall Street Journal* to invite U.S. firms to join it. Some foreign firms complained that regulations governing the new organization would not allow them to conduct research in their home countries but only at Japanese facilities. The Science and Technology Agency, a frequent rival to MITI as government mentor for the development of some new technologies, established a New Superconductor Materials Forum in 1987. This organization is to serve as a clearing house for information. It also is open to foreign members, but of the 140 companies and research organizations that joined, only one (an Italian chemical and engineering company) was foreign.[27] Foreign firms are also allowed to join research groups under the Key Technology Center program mentioned above, but only two U.S. affiliates (IBM Japan and Nihon DEC) were among the firms participating in the first twenty-five long-term projects approved by the government.[28]

While U.S. firms have sought access to technology controlled by the Japanese government, the U.S. government has also sought technology controlled by Japanese firms. A major interest has been in defense-related technologies. The Japanese have been widely criticized by the United States for benefiting from the protection afforded by U.S. technology in defense while withholding technology that might contribute to the U.S. defense effort. In January 1983 Prime Minister Nakasone's government agreed to modify Japan's ban on exports of defense-related technologies to allow certain technologies that might have military applications to be transferred to the United States. Actual transfers, however, appear to have occurred more slowly than Washington had hoped.[29]

The U.S. Department of Defense also strongly encouraged Japan to become involved in the Strategic Defense Initiative (SDI). After considerable study (including three tours of the United States by Japanese delegations of businesspeople and government officials), the government of Japan formally announced that it would participate and signed an agreement to so do in July 1987. The agreement allows Japanese firms to develop parts of the SDI technology in equal competition with other firms. This development marks the first time Japanese government ministries have worked with private companies taking part in the Pentagon procurement process.[30]

The Problem of Access and the Future of U.S.-Japanese Relations in Technology

Much of the problem in the U.S.-Japanese relationship in technology, as in economic issues, is that both Americans and Japanese were slow to recognize the rising importance of Japan. This recognition came as a shock to Americans, who belatedly realized that even in their areas of traditional strength they could no longer ignore Japan and maintain international competitiveness. All at once they decided they needed broader access to Japanese science and technology, and they wanted it at once. Part of the problem was that Japanese institutions and attitudes had not "internationalized" in pace with the rapid growth in the importance of Japanese technology. Excessive Japanese modesty over their achievements, combined with still deeply ingrained attitudes that foreigners have great difficulty working in Japan, have resulted in the maintenance of anachronistic barriers. An added irritant to Americans who experience these barriers is that Japan has acquired an image of being one of the most aggressive and effective societies in the world at drawing on the science and technology of other countries.

So part of the problem has been a system of administrative barriers that has made it very difficult for foreign researchers to work in Japan and difficult for U.S. and other foreign firms to move into the Japanese R&D community. Foreign pressure, combined with genuine desires to internationalize by some Japanese, has resulted in considerable progress in this area. Unfortunately, the problem of U.S. access to Japanese technology is deeper. Another key component is that the U.S. capability to enter the Japanese R&D system is very weak.

Until recently, few American technical personnel knew much about the kinds of research being done in Japan and who was doing it. In contrast, the Japanese, through a variety of mechanisms, are very well versed on what is going on in the United States and on who the key researchers are.[31] Few Americans, and even fewer American scientists and engineers, speak Japanese well enough to work on an equal footing with Japanese in Japan. Most Japanese researchers have studied English a number of years, and many attain a level enabling them to function quite well in the United States. U.S. businesses have made progress in the past few years, but they still are not well equipped to find out what is happening in technical fields in Japan. Japanese firms routinely send their employees to U.S. universities and to technical conferences, and some have special offices to watch technology development in the United States. Japanese trade associations, general trading companies, and other organizations also support the firms in the collection of information.

The solution to this problem is not to engage in an orgy of "Japan-bashing" until an acceptable balance is achieved in terms of the numbers of U.S. researchers in Japan. If some sort of symmetrical access is to be achieved, Americans will have to do much more to improve the U.S. ability to function in Japan. This chapter has described some of the steps U.S. businesses have taken in the past few years to establish research facilities in Japan. One could also point to programs at MIT, North Carolina, Lehigh, and other universities designed to facilitate the ability of U.S. researchers to draw on the Japanese R&D system. These programs deserve broader support than they are now getting.[32] Similarly, the efforts of the NSF to help U.S. researchers find places in private Japanese research laboratories are certainly commendable. The risk is that these efforts will not be enough and will not show results quickly. The consequences would be a loss for both countries, but probably a greater loss for the United States than for Japan.

Notes

Some sections of this chapter draw on material published in Leonard H. Lynn, "Research and Development in Japan," *Current History* (April 1988):165–168, 180.

1. *JEI Report* 35B (18 September 1987).

2. Gene Bylinsky, "The High Tech Race: Who's Ahead," *Fortune* 114 (13 October 1986):26–57.

3. A more recent survey of 100 Japanese research executives reached similar conclusions on the overall status of Japanese technology. See Junichi Taki, "Japan Leads in Optics, U.S. in Life Science," *Japan Economic Journal*, 23 January 1988.

4. "Japan Shoots for the Stars," *JEI Report* 40A (23 October 1987); and Barbara Buell, "Blast-off: Japan Inc. is Joining the Space Race," *Business Week* (24 August 1987):84–85.

5. "Foreign Patents up Again," *Research Management* 30 (July/August 1987):4.

6. See Leonard H. Lynn, "Multinational Joint Ventures in the U.S. Steel Industry," in David Mowery, ed., *International Collaborative Ventures in U.S. Manufacturing* (Cambridge: Ballinger, 1988).

7. Mowery, *International Collaborative Ventures*, also discusses technology transfer in the automobile, pharmaceutical, aircraft, robotics, and electronics industries.

8. Justin Bloom, "Bilateral Cooperative Programs: A Case Study—the United States and Japan," *Journal of the Washington Academy of Sciences* 77 (September 1987):87-93.

9. Ibid.

10. Richard N. Cooper and Philip B. Jones, "The Long-term Outlook for United States–Japanese Cooperation," in *U.S.-Japan Relations: Towards a New Equilibrium* (Cambridge: Center for International Affairs, Harvard University, 1983), pp. 31–47.

11. Eduardo Lachica, "U.S., Japanese Negotiators Deadlocked on Tapping Each Other's Technology," *Wall Street Journal*, 22 January 1988.

12. Marjorie Sun, "Strains in U.S.-Japan Exchanges," *Science* 237 (31 July 1987).

13. Yuko Inoue, "Negotiators Reach Basic Agreement on Science and Technology Pact," *Japan Economic Journal* (16 January 1988):2; and Marjorie Sun, "Down to the Wire on U.S.-Japan Agreement," *Science* 239 (1 January 1988):13-14.

14. For a general description of the Council for Science and Technology and other Japanese government agencies involved in research, see Leonard H. Lynn, "Japanese Research and Technology Policy," *Science* 233 (18 July 1986):296-301.

15. The Tokyo Office of the U.S. National Science Foundation, *Report Memorandum #96*, 7 April 1986.

16. The official English name of the Ministry of Education is "Ministry of Education, Science and Culture." On this program, see *Japan Economic Journal*, 14 November 1987.

17. The Tokyo Office of the U.S. National Science Foundation, *Report Memorandum #97*, 18 April 1986; Riken, *Frontier Research Program* (Tokyo: Riken, undated); and Alan K. Engel, "Japan Adds Flexibility to R&D Effort," *The Scientist* 1 (17 September 1987):1ff.

18. The Tokyo Office of the U.S. National Science Foundation, "Japan Key Technology Center," *Report Memorandum #91*, 16 January 1986.

19. See Hugh Patrick, ed., *Japan's High Technology Industries: Lessons and Limitations of Industrial Policy* (Seattle: University of Washington Press, 1986).

20. The Tokyo Office of the U.S. National Science Foundation, *Report Memorandum #93*, 25 February 1986.

21. Paul Ingrassia, "Global Reach: Industry is Shopping Abroad for Good Ideas to Apply to Products," *Wall Street Journal*, 29 April 1985.

22. See Igor Ansoff, *Implanting Strategic Management* (Englewood Cliffs, NJ: Prentice Hall, 1984); and James C. Abegglen and George Stalk, Jr., *Kaisha: The Japanese Corporation* (New York: Basic Books, 1985).

23. "Foreign Firms Set Up Research Beachheads," *Japan Economic Journal*, 14 November 1987; and Hitoshi Sakurazawa, "Nippon kigyo no kenkyu kaihatsu no gurobarizeshon," The Globalization of Developmental Studies by Japanese Industries, *The Journal of Science Policy and Research Management* 2 (1987):131–141.

24. "Japanese Support More Academic Research in the United States," *Research Management* 30 (March/April 1987):3.

25. See Ministry of International Trade and Industry, *Sangyo gitjutsu kaihatsu seisaku to kiban gijutsu kenkyu enkatsu ho*, Industrial Technology Development Policy and the Law for the Facilitation of Research on Fundamental Technologies (Tokyo: MITI, 1985), p. 184; "Foreigners Recruited to Boost Basic Research," *The Japan Economic Journal*, 30 January 1988; and "Start-ups in Need of Capable Technicians and Researchers," *The Japan Economic Journal*, 12 October 1985.

26. See Leonard H. Lynn and Timothy J. McKeown, *Organizing Business: Trade Associations in America and Japan* (Washington, D.C.: American Enterprise Institute and University Press of America, 1988).

27. Stephen Yoder, "Americans Spurn Japan's Research Offer," *Wall Street Journal*, 30 December 1987.

28. These two firms, however, were each in more than one consortia. The Tokyo Office of the U.S. National Science Foundation, "Japan Key Technology Center," *Report Memorandum #91*, 16 January 1986.

29. "Whatever Happened to Defense Technology Transfers?" *JEI Report* 30A (7 August 1987).

30. Ibid.

31. See Lynn and McKeown, *Organizing Business*; and Leonard H. Lynn, "Japanese Technology: Success and Strategies," *Current History* (November 1983):366–370, 390.

32. The MIT-Japan Program on Science and Technology, for example, offers applied Japanese studies for scientists and engineers. It includes language training and opportunities to spend a year or more working in Japanese research laboratories. On MIT see *JEI Report* 1A (8 January 1988). More generally see Ronald A. Morse and Richard J. Samuels, eds., *Getting America Ready for Japanese Science and Technology* (Washington, D.C.: Asia Program of the Woodrow Wilson International Center for Scholars, 1985).

11

Managing Cooperation Toward the Twenty-first Century

Ronald A. Morse

Given what we know of the interrelationship between national economic vitality, political clout, and military strength, it is highly likely that Japan will equal or surpass the United States as a powerful free-world nation during the first decade of the twenty-first century. Japan's remarkable successes since 1945 have been a major surprise to the rest of the world, and now given Tokyo's key leadership position in a dynamic Asia, there is good reason to assume that it will be able to respond to the many requests for it to take a greater leadership role. But between now and 2015 the major concern in Japan will be to manage the transition to ensure that the emerging Japanese superstate is supportive of the free-world interests that the .United States and other advanced nations have defended.

While the Japanese elites understand that their current economic miracle is impressive, they also have come to recognize that an essential component of national greatness is the ability of a country and its people to articulate a social design, a vision of a functioning society that other nations can accept and even emulate. Achieving this objective will be a major step for a culturally and linguistically isolated Japan. The change in spirit toward greater openness, which the Japanese call internationalization, will represent the final step toward modernity and responsibility. This is the challenge that the Japanese will have to meet in the next twenty years if they want to become leaders in the community of nations. They acknowledge this challenge but still look to the United States to help them make the transition. But as I will suggest later, Americans and Japanese have quite different views on how this goal can be achieved.

As Japanese leaders grope toward their new role as an international leader, they are deeply concerned that the United States might not be able to maintain its own leadership position in the meantime. How the two powers together manage this transition will be linked to their ability to provide effective leadership as well as to Japan's preparedness to replace the United States as the dominant leader and hegemonic power. As one writer has reflected on this subject, "Japan remains unwilling—and probably unable—to shoulder many of the responsibilities that have traditionally gone with global leadership."[1]

Before looking at some management and institutional options that have been proposed to smooth out this restructuring of global power relationships, it is useful to consider some recent ideas about how to reach the twenty-first century without encountering serious problems between the two nations. Other contributors to this book have made their own suggestions in this regard. They rightly point to significant changes taking place in the economic, security, and political relations between the two nations, and by extension, in the rest of the world. On the one hand, recent trade disputes and increasing foreign demands on Tokyo for greater economic and sometimes security and defense expenditures have raised questions about a widening gulf in the policies of the two nations, and even a possible "divergence" in their relations. Most people, however, downplay these differences and emphasize the "convergence" of interests brought about by the interpenetration, interdependence, and interrelatedness of the two economies and societies. A complex set of relationships on a broad range of issues has, they would argue, only brought bilateral differences into greater prominence, implying far more divergence than is in fact really the case.

For better or worse, there is no denying that there have indeed been significant changes during the past forty years and that these changes have led to a more realistic, if often confrontational, relationship between Tokyo and Washington. While both sides are aware of this changing situation and have tried to articulate a new framework for a different set of relationships, few practical solutions have been found to date.

Interpreting Change

The Japanese, for example, sensitive to the traditional Asian astrological cycles, were quick to identify one historical trend—that 1988 was the Year of the Dragon, a sign in the cycle of events of significant importance. The dragon, an auspicious and formidable animal, is usually associated with years of dramatic change. The next Year of the Dragon will occur in the year 2000, the turn of the century. Japan's drive toward modernization began in 1868—120 years ago—and that too was the Year of the Dragon. The Russo-Japanese War and the start of World War II also took place in Years of the Dragon. Equally important, for nearly four years now the Japanese have been speculating, largely because of the huge U.S. trade deficit with Japan but also in connection with their study of economic history, that the two countries are at a historical crossroads of major importance. If there has been significant economic change, however, an even more important question concerns its implications for the broader global aspects of the relationship.

For example, some observers have suggested that Japan turned a corner in its postwar development in 1987 when Noboru Takeshita became the prime minister. All of the elements for new leadership were in place. The political revolution more or less imposed on Japan by the U.S. postwar occupation successfully put a political system in place and made democracy the vital force in Japan that it is today. An unprecedented development in Japanese economic growth, production, and trade took place in the 1960s and early 1970s. Today Japan is poised for its "third revolution" after the political and economic ones—an intellectual or ideological revolution that articulates a vision, the final step toward the transformation of Japan into a global leader. The difficulty Japan has in accomplishing this goal stems in part from its long and intimate junior partner relationship with the United States. In defining its new status vis-à-vis the United States, Tokyo will gain the capacity to have more mature relations with other nations—most significantly with the Soviet Union.

As one would expect, Japanese thoughts on the twenty-first century are closely linked to this rethinking of Japan's national image. The year 1987 was just halfway between the early 1970s and the year 2000. Japan came to economic and political maturity about thirteen years ago, and in another twelve years it will enter the new century a far more powerful country than it is even today. Sandwiched halfway between the political and economic recovery of the 1970s and what the Japanese see as the full flowering of their national autonomy in the twenty-first century, their fate is bracketed between a past where they were a junior partner to the United States and a future when they will be strong, independent, and equal to the United States in many respects.

Three concerns of the Japanese emphasize the fact that they see themselves at a turning point in their own history. In the first place, when former Prime Minister Nakasone ended his five-year term in November 1987, he left the Japanese with a sense that their recent successes had established a brilliant benchmark and that their new task was to consolidate the postwar economic and institutional achievements and then blaze a "Japanese path" into the future. "We need a noble goal," he said in one speech. "Standing on that philosophy, we must make an effort not to fall behind in the second industrial revolution of this century."[2]

The second concern has been with the illness and death in January 1989 of Hirohito, the Showa Era Emperor, which has caused considerable speculation about what will happen to Japan with his passing. He was named emperor in 1925 and ruled during periods still vivid in memory. With his death and the accession of his son Akihito, the Japanese sense they are making a definite historical break with their past.

The third issue has to do with Japan's changing demographic situation. A new, self-confident technocratic elite, imbued with a feeling that Japan has achieved its postwar success on its own, is moving into the key positions of political power. This post-1945 generation feels that the nation is indebted to no particular outside source for its success; rather, it has earned the power it has achieved. This new confidence, which many misinterpret as arrogance, is changing the traditional style of Japanese relationships with foreign elites into a style that incorporates a new willingness to engage in confrontational interchanges.

Like other writers and statesmen before him, Nakasone has attempted to position himself as an interpreter of the tea-leaves of Japan's modern history. Since leaving office he has become the spokesman for a new "international era" of Japanese prominence, a notion that has a significant basis in Japan's economic achievements. Nakasone undoubtedly will use his new "think tank" as a platform to articulate what he sees as Japan's leadership position in the Pacific Basin and elsewhere.

Indeed, "the twenty-first century" has become the most popular Japanese phrase for defining "the future."[3] In the last three years from 1986 through 1988 there have been more than 100 books and thousands of Japanese articles on Tokyo and its role in the next century. These reports, literally pouring out of some 250 corporate and public policy institutes, deal with nearly every dimension of Western economic and social history and the implications for Japan's future. They have a common theme: The challenge to Japan is to focus its educational, technological, and economic talent and gain momentum toward the twenty-first century ahead of the United States and everyone else. It is interesting to note that these studies delineate a future that extrapolates from the political, social, and economic achievements already in place. The Japanese vision of the twenty-first century is, as one might expect, not radically different from U.S. or European views on the subject. One difference is perhaps the intensity of Japan's preoccupation with the future and the proper role for Japan on the international scene. If there is one weakness in all of this speculation, it is that the Japanese leadership might be reluctant to tinker with what has so far been a winning strategy. They thereby run the risk of not having the flexibility and adaptability that has been a major strength thus far.

In this context, Japanese sociologists have argued that a cultural "future orientation" is a national characteristic. Studies show that anticipating the future has been a key feature of the Japanese technocratic mind since 1945 and that strategies for change have often been structured around official public policy white papers with a very practical, orderly, and programmatic character. Once an internal consensus is reached on a policy, the Japanese leadership generally takes a disciplined approach toward its implementation, exhibiting what Herman Kahn called the "unsurpassed [Japanese] capacity for purposive, dedicated, and communal action."[4]

Leaders of the Japanese private sector as well as policymakers have focused attention for years on how Japan can continue to maintain its competitive edge through a series of quasi-official "vision" statements. A few of the points that this extensive Japanese literature makes about the rather cautious path to the year 2000 for manufacturing and trade are: continued annual growth rates of 3 to 4%; exploitation of emerging trends and opportunities in the world economy; continued emphasis on managed trade relations with all countries; growth in overseas subsidiaries from 4 to 20% of total domestic manufacturing sales; and a continued avoidance of structural dependence on imports by holding onto a domestic manufacturing base of 30% of the work force.[5]

But Japan's policies of the twenty-first century will have to represent something more than just a resolution of recent economic problems if they are to speak to the larger question of Japan's leadership role. Japan has already faced this issue twice since the mid-1850s. It now has moved a long way from passive emulation of Western imperialism or the expansive militarism of the prewar era. The slogans of the Meiji regime (1868–1912), which ended 300 years of complete national isolation, included "Expel the barbarians," "Build a strong and wealthy nation," and "Restore the Emperor to his rightful position." These goals too were pursued at considerable cost in the 1930s, and the leadership in Japan does not want to repeat the past.

The Japanese are now convinced that they must move to the next phase in leadership. Japan is now wealthy: Where young men in the Meiji era were admonished to be ambitious, today Japanese youth are encouraged to relax, enjoy leisure activities, and become consumers. A representative and democratic political system has replaced the old authoritarian regime. As The Age of the Pacific begins to unfold, Japanese leaders are advocating less dependence on the West and more creativity at home. Japanese development strategy up to the present has been to graft Western educational, political, and technological institutions onto Japanese culture and society to produce a hybrid civilization stronger and more enduring than anything that has come before. The fruits of that effort are finally evident. Now the issue of articulating a leadership framework is central to Japan's policy debate.

Identifying a Framework for Cooperation

If the Japanese have been future-oriented in redefining their relationship with the United States, Americans have been historically minded and reflective about the fading of the twentieth century era of U.S. hegemonic rule.[6] Making a "comeback" is on everyone's mind in the United States; soaring ahead is on everyone's lips in Tokyo. If, as seems likely, the Japanese continue to plan their historic rise as Americans become introspective and resentful, then the implications are profound.

The Japanese literature on America's ability to manage its own future successfully is not very positive. Many recent Japanese books start out by analyzing the successes and failures of the United States and go on to discuss how Japan will be able to build on the earlier mistakes of England and the United States. The Japanese of course are not the only ones reflecting on this problem. Americans also feel that the easy times of the postwar era are over. Increasingly in American households, both husbands and wives must work in order to maintain their earlier standard of living; young people are more practical and serious about their work; and a sense of survival has replaced the risk-taking and job-hopping of workers in the past.

But what have Japanese and Americans had to say about a possible framework for the alliance that will strengthen ties during the interim? And has the approach on both sides been consistent? Answers must be tentative, but an examination of the literature on both sides suggests various options.

The most common Japanese categorization of the "rise and fall" of America is as follows:

1. *Pax Americana I*: The era up until the 1980s spanning the rise of the United States to a world leadership role—economically, politically, and strategically.
2. *Pax Americana II*: The period beginning with the current relative decline of the U.S. hegemony and the transformation of the United States into a debtor nation suffering from what Yale Professor Paul Kennedy termed "imperial overstretch" in his book, *The Rise and Fall of the Great Powers.*[7]

As U.S. dominance has come into question, new forms of shared or even "trilateral" or "pluralistic management" strategies have been suggested. These include:

1. *Pax Ameripponica*: A grand historical venture—a leadership coalition or condominium style of U.S. and Japanese rule with Japan's role being primarily economic and the United States retaining a strategic and political leadership role. How economic competition would be managed is unclear. (Nations leery of Japan assuming a major military burden prefer this arrangement.)[8]
2. *Pax Consortium*: A more loosely defined alliance structure including the European Community and some of Asia's newly industrializing countries (NICs). A regional subcategory of this concept could be "Japanics," referring to Japan's leadership role with the Asian NICs.

Those who look to the benefits of interdependent economies are comfortable with an increasingly prominent Japan because they believe that Tokyo will operate within the U.S. orbit of influence and that a Japanese reliance on U.S. markets gives U.S. policymakers leverage in other areas of the relationship. The Japanese also see advantages for their country in such a framework: maintaining a low-posture strategy justifies modest defense expenditures, assures access to the United States market, and encourages favorable treatment worldwide as an ally and friend of the United States and the free world.

But history suggests that the concept of mutually beneficial interdependence may be tactically useful but shortsighted in strategic terms. It seems almost inevitable that Japan at some point will assume positions on economic policies and on political and strategic issues that conflict with those preferred by the United States. Then deeper questions about the relationship will be asked. Experience has shown that once uncertainty surfaces in the United States over how far Japan can be trusted to assume a benign leadership role and take part in an open and fair trading and political relationship, more fundamental problems will be exposed. Beneath the present rhetoric of cooperation, both sides are already observing each other with restraint and caution as they sort out their respective national interests.

There is also the feeling that Japan's interest in "shared power roles" is a temporary strategy on the way to an era of *Pax Nipponica*. As one prominent Japanese thinker expressed this view,

> Friction between Japan and the United States remains unabated because the foundations of Pax Americana have begun to crumble. As a late

entrant to the oil civilization, Japan has a certain advantage over the U.S.: its industrial infrastructure is thoroughly up-to-date and its workers are much more willing to accept new technologies. . . . Given America's decline and Japan's continued growth, it is realistic to assume that Japan will acquire a greater voice in the world community.[9]

Or, as an American observer put it, "The prospects for the next few years, therefore, are for a pattern of limited and uneven *Pax Nipponica*, led by a country of modest military strength, of limited ability to attract a foreign following and to give foreign aid, but of great economic leverage."[10]

No Easy Solutions

Japanese competitive instincts will continue to challenge U.S. leadership in financial services, as dramatic Japanese investment has taken place in trading companies, banks, insurance, financing, leasing, and real estate. The returns flowing from Japanese investments and assets abroad will fuel further increases in Japan's national wealth, even as economic growth rates decline, well into the twenty-first century.

If foreign economic ties pull Japan "laterally" toward other nations, science and technology have forced its leaders to think of "vertical" integration of human and technical resources within their own country. Japan is striving to be an independent center for technology. It is aggressively exploring all areas of technology acquisition, training scientists and engineers, pursuing joint ventures to collect technical knowledge, purchasing and licensing technology, and looking into reverse engineering.

Perhaps the least discussed but most hotly contended issue with regard to Japan's future leadership role is whether Japan eventually will seek a strong military and acquire a nuclear weapons capability in order to bolster its own interests. While China and other Asian neighbors are worried that the United States already has pushed Japan too far toward military rearmament, some U.S. defense officials and congressional leaders complain that Tokyo is still doing too little too slowly in the military field.

Neither Soviet threats nor U.S. pressures have been decisive factors in Japan's gradual buildup of its defense capabilities. Japan's own uneasiness that it can no longer fully rely on the United States has driven it to consider various options, but as long as U.S. actions pose no major threat to Japanese national interests, Tokyo will remain aligned with Washington. Already, however, there are signs that in the years ahead most Japanese will support policies that give Japan greater flexibility in the pursuit of its own interests. Today a majority of Japanese would reject any high-cost, high-risk, unilateral option.

Patchwork solutions and temporary mechanisms have not worked well, although they have at times eased bilateral problems. Over the years a number of strategies have been tried to deepen and widen the bilateral consultative process—policy planning groups in economic, political, and strategic areas; bilateral business organizations; public/private Wisemen's Groups (as discussed earlier in this volume by Akio Morita); and a vast array of cultural and academic exchanges and meetings, to say nothing of cultural projects and discussion forums. A few people have advised the creation of special U.S.-Japanese policy secretariats to give more coordinated and focused policy attention to each other's policies.[11] Most recently, a cabinet-level forum and an America-Japan Council, a permanent, nongovernmental institute designed to anticipate long-term issues and advise government leaders, have been proposed.[12]

These institutional arrangements are useful in providing forums for consultation, but understanding the differences between the perspectives of the two leadership elites is of more importance to the success of bilateral relations. U.S. leaders concentrate on political and military issues, and focus mainly on the Soviet Union and Eastern Europe. Their outlook is short-term, multilateral, and pragmatic. When they examine relations with Japan it is in a nonthreatening economic context, and problems in the U.S.-Japanese relationship are usually not invested with major day-to-day importance. U.S. leaders encourage Japan to be strong, democratic, and independent. They want a Japan that carries its own weight on the international scene. They would prefer an autonomous Japan that is consultative and cooperative but driven by its own "independent" agenda.

The Japanese approach to cooperation is quite different. Japanese leaders would prefer to avoid an "independent" agenda. Relationships of shared dependence or interdependence are preferred, both culturally and psychologically. The Japanese feel most comfortable in a world characterized by strong U.S.-Japanese involvement where the United States feels linked to Japan, and they seek to foster such ties through the cooperative schemes discussed earlier.

None of the problems examined here will go away, largely because they are rooted in historical, cultural, economic, and political traditions that are very different in the two countries. But the search for new and more complex ways of conceptualizing the relationship under changing circumstances is still important to both sides. It is essential for both sides to remain open to dialogue and to maintain an appropriate level of consultation at various levels. And out of this debate over consultative frameworks some good ideas are likely to emerge that will ease the transition toward the twenty-first century.

Notes

1. Louis Uchitells, "When the World Lacks a Leader," *New York Times*, 31 January 1988.

2. *Chuo Koron* (November 1986):146–162.

3. For greater detail see Ronald A. Morse, "Japan's Drive to Pre-eminence," *Foreign Policy* 69 (Winter 1987–1988):3–21.

4. Herman Kahn, *The Emerging Japanese Superstate* (Englewood Cliffs, NJ: Prentice-Hall, 1970), p. 8.

5. For a recent economic study, see The Japan Development Bank, *Economic Projections on Japan's Economy to the Year 2000* (February 1986). Also see National Institute for Research Advancement, *United States Industry and Trade: Trends and Perspectives—Japan* (March 1988).

6. On shifting power relationships, see "The Ascent of Books on Decline of U.S.," *New York Times*, 10 April 1988; "Japan's Doom: Always Near, Never Here," *Wall Street Journal*, 9 February 1988; "Is America in Decline?" *New York Times Magazine*, 17 April 1988; and "America's 'Decline': Illusion and Reality," *Wall Street Journal*, 12 May 1988.

7. Paul Kennedy, *The Rise and Fall of the Great Powers: Economic Change and Military Conflict from 1500 to 2000* (New York: Random House, 1987).

8. Zbigniew Brzezinski, "How About an Informal U.S.-Japan Inc.?" *New York Times*, 28 April 1987.

9. Amaya Naohiro, "America in Decline," *Look Japan* (May 1988):4–6.

10. Ezra Vogel, "Pax Nipponica?" *Foreign Affairs* 64 (Spring 1986):752–767.

11. Ronald A. Morse and Edward A. Olsen, "Japan's Bureaucratic Edge," *Foreign Policy* 52 (Fall 1983):167–180.

12. Pacific Forum, *Creative Engagement: Strategies for United States–Japan Global Cooperation Toward the 21st Century* (Honolulu: Pacific Forum, June 1988).

Bibliography

Abegglen, James, and George Stalk, Jr. *Kaisha, the Japanese Corporation.* New York: Basic Books, 1985.

Aho, Michael, and Jonathan Aronson. *Trade Talks.* New York: Council on Foreign Relations, 1985.

Asahi, Shimbun, comp. *The Pacific Rivals: A Japanese View of Japanese-American Relations.* New York: Weatherhill, 1971.

Austin, Lewis. *Saints and Samurai: The Political Culture of American and Japanese Elites.* New Haven: Yale University Press, 1975.

Azuma, Hiroshi, et al. *Child Development and Education in Japan.* New York: W. H. Freeman, 1986.

Barnett, Robert W. *Beyond War: Japan's Concept of Comprehensive National Security.* Elmsford, NY: Pergamon-Bassey's, 1984.

Beauchamp, Edward R. *Learning to Be Japanese: Selected Readings on Japanese Society and Education.* Hamden, CT: Shoe String Press, 1978.

Bendahmane, Diane B., and Leo Moser, eds. *Toward a Better Understanding: U.S.-Japan Relations.* Washington, D.C.: Foreign Service Institute, U.S. Department of State, 1986.

Bergsten, C. Fred, and William R. Cline. *The United States– Japan Economic Problem.* Washington, D.C.: Institute for International Economics, 1985.

Blaker, Michael, ed. *The Politics of Trade: U.S. and Japanese Policymaking for the GATT Negotiations.* New York: The East Asian Institute, Columbia University, 1978.

Bloom, Justin L. "Bilateral Cooperative Programs: A Case Study—the United States and Japan." *Journal of the Washington Academy of Science* 77 (September 1987):87–93.

Bowman, Mary J. *Educational Choice and Labor Markets in Japan.* Chicago: University of Chicago Press, 1981.

Buck, James H., ed. *The Modern Japanese Military System.* Beverly Hills, CA: Sage, 1975.

Burks, Ardath. *Japan: A Postindustrial Power.* Boulder, CO: Westview Press, 1984.

Buruma, Ian. "A New Japanese Nationalism." *New York Times Magazine,* 12 April 1987.

Buss, Claude A., ed. *National Security Interests in the Pacific Basin.* Stanford, CA: Hoover Institution, 1985.

Chapman, J.W.M., R. Drifte, and I.T.M. Gow. *Japan's Quest for Comprehensive Security.* New York: St. Martin's, 1982.

Choy, Jon K.T., ed. *Japan: Exploring New Paths*. Washington, D.C.: Japan Economic Institute, 1988.

Christopher, Robert C. *The Japanese Mind: The Goliath Explained*. New York: Linden, 1983.

_____ . *Second to None: American Companies in Japan*. New York: Crown, 1987.

Copper, John F. *The U.S. and East Asia: Problems and Dilemmas for the 1980s*. Washington, D.C.: Heritage Foundation, 1984.

Crane, Donald. *The ASEAN States: Coping with Dependence*. New York: Praeger, 1983.

Cummings, William K. *Educational Equality in Japan*. Princeton: Princeton University Press, 1980.

_____ . *Educational Policies in Crisis: Japanese and American Perspectives*. New York: Praeger, 1986.

Destler, I. M., and Hideo Sato. *Coping with U.S.-Japanese Economic Conflicts*. Lexington, MA: Lexington Books, 1982.

Dore, Ronald P. *Education in Tokugawa Japan*. London: Rutledge and Kegan Paul, 1965.

Drucker, Peter. "The Changed World Economy." *Foreign Affairs* 64 (Spring 1986):758–791.

Endicott, John E. *Japan's Nuclear Option: Political, Technological and Strategic Factors*. New York: Praeger, 1975.

Fallows, James. "Japan: Playing by Different Rules." *The Atlantic* (September 1987):22–32.

Feldstein, Martin. "Correcting the Trade Deficit." *Foreign Affairs* 65 (Spring 1987).

Frost, Ellen. *For Richer, for Poorer: The New U.S.-Japan Relationship*. New York: Council on Foreign Relations, 1987.

Greene, Fred. *Stresses in U.S.-Japanese Security Relations*. Washington, D.C.: Brookings Institution, 1975.

Gregor, James, and Maria Hsia Chang. *The Iron Triangle: A U.S. Security Policy for Northeast Asia*, Stanford, CA: Hoover Institution, 1984.

Hall, John Whitney. *Japan: From Prehistory to Modern Times*. Tokyo: Tuttle, 1983.

Hofheinz, Roy, Jr., and Kent E. Calder. *The Eastasia Edge*. New York: Basic Books, 1982.

Homma, Nagayo. "Beyond Bashing: Toward Sounder Japan-U.S. Ties." *Japan Review of International Affairs* 1 (Fall/Winter 1987):154–169.

Iriye, Akira, ed. *Mutual Images: Essays in American-Japanese Relations*. Cambridge, MA: Harvard University Press, 1972.

Jansen, Marius B. *Japan and Its World*. Princeton: Princeton University Press, 1980.

Japan Defense Agency. *Defense of Japan, 1987*. Tokyo: Japan Times, 1987.

Japan-U.S. Businessmen's Conference. *Understanding the Industrial Policies and Practices of Japan and the United States: A Business Perspective*. Tokyo and Washington, D.C.: The Japan-U.S. Businessmen's Conference, 1984.

Johnson, Alexis U., and George R. Packard. *The Common Security Interests of Japan, the United States, and NATO.* Cambridge, MA: Ballinger, 1981.

Kahn, Herman. *The Emerging Japanese Superstate.* Englewood Cliffs, NJ: Prentice-Hall, 1970.

Kaplan, Morton A., and Mushakoji Kinhide. *Japan, America, and the Future World Order.* New York: Free Press, 1976.

Kataoka, Tetsuya, and Ramon Myers. *Defending an Economic Superpower.* Boulder, CO: Westview Press, 1989.

Katz, Joshua D., and Tilly C. Friedman-Lichtschein. *Japan's New World Role.* Boulder, CO: Westview Press, 1983.

Kennedy, Paul. *The Rise and Fall of the Great Powers.* New York: Random House, 1987.

Kihl, Young Whan, and Lawrence E. Grinter, eds. *Asian-Pacific Security: Emerging Challenges and Responses.* Boulder, CO: Lynne Rienner Publishers, 1986.

Kitamura, Hiroshi. *Psychological Dimensions of U.S. Japanese Relations.* New York: Cambridge University Press, 1971.

Kitamura, Hiroshi, et al. *Between Friends: Japanese Diplomats Look at Japan-U.S. Relations.* Tokyo: Weatherhill, 1985.

Krause, Lawrence B. *U.S. Economic Policy Toward the Association of Southeast Asian Nations: Meeting the Japanese Challenge.* Washington, D.C.: Brookings Institution, 1982.

Langer, Paul F., and Richard Moorsten. *The U.S.-Japanese Military Alliance.* Santa Monica, CA: Rand Corporation, 1975.

Lauren, Paul Gordon. *Power and Prejudice: The Politics and Diplomacy of Racial Discrimination.* Boulder, CO: Westview Press, 1988.

Lebra, Takie Sugiyama. *Japanese Patterns of Behavior.* Honolulu: University of Hawaii Press, 1976.

Lynn, Leonard H., and Timothy J. McKeown. *Organizing Business: Trade Associations in America and Japan.* Washington, D.C.: University Press of America, 1988.

McGraw, Thomas K., ed. *America Versus Japan.* Boston: Harvard Business School Press, 1986.

Maekawa, Haruo, et al. "The Report of the Advisory Group on Economic Structural Adjustment for International Harmony. Submitted to the Prime Minister, Mr. Yasuhiro Nakasone, on 7 April 1986" (Maekawa Report).

Mannari, Hiroshi, and Harumi Befu, eds. *The Challenge of Japan's Internationalization.* New York: Kodansha International, 1983.

Mansfield, Mike. *No Country More Important: Trials in a Maturing Japan-U.S. Relationship.* Tokyo: Simul Press, 1984.

Marris, Stephen. *Deficits and the Dollar Revisited.* Washington, D.C.: Institute for International Economics, 1987.

Morita, Akio. *Made in Japan: Akio Morita and SONY.* New York: Dutton, 1986.

Morley, James W., ed. *The Pacific Basin: New Challenges for the United States.* New York: Academy of Political Science, 1986.

——. *Security Interdependence in the Asia Pacific Region.* Lexington, MA: Lexington Books, 1986.

Morrison, Charles. *Japan, the United States, and a Changing Southeast Asia.* Washington, D.C.: University Press of America, 1985.

Morse, Ronald A., and Richard J. Samuels. *Getting America Ready for Japanese Science and Technology.* Washington, D.C.: Woodrow Wilson International Center, 1985.

Morse, Ronald A., and Shigenobu Yoshida, eds. *Blind Partners: American and Japanese Responses to an Unknown Future.* Washington, D.C.: University Press of America, 1985.

Mowery, David, ed. *International Collaborative Ventures in U.S. Manufacturing.* Cambridge, MA: Ballinger, 1988.

Nishihara, Masashi. *East Asian Security and the Trilateral Countries.* New York: New York University Press, 1985.

Ogura, Kazuo. *Trade Conflict: A View from Japan.* Washington, D.C.: Japan Economic Institute, 1982.

Okimoto, Daniel, ed. *Japan's Economy: Coping with Change in the International Environment.* Boulder, CO: Westview Press, 1982.

Okita, Saburo. *Japan's Challenging Years: Reflections on My Lifetime.* Canberra: Australian National University, 1983.

_____ . "The Outlook for Pacific Cooperation and the Role of Japan." *Japan Review of International Affairs* 1 (Spring/Summer 1987):2–16.

Olsen, Edward A. *U.S.-Japan Strategic Reciprocity: A Neo-Internationalist View.* Stanford, CA: Hoover Institution Press, 1985.

Passin, Herbert. *Society and Education in Japan.* New York: Kodansha International, 1983.

Patrick, Hugh, ed. *Japan's High Technology Industries: Lessons and Limitations of Industrial Policy.* Seattle: University of Washington Press, 1986.

Pempel, T. J. *Patterns of Japanese Policy-Making: Experience from Higher Education.* Boulder, CO: Westview Press, 1978.

Peters, Lois. *Technical Network Between U.S. and Japanese Industry.* Troy, NY: Rensselaer Polytechnic Institute, 1987.

Prestowitz, Clyde V., Jr. *Trading Places: How We Allowed Japan to Take the Lead.* New York: Basic Books, 1988.

Pugel, Thomas, and Robert Hawkins, eds. *Fragile Interdependence.* Lexington, MA: Lexington Books, 1986.

Pyle, Kenneth B., ed. *The Trade Crisis: How Will Japan Respond?* Seattle: Society for Japanese Studies, 1987.

Reischauer, Edwin O. *The Japanese.* Cambridge, MA: Belknap Press, 1981.

Rohlen, Thomas P. *Japan's High Schools.* Berkeley: University of California Press, 1983.

Romberg, Alan D., ed. *The United States and Japan: Changing Societies in a Changing Relationship.* New York: Council on Foreign Relations, 1987.

Satoh, Yukio. *The Evolution of Japanese Security Policy.* Adelphi Paper No. 178. London: International Institute for Strategic Studies, 1982.

Scalapino, Robert A., ed. *The Foreign Policy of Modern Japan.* Berkeley: University of California Press, 1977.

Shibusawa, Masahide. *Japan and the Asian Pacific Region: Profile of Change.* New York: St. Martin's, 1984.

Shimahara, Nobuo. *Adaptation and Education in Japan.* New York: Praeger, 1979.

Shishido, Toshio, and Ryuzo Sato, eds. *Economic Policy and Development: New Perspectives.* Dover, DE: Auburn House, 1985.

Sigur, Gaston, "Current Reflections on U.S.-Japan Relations," U.S. Department of State, *Current Policy No. 1056* (Washington, D.C.: Government Printing Office, 1988).

Sigur, Gaston, and Y. C. Kim. *Japanese and U.S. Policy in Asia.* New York: Praeger, 1982.

Simon, Sheldon W. *The ASEAN States and Regional Security.* Stanford: Hoover Institution, 1982.

Singleton, John. *Nichu: A Japanese School.* New York: Irvington, 1982.

Sinha, Radha. *Japan's Options for the 1980s.* London: Croom Helm, 1982.

Sneider, Richard L. *U.S.-Japanese Security Relations: A Historical Perspective.* New York: Columbia University, East Asian Institute, Toyota Research Program, 1982.

"SONY's Challenge." *Business Week* (1 June 1987):64-69.

Sudershan, Chawla, and D. R. Sardesai, eds. *Changing Patterns of Security and Stability in Asia.* New York, Praeger, 1980.

Suriyamongkol, Marjorie L. *Politics of ASEAN Economic Cooperation.* New York: Oxford University Press, 1988.

Thomas, Raju G.C., ed. *The Great-Power Triangle and Asian Security.* Lexington, MA: Lexington Books, 1983.

Thurow, Lester C., ed. *The Management Challenge: Japanese Views.* Cambridge: MIT Press, 1985.

Tsurutani, Taketsugu. *Japanese Policy and East Asian Security.* New York: Praeger, 1981.

United States Congress. House Committee on Ways and Means, Subcommittee on Trade, United States-Japan Trade Task Force. *Task Force Report on United States-Japan Trade.* Washington, D.C.: Government Printing Office, 1979.

United States-Japan Advisory Commission. *Challenges and Opportunities in United States-Japan Relations: A Report Submitted to the President of the United States and the Prime Minister of Japan.* Washington, D.C.: Government Printing Office, 1984.

Uyehara, Cecil H., ed. *Technological Exchange: The U.S. Japanese Experience.* Washington, D.C.: University Press of America, 1982.

_____. *U.S.-Japan Science and Technology Exchange: Patterns of Interdependence.* Boulder, CO: Westview Press, 1988.

Varley, H. Paul. *Japanese Culture.* Honolulu: University of Hawaii Press, 1984 ed.

Vogel, Ezra E. *Japan as Number One: Lessons for America.* Cambridge, MA: Harvard University Press, 1979.

Watts, William. *The United States and Japan: A Troubled Partnership.* Cambridge, MA: Ballinger, 1984.

Weinstein, Martin E. *Japan's Postwar Defense Policy, 1947-1968.* New York: Columbia University Press, 1971.

West, Philip, and F.A.M. Alting von Geusau, eds. *The Pacific Rim and the Western World: Strategic, Economic, and Cultural Perspectives.* Boulder, CO: Westview Press, 1987.

White, Merry. *The Japanese Educational Challenge: A Commitment to Children.* New York: Free Press, 1987.

Yoshida, Kenichi. *Japan is a Circle: A Tour Round the Mind of Modern Japan.* New York: Kodansha International, 1976.

Zagoria, Donald. "Soviet Policy in East Asia: A New Beginning?" *Foreign Affairs* 68 (Winter 1988/1989):120–138.

About the Contributors and Editors

Michael H. Armacost, a native of Ohio, studied at Carleton College and Columbia University, where he earned the Ph.D. degree. During his academic career, he taught political science and East Asian affairs at Johns Hopkins University and the International Christian University in Japan. He joined the Department of State in 1969 and has since served in a variety of posts, including that of ambassador to the Philippines from 1980–1982. In 1984, he was appointed under secretary of state for political affairs, the highest career position in the State Department. Armacost was named as U.S. ambassador-designate to Japan in early 1989. His scholarly writings include *The Foreign Relations of the United States* (1969) and numerous articles.

Robert C. Christopher, born in Connecticut, graduated in Oriental studies from Yale University. After serving as a Japanese language officer in the U.S. Army during World War II and an intelligence officer in the Korean War, he embarked on a career in journalism, occupying a number of senior positions at *Time, Newsweek,* and other well-known news magazines. A long-term resident in Japan, he gained widespread recognition for his 1983 book, *The Japanese Mind.* At present, he is the administrator of the Pulitzer Prizes at Columbia University's School of Journalism. His most recent work is *Second to None: American Companies in Japan* (1987).

William K. Cummings spent part of his early life in India. After graduating in engineering from Clarkson University, he gained his Ph.D. from Harvard University. He has taught and researched at a number of institutions around the world, including the National Science Foundation and Tsuda College in Japan. Currently, he is a lecturer in international education at the Graduate School of Educaton, Harvard Universty. A specialist in Japanese education, his many publications include *Education and Equality in Japan* (1980) and *Education Policies in Crisis* (1986). He has also served as a member of the advisory committee on a study of Japanese education undertaken by the U.S. Department of Education.

Tommy T.B. Koh is a native of Singapore and currently serves as his country's ambassador to the United States. A graduate in law at the National University of Singapore, Professor Koh undertook advanced studies at Harvard University and later Cambridge University in England. He taught at the University of

Singapore for several years, serving as the dean of the faculty of law during 1971–1974. He was later appointed Singapore's permanent representative to the United Nations, serving in that post until 1984, when he assumed his present position. Among his many awards is the honorary degree of doctor of laws from Yale University.

Paul Gordon Lauren earned his Ph.D. from Stanford University, where he was a Woodrow Wilson Fellow and where he has taught on several occasions. He joined the Department of History at the University of Montana in 1974, specializing in international relations and diplomatic history. Dr. Lauren has been a National Peace Fellow, a Social Science Research Council Fellow, and a Rockefeller Foundation Humanities Fellow. Besides numerous articles, his books include *Diplomats and Bureaucrats* (1976), *Diplomacy: New Approaches in History, Theory, and Policy* (1979), *The China Hand's Legacy* (1987), and *Power and Prejudice: The Politics and Diplomacy of Racial Discrimination* (1988). Since 1985 he has been the director of the Maureen and Mike Mansfield Center at the University of Montana.

Leonard H. Lynn received his B.A. and M.A. in Asian studies from the University of Oregon, after which he lived and worked in Japan for a number of years. He then pursued graduate studies in sociology at the University of Michigan, where he received his Ph.D. Currently he is an associate professor in the Management Policy Division, Weatherhead School of Management, Case Western Reserve University. Dr. Lynn has published widely on a range of comparative U.S.-Japanese technology-related topics, including a study of *How Japan Innovates: A Comparison with the U.S. in the Case of Oxygen Steelmaking* (1982). Most recently, he coedited a book on *Organizing Business: Trade Associations in America and Japan* (1988).

Mike Mansfield was raised in the state of Montana and has served in the U.S. Navy, Army, and Marine Corps. He graduated from the University of Montana and later taught there from 1933 to 1943 as a professor of Far Eastern history. Mansfield served for ten years in the U.S. House of Representatives and for twenty-four years in the Senate, often receiving foreign policy assignments from both Democratic and Republican presidents. He became Senate majority leader in 1961 and served in that capacity longer than anyone else in U.S. history. President Jimmy Carter appointed him as U.S. ambassador to Japan in 1977, and President Ronald Reagan subsequently renewed the appointment. Mansfield retired from his position in January 1989, having served in this ambassadorial capacity longer than any other individual.

Akio Morita, a graduate of Osaka Imperial University in Japan, is chairman and chief executive officer of the SONY Corporation. A cofounder of the company, he was active in both technical innovation and sales promotion. In particular, he has been responsible for establishing SONY's worldwide marketing network. The recipient of many international awards, including the Albert

Medal of the Royal Society of Arts in Great Britain, Mr. Morita has been described as the "exemplar and leader of Japan's new generation of inventive, competitive executives." He is also the author of a best-selling book, *Made in Japan* (1986).

Ronald A. Morse, a native of New York City, gained his B.A. and M.A. at the University of California at Berkeley and his Ph.D. at Princeton University. Until recently he was the secretary of the Asia Program at the Woodrow Wilson International Center for Scholars in Washington, D.C. Currently, he is development officer at the Library of Congress. A specialist in modern Japanese politics and foreign policy, he has written or edited a number of books, including *U.S.-Japanese Energy Relations: Cooperation and Competition* (1984) and *Getting America Ready for Japanese Science and Technology* (1984).

Dennis J. O'Donnell, born in Colorado, received his Ph.D. in economics from Penn State University, where his dissertation focused on modeling and statistical analysis of fertility. He has presented professional papers in Asia, Latin America, and Europe. O'Donnell's research centers upon development and trade issues dealing with the Pacific rim, Thailand, and Nepal. He is currently professor of economics, former chair of the Asian Studies Committee, and an affiliate of the Public Policy Research Institute of the University of Montana. Dr. O'Donnell is currently working on a book entitled *Crossings: Crisis and Opportunity in the Asian Era* concerning Asian development issues.

Saburo Okita is the president of International University of Japan. In a lengthy career, he has served in a wide variety of economic posts in the Japanese government, including that of director-general of the Development Bureau, Japanese Economic Planning Agency. Recognized as one of Japan's leading economists, Okita served as his country's minister for foreign affairs from 1979–1980. He has also been actively involved in economic affairs in the United Nations and other international organizations. Among his many publications are *Japan's Postwar Economic Policy* (1961) and *Japan and the World Economy* (1975).

Raymond F. Wylie was born in Northern Ireland and educated at the University of Toronto (B.A., M.A.) and the University of London (Ph.D.). Currently, he is professor of international relations and director of the East Asian Studies Program at Lehigh University. He served as the first Mansfield Professor of Modern Asian Affairs at the Mansfield Center, University of Montana, during 1985–1987. He is a member of the Royal Institute of International Affairs and has a broad interest in international relations and East Asia. Wylie's works include *The Emergence of Maoism, 1935–45* (1980) and articles in the *Bulletin of the Atomic Scientists,* the *China Quarterly,* the *Far Eastern Economic Review,* and other academic publications.

Index

Adams, Robert McCormick, 9–10
Advanced Micro Devices, Inc., 167
Age of the Pacific, 14, 41, 55, 99, 177
Akihito, Emperor, 12, 176
Any Person, Any Study (Ashby), 146
ANZUS pact, 69
ASEAN. *See* Association of Southeast Asian Nations
Ashby, Eric, 146
Asian Development Bank, 90, 94, 137
Association of Southeast Asian Nations (ASEAN), 93, 118, 135–136
Athos, Anthony G., 152
Atlantic, The, 4, 151
Atoms for Peace program, 162
Australia, 69
AZT compound, 154

Baker, James A., 132, 138
Basic Policy for National Defense, 61
Belgium, 165–166
Bennett, William, 153
Bloom, Justin, 162
Boeing, 167
Boggs, Hale, 79
Boorstein, Daniel, 151
Boyer, Ernest, 145
Bradley, Bill, 135
Brock, William, 83
Buruma, Ian, 31, 67
Bush, George, 46, 71, 131. *See also* Bush administration
Bush administration, 74(n13). *See also* Bush, George

California's Proposition 13, 147
Canada, 68, 100
Carter, Jimmy, 71, 105. *See also* Carter administration
Carter administration, 28. *See also* Carter, Jimmy
Central America, 50
Chace, James, 72
Chicago Commodities Exchange, 43
China, 21, 28. *See also* People's Republic of China
Chrysler, 103
Churchill, Winston, 51
Ciba-Geigy, 166
Clark, William S., 20
Coca Cola, 100
COCOM. *See* Coordinating Committee for Export Control
Cogan, John, 151
Columbia Business School, 38
Columbia Journalism School, 38

Comprehensive security. *See* Japan, comprehensive security doctrine of
Conference on Security and Cooperation (1975), 72
Confucianism, 154
Congressional Record, 2
Coordinating Committee for Export Control (COCOM), 7
Cummins, 167

Defense Science Board, 159
Deficits and the Dollar Revisited (Marris), 114
Deficits and the Dollar: The World Economy at Risk (Marris), 114
Depression. *See* Great Depression
Developing countries. *See* Third World
Dewey, John, 143
Dollar, 45, 59, 101, 102, 103, 127
 and Asian NICs, 91
 devaluation of, 119, 122, 123
 and Japanese foreign assets, 114
 overvaluation of, 87–88, 134
 and world economy, 104, 113, 114, 116
Drucker, Peter, 109, 111, 122, 123–124, 133
Dulles, John Foster, 2
Dupont, 166

Economist, The, 112
Edo Bay, 19
EEC. *See* European Economic Community
Egypt, 50
England. *See* Great Britain
Eurobonds, 42
European Community. *See* European Economic Community
European Economic Community (EEC), 86, 94, 179
Export Import Bank of Japan, 90

Fairchild Semiconductor Corporation, 157
Fallows, James, 4, 151
Fanuc, 167
Far Eastern Economic Review, 124
FBI. *See* United States, Federal Bureau of Investigation
Federal Republic of Germany (FRG), 88, 90, 102, 111
 manufactured exports of, 123
 research and development in, 158(table)
 See also Germany
Feldstein, Martin, 95, 134
Ford (Motor Company), 123
Foreign Affairs, 83
Fortune, 159
Fortune 500 companies, 100
France, 158(table)
Fraser, Malcolm, 94